Creating t... ...

ALSO BY TIMOTHY B. RIORDAN

Prince of Quacks: The Notorious Life
of Dr. Francis Tumblety, Charlatan
and Jack the Ripper Suspect (McFarland, 2009)

Creating the Boston Police

*Francis Tukey and the Invention
of Modern Crime Fighting*

TIMOTHY B. RIORDAN

Exposit

Jefferson, North Carolina

ISBN (print) 978-1-4766-8941-8 ∞
ISBN (ebook) 978-1-4766-4699-2

LIBRARY OF CONGRESS AND BRITISH LIBRARY
CATALOGUING DATA ARE AVAILABLE

On the cover: Engraving of Francis Tukey, 1851
(*Gleason's Pictorial Drawing-Room Companion*)

Printed in the United States of America

Exposit is an imprint of McFarland & Company, Inc., Publishers

Exposit
Box 611, Jefferson, North Carolina 28640
www.expositbooks.com

To Trish—whose love and support helped get this done

Table of Contents

Preface

    This study is a biography of Francis Tukey, city marshal of Boston from 1846 to 1852 and, by default, the first police chief for the city. In many ways, Tukey invented the modern police system in the United States. Charged with creating an active force rather than a reactive one, he used what was then known as the "London system," assigning men to walk specific beats within the city and having twice daily roll calls at headquarters. In addition, he hired the first professional police detectives in the country. Together, they matched wits with many of the most famous criminals of the 1840s and 1850s. In the course of these activities, Tukey became a national celebrity and the Boston Police Department was used as a model for police forces all across the county.

    My interest in Francis Tukey was sparked while doing research for another project where I discovered that Tukey's early life was anything but what would be expected of a future police chief. Leaving his home in Maine in his late teenage years, he first set up as a baker in Salem but soon lost the business. Trying again in Chelsea, he was soon bankrupt and looking for a job. He ended up running a barroom in the North End of Boston, close to the docks. This was the worst section of Boston, known at the time as the "Black Sea." He was arrested twice for assault, declared himself insolvent and was headed for oblivion. Turning his life around and becoming city marshal seemed to me to be an amazing story and one I was eager to tell.

    The study covers Tukey's development of tactics to deal with well-known names such as "Black Bill" Henderson, "One-Eyed" Thompson, and "Bristol Bill" Darlington, criminals with international reputations. His most famous case was the murder of Dr.

George B. Parkman by John Webster, a professor at Harvard's Massachusetts Medical College. Tukey was deeply involved in the discovery of his remains, and the conviction of Prof. Webster. He and his detectives were involved in developing the first forensic evidence used in court. The police under Tukey became famous for their organized "descents" on gamblers, rum-sellers and prostitutes. Besides normal police work, Tukey was forced to confront the major social movements that swept through Boston in the mid–19th century, including the temperance movement, the reaction to the Fugitive Slave Law of 1850 and the many problems associated with the great influx of immigrants fleeing the Great Potato Famine in Ireland. On top of all this, he and his men were primarily responsible for dealing with the victims of the cholera epidemic of 1849. While this story is primarily about Francis Tukey, it touches on many important issues in Boston's history.

This is the first in-depth study of the beginning of policing in Boston. Other studies have touched on the subject as part of a larger history of policing in Boston. Particularly important was Roger Lane's *Policing the City: Boston 1822–1885* that was published in 1967. Within the scope of such a time period, he was not able to devote much time to the details of the establishment of the Tukey's department nor to the successes and failures of it. To conduct this research, I perused thousands of pages of newsprint, many manuscript letters, numerous published diaries and hundreds of secondary sources to try to get the details of this fascinating story.

Introduction

In the late 19th century, Horatio Alger, Jr., wrote novels about impoverished boys who, through hard work and virtue, rose from poverty to "middle class respectability." It was said that this typified the American experience. His novels remained popular well into the 20th century and have been reprinted as late as 2015. The stories were so popular that the phrase "Horatio Alger story" now stands for just such a theme. His heroes are part of any discussion of upward mobility based on self-determination, personal responsibility and self-reliance. Critics have long since ridiculed his plots, his themes and his heroes, yet the myth endures. Perhaps the myth continues because there was more truth in it than the critics were willing to admit.

This biography of Francis Tukey can be seen as a real-life Horatio Alger story. Tukey was born to respectable but poor parents in Portland, Maine, left home as a teenager and became an independent baker in Salem and in Chelsea, Massachusetts. He failed in this business and became the manager of his brother-in-law's bar in the worst section of Boston. He was impulsive and prone to violence when opposed, things his later opponents would always hold against him. In the bar business, he also failed. It looked like he was heading for an obscurity that he richly deserved. Somehow, Tukey got accepted to Harvard Law School and there he flourished. He passed the course and attained a law degree. He was so involved with the law school that after he graduated he named his second son, Greenleaf Story Tukey, after his two professors, Simon Greenleaf and Joseph Story.

There are no known photographs of the subject of this biography but Francis Tukey was prominent enough that several etched portraits were completed. While short by modern standards, he was of average height for his time. Tukey was described as stocky and later, probably tended to chubbiness. His hair was short and black and he combed it back. People remembered his face as being angular and built around a prominent nose. This last feature was what gave him such a distinctive "downeast accent" and a commanding voice that could be heard over the noise of the largest crowds. The feature which people most often commented on was his eyes. It was said that he had black, piercing eyes and a stare that made many a criminal regret ever coming to Boston.

It is likely that while he was at Harvard, Tukey was befriended by Josiah Quincy, Jr., who would be a major influence on him and would remain a friend for the rest of his life. When Quincy was elected mayor of Boston, he chose Tukey for the position of city marshal and charged him with changing the Boston Police Department from a reactive force against riots to an active, patrolling, law-enforcement organization. Quincy believed that the police should not just catch criminals but actively work to improve the moral character of the city. Tukey molded the police to what we know today and set the standard for departments across the country. His patrolmen were not to wait at the office until a crime was reported but to be out in the community looking to stop crime. He matched wits with some of the most notorious criminals in the United States. In the process, his exploits as city marshal made him a national celebrity.

Like many men in the 19th

FRANCIS TUKEY, ESQ., CITY MARSHAL OF BOSTON.

Portrait of Francis Tukey that appeared in *Gleason's Pictorial Drawing Room Companion* in 1851. The engraving was based on a daguerreotype taken by Luther H. Hale. It is not known if the daguerreotype survives. This is the only illustration of Tukey taken from life.

century, Tukey tried very hard to become both financially successful and respectable. In the process, he went broke three times, twice
as city marshal, and yet always came back. If he was not rich when
he died, he was financially secure. The quest for respectability was
even more difficult. While he was useful to Boston's elite, he was
not accepted by them. His opponents published vilifications of him
that make today's scandals seem pale in comparison. Through it all,
Tukey maintained his own code of conduct. He was often described
as imperious and when he gave orders, they were short, to the point
and he expected them to be obeyed. If his men followed his orders,
he backed them fully against all criticism. In the same way, Tukey
carried out the orders given to him by the mayors under whom he
served with precision and care, even if he did not agree with them.

Yet there was an underlying streak of rebellion in Tukey that
sometimes came to the forefront. When told to enforce the city ordinances, he often chose to enforce them not against poor people who
were trying to make a living, but against the elite who felt they did
not have to comply simply because of their position. This naturally
made him less popular with those in power. Bringing a city alderman
to court for not shoveling his sidewalk was not what the elite meant
when they decided to enforce the ordinances.

Under Tukey's leadership, the Boston police became an active
force. Using the "London system," where each officer had an assigned
beat, the police became part of the community and were able to seek
out crimes rather than wait for them to be reported. Sometimes
those crimes were as simple as someone blocking a street with their
goods or parking a cab where they should not. At other times, the
police were able to arrest burglars in the act of robbing a store or bar
owners selling alcohol on a Sunday. In addition to the patrol force,
Tukey made a number of innovations. One of the most important
was that he hired the first police detectives in the country and taught
them to be on the lookout for pickpockets, forgers and other known
criminals. The detectives kept records of crimes and criminals and
used these to inform other police departments across the country.
Tukey was one of the first to realize that criminal behavior was not
confined to one town but that to fight criminals, one had to be aware
of what was going on in surrounding towns and be familiar with a
developing national criminal culture.

Because photography was in its infancy and there was no reliable way to keep track of individual criminals, many of whom had multiple aliases, Tukey began what was known as the "show-up." When an individual was arrested, he would be presented to the entire police force at roll call and Tukey would explain his criminal history. The men were instructed to keep an eye out for this individual as they went about town. As time went on, this process was subject to abuse. Known criminals were sometimes brought before the police for a show-up before they had been arrested for any crime in Boston

Having an active police force for the first time, the city authorities felt that they could use it against those who seemed to violate the moral fabric of the community. Tukey and his men made several famous "descents" against gamblers, rum-sellers, and brothels. These were organized as military style raids, most often with Tukey directly in charge, that gathered not only the owners but their customers as well. These highly publicized raids filled the Police Court with defendants but they were essentially given a slap on the wrist and let go. Tukey pointed out that none of what he did would have any effect if the judicial system did not impose stricter penalties.

The early 19th century was a time of great social movements and Tukey and his department were caught up in several of these which usually began in Boston and spread to the rest of the country. One of the first of these was the temperance crusade. Tukey, who in his early life was himself a rum-seller, joined the temperance movement and his police were used by the city in an attempt to curtail the trade. Through the late 1840s and into the 1850s, arrests for violating the alcohol laws and for drunkenness were the largest percentage of the total number of crimes. When it became apparent that the Massachusetts Legislature was about to pass a Draconian prohibition law, the alcohol interests in Boston knew that had to get rid of Tukey and managed to maneuver him out of office.

One of the social movements that the police reluctantly got involved with was the developing Abolition crusade. During the Fugitive Slave crisis of the early 1850s, Tukey and his police force, having no direct orders to get involved, stood by and ignored the rescue and escape of several runaway slaves who had been sought or taken by the U.S. marshals. Only after the federal government began to apply pressure to the city fathers, who in turn ordered Tukey to take charge, did he get reluctantly get involved and, much to his displeasure, aided in the process of sending a runaway back to the South.

Tukey's time as city marshal coincided with one of the great population movements of the 19th century. The Potato Famine in Ireland began just when he was becoming city marshal. Within a few years, thousands of Irish men and women crossed the Atlantic and flooded into Boston, forever changing the nature of the city. As a whole, the Irish were from rural backgrounds and were not familiar with city living. This lack of knowledge, their poverty and their Catholic religion made living in Boston difficult. They often sought solace in alcohol and this led to confrontations with the police. Tukey and his men were not unsympathetic to the plight of the Irish. They often aided them by finding food and charity. Tukey even took two small children into his own home when he arrested their single father and no one else stepped forward to look after them.

Tukey is often criticized for his opposition to hiring the first Irish policeman. However, his problem was not so much that he was Irish but that the City Council broke a promise they made to Tukey. A year before, several policemen had been arrested for crimes. Tukey pointed out that he had not recommended these men before they were hired and forced the Council to agree that anyone to be hired on the police had to have his approval. In a very tight mayoral race, the mayor and Board of Aldermen decided to seek the Irish vote by hiring an Irishman for the police without seeking Tukey's approval. He looked on this move as a betrayal and strongly opposed this appointment. Ultimately, this was one more thing the elite used to maneuver him out of office.

Even before he was forced from office, Tukey was engaged in supporting and profiting from the California Gold Rush. He shipped supplies on speculation to San Francisco in the early days, arranged support of parties leaving Boston for the gold fields and invested in mining companies. He married his second wife, Caesilla Haycock, in 1851, and she was the widow of an early emigrant to California who had struck it rich and invested heavily in land near Sacramento. When he ceased to be city marshal of Boston, Tukey fulfilled a long held wish and moved to that city, where he became a successful businessman, lawyer and politician. During the Civil War, he became a leader of the Union forces in Sacramento and was elected to the State Assembly in 1863.

During his active life, Tukey exemplified the real underpinning of the Horatio Alger myth. Although vilified by many, he kept to his own code of virtue and eventually succeeded. Despite many setbacks, he persevered and overcame all challenges. In his personal life, he rose from poverty, business failure and obscurity to a competent security, a successful career and national celebrity. His greatest legacy is his contribution to the formation of the Boston Police Department which still carries on the traditions he laid out.

1

"A dirty, troublesome, brutish little whelp"

Throughout the early 19th century, from all over New England, young men left their farms, villages and small towns to flood into Boston in search of economic success. In one study of these "in-migrants," that is native-born men from New England, about 40 percent were from other places in Massachusetts but 25 percent came from Maine. Perhaps this is to be expected as Maine was part of Massachusetts until 1820 and maintained strong economic ties with the Bay State throughout the 1830s. One of the migrants from Maine to Massachusetts in this time period was Francis Tukey.[1]

He was originally from Portland but there is not much certainty about his early years. His father, Benjamin Tukey, was a pump and block maker servicing Portland's commercial fleet from a location on Titcomb's Wharf. This was adjacent to Clay Cove, which by the late 1840s would acquire a nefarious reputation. A much later, and entirely scurrilous, pamphlet attempted to portray the area as equivalent to the Five Points Neighborhood in New York. There is no indication that it was that way when Francis was born in 1815 or when he was growing up. Aside from the above mentioned document, there are no recollections of his boyhood. In keeping with the pamphlet's intention to smear him, it described him as "a dirty, troublesome, brutish little whelp, whom no kindness could effect, no correction reclaim." In between all the hyperbole about his character and actions, there are a few interesting items that might have some validity. The pamphlet suggests that his parents were "humble but respectable." In addition, it reports that he apprenticed as a baker in Portland, which is the profession he first pursued in Boston.[2]

9

When Francis Tukey chose to leave Portland and join the tide swelling into Boston is unknown. He is not listed in the 1830 census of his father's household. However, he may have been listed in the household of the baker to whom he was attached, but there is no way to ascertain this. The earliest reference to him in Boston is in a list of letters left at the Boston Post Office in early July 1833. In any case, he was on his own in Boston by the time he was 18 years old.[3]

A little over a year later, we find him in Salem running his own bakery. Why he chose Salem is unknown but by October 28, 1834, he was advertising in the *Salem Gazette*. The notice announces his new bakery on Court St. in Salem. It reveals that he had been in Boston and had "lately removed" from there and purchased the "baking establishment of Mr. Samuel Berry." This was a well-known bakery that had been established in 1815. Samuel Berry was famous in Salem for being an organizer of the first Methodist Church in the town. In his long life in Salem, he was active in both religious and civil spheres. By the time he sold the bakery to Tukey, he was 73 years old. He continued to be active in the community until his death, at 90, in 1852.[4]

Tukey advised his patrons that he would have bread of all descriptions and the best quality, as well as fancy bread and cake. Ship bread would be baked to order. Finally, he offered free delivery to any part of Salem. His shop was prominently located in the center of Salem by the town market. As Tukey continued to advertise in the *Gazette*, the editor repaid his patronage with a notice in the paper. The notice was entitled "Mr. Tukey's Cake" and was published on November 11. It stated that the editor had been provided with various samples of cake from the new business but, it being election time, they were too busy to fully test them. So, to be fair, they set up three juries to taste them: one of matrons, one of schoolboys and the last of workingmen and all three juries deemed the cakes "first rate."[5]

After not advertising for six months, Tukey put out a new notice on June 12, 1835, which began with the headline "Dyspepsia Bread" and stated that it was available at his bread store. Dyspepsia was the 19th-century description of indigestion but carried many other implications. Because the American diet, in the 19th century, was based on meat with very little vegetable fiber, indigestion was a common complaint. The recipe for dyspepsia bread called for unsifted flour, which left the fibrous parts and was thought to aid digestion. It was basically a brown bread as opposed to the white bread normally preferred by Americans. The dyspepsia bread, as recorded in cookbooks of the time, included a significant amount of molasses. This was the first time that sweetness became associated with bread and would lend healthful connotations to sugar for the rest of the century.[6]

Certainly indigestion was a serious condition but there were other reasons why Tukey might begin to advertise this type of bread. Beginning in 1832, Asiatic cholera arrived on the East Coast of the United States and for the rest of the decade ravaged coastal cities, mostly during the hot summer months. Various attempts were made to study the disease and the conclusion was that it was related to diet. Specifically, experts recommended drinking port wine, avoiding fruits and vegetables and increasing the amount of meat consumed. These recommendations were guaranteed to increase the prevalence of indigestion. There was no real understanding of the cause of this disease but it was widely believed to begin with stomach problems and bowel complaints. Anything which claimed to aid in digestion, the main reason for dyspepsia bread, was seen as a preventive.[7]

Into this atmosphere stepped Sylvester Graham, part religious fanatic, part dietary reformer and full-time temperance advocate. Contrary to accepted wisdom, Graham stated that eating meat and drinking alcohol were the main reasons for the spread of cholera. His dietary reform focused on plant foods exclusively. He advocated a diet based on vegetables and fibrous plants without alcohol, tobacco, coffee, tea or spices. As part of this dietary reform, he came to champion brown bread made from unsifted flour, preferably coarsely ground at home, which became known as dyspepsia bread. In 1832, he lectured in New York City on this diet as a preventive to cholera but was derided by medical authorities. When the disease did reach New York, his followers seemed to be spared and his reputation was made. He emphasized drinking pure water as part of this diet. Of course, as cholera is most often spread through infected water supplies, his diet might have actually helped some people.

There is no indication of why Tukey began to advertise dyspepsia bread in 1835 but Sylvester Graham was travelling in New England in the summer of 1835, lecturing in Boston in October and in Salem by

November that year. His fame was only beginning to grow. The previous year, cholera had been in Boston and New Bedford and would extend to other Massachusetts cites in towns in 1835. Tukey, as a good entrepreneur, tried to capitalize on this trend and continued to advertise his dyspepsia bread until the last of his ads in Salem in August 1835.[8]

A much later article in the *Salem Register* looked back on Tukey's time as a baker. It described him as a "dashing and energetic Baker in the city." Further, it reported that he had a "large reputation for smartness and activity" but commented that he was "a more promising subject for a police court then candidate for police officer. Almost a decade after he left Salem, the memory of his time there was at best ambivalent."[9]

However, by this time, his mind was on other things. In February 1835, Tukey married Mary S. Gay in Boston. Her family was from Quincy but her brother, Charles E. Gay, was living at 1 Fleet St., in the North End of Boston. He was described as a grocer but kept a barroom. Charles Gay was in Boston as early as 1830 and Mary may have met Tukey before he moved to Salem. The minister who performed the marriage was George W. Blagden, then pastor of the Salem St. Congregational Church at the corner of Salem and North Bennett Streets in the North End. Tukey was described as "of Salem" and he continued to bake bread there through much of 1835. He, and his new bride returned to Salem and in January 1836, their daughter Adelaide was born.

Why and when they chose to leave Salem remains unknown but in 1837, they were living in Chelsea. What happened to the Salem bakery is also unknown but it may have gone bankrupt. In the 1837 Salem City Directory, Tukey is not listed but Samuel Berry is listed as a baker. In all subsequent city directories, Berry is listed as a farmer. It may be that he took the bakery back from Tukey. In Chelsea, Tukey appears also to have been a baker but there is no information available on where his bakery was nor what he sold. One of the few pieces of evidence from his time in Chelsea is the birth of another daughter, Sarah Elizabeth, in July 1837. According to the 1848 pamphlet, a poor source to go on, Tukey again lost the bakery in Chelsea and was forced to move to Boston.[10]

In moving to Boston, Tukey was entering a profession for which he is not known to have any experience. Having failed twice at being a baker, Tukey took up the running of a "grocery store" in the North End. At least in this instance, there was someone he could turn to for advice. Charles E. Gay, his brother-in-law, had been in business as a "grocer" since 1830, when he began as a partner in the firm of Howard & Gay, 237 Ann St. By the end of that year, Eleazer Howard, Jr., would leave the business and Gay would be the sole proprietor. Despite a major fire in 1839, Gay would continue to run the grocery business on Ann St. until 1840.

Under the licensing law in the early 1830s, there were two types of places that could legally sell spirituous liquors. The first were inns or taverns that offered lodging. The other, much more common in Boston, were grocery stores. By acquiring a grocery license, proprietors were able to open a barroom, which also sold other goods. Boston's "grocers" became an important political force in the 1830s in order to protect this type of arrangement.

When Tukey moved to Boston, he opened or took over a barroom and eating place located at the corner of Commercial and Fleet streets. At the time, this was on the waterfront across from Snow's Wharf between Lewis and Sargent's Wharf's. This establishment was in the heart of what was described as the Black Sea, the city's red-light district. Fleet Street, was adjacent to many of the wharfs on the waterfront of the North End. It was a place where sailors released from their ships found lodging and entertainment. It was reported that over half of Boston's brothels were located in this area. The entry for the Black Sea in *Bacon's Dictionary of Boston,* though written in 1886, long after its heyday, gives some of the flavor of this district:

> But a few years ago, comparatively these streets, particularly North (more anciently Ann Street) were almost wholly devoted to sailors' boarding-houses and to dance-halls and other dens of iniquity. Every ground-floor, and many a cellar, was a bar-room and dancing-hall combined.... Down North Street, every door stood invitingly open; sounds of revelry and music issued from within; and floods of light streamed over the brightness of the bar and the brilliant attire and meretricious charms of the painted sirens along the walls.[11]

Tukey secured lodging for his family in the rear of 107 Hanover St., which was being used as an auction yard. This part of Hanover St. was well away from the debauchery of his business location, being over half a mile distant. His neighbors were lawyers and merchants.

By operating a barroom or restaurant selling alcohol, Tukey became embroiled in one of the major reform movements of the early 19th century. The temperance movement was on the ascendency in the 1830s and Massachusetts was the center of the development. At the beginning of the 19th century, the state required a license for anyone who sold spirituous liquors. The requirements for the license were very rigid and stated that any business that sold liquor had to be in a prominent location, could not offer credit above 10 shillings, and must offer accommodation and stabling to travelers. All of these required a large capital investment and made obtaining licenses a difficult process. By 1816, the legislature, responding to pressure, granted the grocers of Boston an exemption from providing accommodations and stabling. The number of licenses in Boston quickly rose, increasing by over 1000 percent from what had been before. This was not a sudden increase in drinking but rather an acknowledgment that most grocers had previously chosen to ignore the law and there was no effective means of enforcement.[12]

These developments did not go unobserved by those concerned with the effect of alcohol on the public good. In the mid–1820s, the American Society for the Promotion of Temperance was founded in Boston and shortly became a national organization. The Boston Board of Aldermen responded to the growing movement in 1833 by again tightening the conditions for a license, including requiring lodging and stabling nearby, if not on the premises. This effectively cut the number of licenses in half. This was the situation when Tukey began running his tavern on the waterfront. It is likely that he did not have a license and he relied on the fact that there was no effective method of enforcing the law.

By 1838, there were few politicians who would stand against temperance and, at the meeting of the State Temperance Union, the body declared itself in favor of total prohibition. In April, the General Court passed a law entitled "An act regulating the sale of spirituous liquors" which, though it never stated it directly, was designed to completely prohibit the sale of liquor as a beverage. The central tenet of this law was that no liquor or wine could be sold in quantities of less than 15 gallons, which gave the law its popular name. If anyone was convicted of breaking the law, a fine of ten to twenty dollars was to be assessed for each drink sold. The "15 gallon" law went into effect in July 1838.[13]

Various ploys were tried to get around this law, some were quite unique. It was reported in September, at the Dedham muster, an entrepreneur applied to the selectmen for a permit to exhibit a "rare striped pig." On the day of the muster, he set up a tent in the open field, painted stripes on a pig, and began to advertise this attraction. Admittance was a low price of six and a quarter cents. When a patron was admitted, after paying his fee, to see the pig, he was offered his choice of a free drink of brandy or gin. It appears that the "exhibit" was undisturbed by the authorities and was an outstanding success. The concept of the striped pig captured the imagination of the public and was soon translated into other areas. A play was put on in Boston with the title "The Striped Pig" and it was reported that in New York, several establishments were offering drinks called a "striped pig." Politicians who opposed the 15 gallon law were termed the striped pig party.[14]

While the humor of the striped pig widely made the rounds, more serious rumblings were on the horizon. An important objection to the law was that it was discriminatory against the poor. While the rich could afford to buy 15 gallons at a time and carry it home, such was not possible for the average workingman. This discrimination was considered un–American. Opponents also attacked the law as an assault on property rights. However, no aspect of the law was more resented than the way it was enforced.

Like all of the previous legislation on restricting the use of liquor, there was no provision for enforcement of the statue. This was not a problem for the Temperance Societies as they set up "vigilance committees" to see that it was enforced. One way to do this was to hire informers to go to places where it was suspected that sale of liquor was still being carried on and later to testify to the facts. A number of individuals are repeatedly mentioned in newspapers testifying to buying spirituous liquors. This was facilitated because the law punished the seller not the buyer of such goods. Some of the informers did it for the cause of temperance, others received pay for making the complaints. All of them were deeply resented by the public.[15]

One of the earliest prosecutions for violating the law was

brought against Gilbert Cummings, who kept a barroom opposite the National Theater in Boston. Early in April 1839, he was hauled before the Police Court on the charge of selling liquor. The accusers were two paper hangers and a carpenter. From their testimony, it is clear that they were reluctant to admit that they were paid informers. At one point the defense attorney asked one of them "Do you belong to a committee to inform against violations of the law?" The witness replied "I belong to a committee of my own." Later he was asked "Who appointed you to the committee?" and he replied "I appointed myself."

The jury had a problem with the case as well. They deliberated for about an hour and when they came back, they stated they had a special verdict: "We believe that a law exists restricting and forbidding the sale of ardent spirits in quantities less that fifteen gallons and we find that Gilbert Cummings … is guilty of infringing the said law." The implication was that the law was unjust but the defendant was still guilty. The defense attorney objected to this and the Judge instructed them to come to a simple verdict of either guilty or not guilty. After a short meeting, Cummings was found guilty and fined $20. The hearing room was very crowded and when the verdict was given, there was a disturbance.

Later, when the witnesses were ready to leave the courthouse, there were hundreds of men gathered outside, waiting to express their displeasure at the accusers. The newspapers reported that there was some plan to lynch them. The Judge kept the witnesses in a small room for two hours until the crowd had dispersed. When released, they slipped out a side door and escaped. In June, in another case, as the defendant was being brought to the courthouse, a large crowd blocked the door of the courthouse and the sheriff's men were required to keep the peace. In November, someone printed handbills and posted them in public places, trying to incite a mob against the Police Court.[16]

With resentment beginning to boil over, two informers, Asa A. Savels and Ezekiel A. Coleman, participated in 40 indictments before the municipal court in October. The most famous of those accused was Charles Taft, who kept the noted Chelsea House, located near the ferry landing in Chelsea. The indictments also covered John Albee (or Albree) who dealt in West India Goods and Francis Tukey, listed as a grocer, both of whom were from Boston. These informers were infamous for the number of times they testified against tavern keepers and other small businessmen. On the night of the 17th, Savels and Coleman took the 10 o'clock ferry from Boston to Chelsea, going home for the day. As they left the landing, Coleman told Savels that he should run, as he saw John Albee and feared what he might do. Before Savels could react, he was seized by a group of men and dragged to the stable next to the ferry landing. There they stripped him of his coat, beat him, and emptied a bucket of tar over his head then covered him with feathers. He was told "that it good enough for him, and he had better go home and mind his own business." The next day, the police had three suspects brought before the court for aggravated assault. They were John Albee, described as a grocer on Commercial St., Francis Tukey and Josiah Tewksbury, toll keeper of the Chelsea ferry.[17]

This was not treated as a simple case of assault but was looked on as an attack on the 15 gallon law itself. To prosecute, the plaintiffs hired Robert Rantoul, Jr., a well-known politician and lawyer. He began practicing law in 1829 and had acquired a reputation for taking on cases related to the major social movements of the early 19th century, including labor unions and slavery. One of his most important causes was that of temperance. As a member of the Massachusetts General Court in 1838, he was instrumental in getting the 15 gallon law passed. One newspaper claimed that the bill would not have been adopted if he were not in the legislature. Throughout 1839, he was traveling through Massachusetts, giving lectures on temperance and in support of the 15 gallon law. He was motivated to see that assaults on the informers were properly punished because without them there would be no way to enforce the law.[18]

On the defense side, the three men hired John C. Park, another well-known politician and lawyer. Like Rantoul, John C. Park went to Harvard and started practicing law in the 1820s. By 1835, he was on the Boston Common Council and in 1837 he was elected as a representative to the General Court from Boston. Unlike his opponent, Park was often in opposition to many of the major social movements. In 1837, after a riot on Broad Street between Irish immigrants and Yankee firemen, he defended several of the firemen and they were acquitted. Park was a very active defense attorney and appeared frequently in court notices. Like all defense attorneys, his clients were accused of many different crimes including a fraudulent employment office, counterfeiting, embezzling, murder, robbery, assault, and safecracking. Importantly, he seems to have been one of the most important lawyers defending those accused of violating the 15 gallon law.[19]

Before the Police Court, on the 18th, testimony by witnesses for the prosecution began. The first witness was the victim, Asa A. Savels, who described what happened to him but could not identify any of his assailants. His friend Ezekiel A. Coleman was next and he had no problem identifying some people. He claimed to hear Tewksbury point out the victim, saying "There goes Savels" just before he was seized. He testified that the man who actually seized Savels was John Albee, pointing him out in the courtroom. Coleman stated that there were four men assaulting Savels and when he went to help, four other men prevented him. When cross-examined, he stated that he had known Albee for four or five years. When he first saw Albee at the ferry landing, he wore a long tailed coat but when he seized Savels, he was dressed in a short jacket and cap. All of the men wore the same type of clothes and one had a mask on.

The next witness was William Perkins who came over on the ferry with the victim. He confirmed that Coleman had warned Savels about Albee. He saw Albee seize the victim and also tried to help but was stopped by Francis Tukey, who shook a fist in his face. He testified that he had known Tukey for three or four years. After they had finished tarring and feathering the victim, the witness testified that he saw Tukey kick him from behind.

After the prosecution witnesses finished, Park admitted that the testimony against Albee and Tukey, being as yet uncontradicted, was substantial but there was little against Tewksbury. He made a motion that he be discharged so that he could testify for the defense. The prosecution objected to this and the judge decided not to sever the defendants. At this time, court was dismissed for the day as Rantoul had a lecture to give that night in Salem. On the following Monday, the defendants would have their say in court and were put upon a bond of $500 each to appear the next week.

Park began the defense by stating that he had three sets of witnesses, a set for each defendant. He began with witnesses for

Tewksbury, most of whom were fellow employees of the ferry. They all stated that Tewksbury did not participate in the outrage and never went near the stable. Further the men who did assault Savels were all dressed in shabby pea jackets and large boots. One witness stated that they had their faces blackened and another said that he "never saw such a shabby looking set." Several of the witnesses said that they knew either Albee or Tukey but did not see them there that evening.

Next Park called three witnesses to state where Tukey was on that night and what he was doing. Jeremiah Tozier, the first witness was a cooper who lived in Boston. He stated that Tukey kept a bar-room at the corner of Commercial and Fleet Streets. Tozier was there from nine until just before eleven, when they went to Tukey's home. Tukey closed the bar soon after nine and they began making clam chowder at the bar. A second witness, who also had chowder, said that it was their habit, on Thursday nights to get together and make chowder. They finished eating a little after ten and then had a cigar. Park then introduced witnesses that demonstrated that Albee was at a restaurant in the North End, having oysters, at 10 o'clock that night. Given the solid alibis given for each of the defendants, there was little doubt of the outcome and the Judge dismissed them all.

Despite clear testimony, from disinterested witnesses, that Tukey and Albee were responsible for the assault, there seems to have been no attempt by the prosecution to impeach the testimony of their friends to the contrary. Rantoul does not seem to have cross-examined the witnesses, at least there is no mention of any in the newspaper accounts. As one newspaper reported, "...an alibi was made out, or some strange swearing was indulged in...."[20]

A few months after being acquitted in the assault case, on January 6, 1840, Tukey was again in court. However, this time, he was there of his own volition. He petitioned the court to declare him an insolvent debtor. The process of insolvency had changed greatly between the time Tukey was a baker in Salem and when he ran a bar in Boston. In 1838, Massachusetts enacted a major reform of the insolvency laws. Prior to this point, debtors could be arrested and put in jail until their debts were paid. The only restriction was the will of the creditor. The process was always instituted by the creditor not the debtor. Also, a debtor could conspire with one of his creditors to the detriment of all the others. Massachusetts considered this question as early as 1831, producing a report on the issue but little legislative action was taken. However, the widespread depression caused by the Panic of 1837 led to major business failures and the legislature was forced to address the issue.[21]

They passed a law, entitled "an act for the relief of insolvent debtors and for the more equal distribution of their effects," which adopted most of the recommendations in the 1831 report. It regulated the process of insolvency and created an equal division of assets between creditors. More importantly, for the debtor, it granted a discharge certificate from his debts, after giving up all the assets of his estate. Instead of having the debts hanging over his head, usually for the rest of his life, the debtor could begin again. It was under this law that Tukey, owing more than $500, submitted a petition on January 6, 1840, to Edward G. Loring, one of the masters in chancery for the County of Suffolk asking to be declared insolvent and asking that a warrant be issued for the seizure of his estate. At the same time, he submitted a list of his creditors and the debts he owed. Unfortunately, that list was not included in the preserved records.[22]

The warrant which authorized the seizure of his property identified him as a baker, even though he had been running a bar/restaurant for over three years. It may be that the effects of that failed ventures in Salem and Chelsea had finally caught up with him. The notice called for all his creditors to meet on January 27 in the office of Edward G. Loring, who was overseeing the case for the Suffolk County Court. The master appointed Abraham C. Paine to be messenger in the case. It was his job to put notices in the newspapers to alert Tukey's creditors to the upcoming legal events. At the direction of the master, Paine placed notices in the *Boston Morning Post* and the *Boston Daily Advertiser* beginning on January 7 and these were repeated once a week for the next three weeks. As part of the process, Tukey was required to give Paine a list of his creditors and Paine was to write personally to each of them to inform them of the insolvency. The final duty of the messenger was to hold the seized assets until the creditors decided how to divide them.

On January 27, the second meeting was held in Loring's office. The purpose of this meeting was for the creditors to agree to the appointment of one of their number as assignee, who would then oversee the division of the assets. Remarkably, none of Tukey's creditors showed up at the meeting. In lieu of any creditors, the master appointed Paine to be the assignee. On the next day, Charles E. Gay, Tukey's brother-in-law, came forward and swore the oath as assignee. As required by the law, another meeting was held on February 13 and again, none of Tukey's creditors appeared. At that meeting, Tukey swore his oath that he had turned over all of his estate to the assignee and was given a discharge for all of his debts.

Why none of Tukey's creditors would show up at either meeting is a mystery. If no demands were made on his assets, presumably, they were returned to him after he was discharged from his debts. The fact that his brother-in-law stepped in at the last minute to be his assignee, while not being one of his creditors seems rather suspicious.

At the age of 25, Tukey was a penniless failure with a wife and a brood of children to support. His first son was born around this time, although no record of the birth has come to light. His brother-in-law, Charles E. Gay, who so conveniently participated in the insolvency case, again came to his rescue. Tukey took over the grocery/bar at 237 Ann St., previously run by Gay. This establishment was also part of the area called the Black Sea. Ann Street, now renamed North, was adjacent to many of the wharfs on the waterfront of the North End. Gay moved to a slightly more respectable area at 102 Commercial St., where he operated another "grocery."[23]

By this time, changes had occurred in the battle for temperance and the regulation of the liquor trade. The 15 gallon law, enacted by the Whigs, was so unpopular that it had an effect in the election of 1839. The candidate for governor of the Democratic Party, Marcus Morton, ran in part against the 15 gallon law. He won, beating the incumbent Whig governor by one vote. The Democrats had not won in Massachusetts for over a decade. Morton took the oath of office in January 1840 and within a month, the 15 gallon law was repealed. Recognizing that total prohibition was not popular and could continue to cost them elections, the Whig-dominated legislature repealed the law and the bars were back in business.[24]

When the 15 gallon law was repealed, the status of liquor sales in Massachusetts was uncertain. No new law was enacted to regulate liquor sales. It was generally assumed that the legal situation reverted to the older licensing law but many believed that when the 15 gallon law was enacted, it repealed the earlier law, thereby leaving no legal basis for regulating sales. Most towns and cities in Massa-chusetts, despite the uncertainty, went back to the practice of licens-ing liquor sales. In accordance with the old law, the names of those applying for licenses to sell liquor were advertised for public com-ment. On April 8, 1840, Tukey was listed as a retailer on Ann St. His brother-in-law Charles E. Gay was listed as a victualler on Commer-cial Street. While Gay was engaged in selling a wide variety of goods, including alcoholic drinks, Tukey was running a barroom.[25]

However, the temperance movement was far from spent, despite the repeal of the 15 gallon law. The power to grant licenses for sell-ing liquor was granted to local town officials. In Boston, this meant the Board of Aldermen. Just because it was legal to grant a license, does not mean that they had to do so. In 1840, in order to continue restricting the sale of liquor, they chose to deny far more licenses than they granted. While Tukey and his brother-in-law were listed as applying for a liquor license, there is no indication that they were issued any.

Many in Boston thought the arbitrary nature of the licensing law was unfair, that it created a "privileged class" and created a monop-oly for selling liquors. They objected not only to the selective nature of the granted licenses but to the way the Board of Aldermen chose to enforce the restrictions. The Aldermen passed a resolution stating:

> Resolved, That in the opinion of this Board, all fair and honorable, yet ener-getic and determined means, should be used by all public officers, and pri-vate citizens, to put an end to the retail of spirituous liquors by persons not duly licensed.

This was a call for citizens and officers to spy on their fellow citi-zens and was thought to be un–American. One Boston editor fumed about the method chosen to enforce the law. He wrote:

> Besides is it *fair* and *honorable* to withhold licenses from a class of citizens equally as respectable as the licensed class—and then employ individuals at $1.75 a day, to loiter about and within the premises, to discover, if possible, any violation of their—the Mayor and Aldermen's—arbitrary, unjust, and impolitic rule? If the Mayor and Aldermen really think this course is *fair* and *honorable*, why, then their motives of what is fair and honorable differ somewhat from ours, and they are not the men we took them to be.[26]

An editorial published in Hartford, then reprinted in the *Bay State Democrat*, talked about the abuses of using paid informers. The editor decried the unfairness, pointing out that these "spies" would demand bribes from unlicensed sellers and if not given what they wanted, would report them to the authorities, where they then would receive half of the fines collected. The editor also decried the hypocrisy of the whole system, "no liquor shall be sold and the selling of liquor is a crime, and at the same time authorizes the sale of it for the price of a license." Given this system of paid informers, it was not long before large numbers of people were brought up on charges of violating the law.[27]

Early in July 1841, the Grand Jury indicted a large number of individuals for selling liquor without a license. Those who pleaded guilty paid their fine and were released. However, 47 men pleaded not guilty and were granted a continuance on condition that they post bail. Both Francis Tukey and Charles E. Gay, his brother-in-law, were charged before the Municipal Court with selling liquor without a license and pleaded not guilty. They had to post a bond of $150 each that they would show up for their trial. Although posting a bond and, eventually, going to trial was more expensive, it was a risk well worth taking. There were cases being tried that challenged whether the licensing law was repealed by the enactment of the 15 gallon law in 1838. If so, then no licenses were legal and there was no legal basis for prosecution.

Even if the legality of licenses were upheld, pleading not guilty and getting a continuance meant that there would have to be 47 separate trials. With other such indictments, it was reported that there were more than a hundred such trials required. This would create a major roadblock in the Municipal Court and with other continuances, and other delays, a particular trial might be delayed for years. Despite objections from the defense attorney, the court chose to keep the names of the informants secret until the trials.[28]

The first of the trials began on August 21 when Alpheus Grant was called to face the charge of unlicensed sales. Samuel D. Parker, county attorney, began the proceedings with an extensive opening statement, designed not just for this case and jury, but to influence all the juries to come in future cases. He knew that it would be reprinted by the major newspapers and widely circulated and discussed. His critics would later argue that he tainted the jury pool by this statement. In his opening, Parker set out to demonstrate that the authorities acted in a legal way in obtaining evidence. He stated that violators were repeatedly warned to stop selling alcohol without a license. Further, it was unjust to refer to the informants as "pimps and spies" in that they were performing a job for the City in the same way as watchmen or constables. To avoid criticisms leveled at informants under the 15 gallon law, these men were given "express orders not to drink themselves or to treat others, but only see if spirit was sold."

Grant did not have an attorney but chose to defend himself. None of the newspapers report much about what he said in his own defense. The main testimony was from witnesses who were in Grant's establishment and saw gin and brandy being ordered and consumed. Presumably these witnesses were the "pimps and spies" being paid by the government. The jury was unable to reach a verdict with eight in favor of conviction and four against. The four who were against conviction were convinced that the witnesses had seen customers call for spirits, seen it delivered and consumed. However, as the witnesses only saw the liquid but did not taste it, they could not swear it was actually liquor. Clearly this was not something the authorities were expecting but reflects the public reaction against the prosecutions.[29]

After the first of the license law trials, there was a delay due to the absence of the attorney that many of the defendants had hired. Benjamin F. Hallett was a well-known lawyer who was already famous as a Democratic Party organizer and supporter of the little guy against moneyed interests. He was an abolitionist, argued against banking abuses, and defended the rights of the Mashpee Indians against the Commonwealth. Although Hallett was a temperance advocate, he believed in moral suasion rather than governmental coercion. He was one of three who advocated before the legislative committee investigating the repeal of the 15 gallon law. He was an active public speaker and may have been on a tour in late August.

Hallett had returned in September and was present on the 21st when the trial of Charles Pfaff began. Pfaff ran the German Coffee House on Pleasant Street. The county attorney had learned much from the previous trial. Pfaff was specifically charged with two counts of breaking the original license law. The first section called for a $100 fine for selling without a license and the second for a fine of $20 for each drink so sold. Parker, the County Attorney, went straight to the heart of the problem which caused the last jury problems. The agent who saw the sale had not tasted the drink and so could not swear that it was liquor. Parker argued that if liquor was called for, mixed, and handed to a buyer, who then paid for it without complaint, that it was only logical that it was liquor that was sold. Further, he said that if the seller served a drink, no matter what it was called, that was not really liquor, he could testify to that under oath which the defendant did not do.[30]

Hallett, for the defense, argued that there was no legal requirement for a license as the 15 gallon law, when enacted, had repealed the previous law. Now that the 15 gallon law had been, in turn repealed, there was no license law. He also argued that, even if there was a license law, it was unconstitutional as it granted monopolies to a favored class. Parker was ready for both of these arguments. He pointed out that the Massachusetts Supreme Court had already decided, in 1839, that the 15 gallon law had not repealed the previous statutes and they were still in effect. Therefore, even though the 15 gallon law had been repealed, it did not affect the earlier law. As to the unconstitutionality of the license law, numerous cases had been judged under the previous law and it had never been challenged. The jury was out three hours and came back with a verdict of guilty and Pfaff was fined $100.

Given that the Massachusetts Supreme Court had decided the license law was still in effect and constitutional, it would seem the issue was settled. However, Boston juries continued to have problems with the issue to the point that the Municipal Court Judge, Peter O. Thatcher, took to asking potential jurors if they had already formed a negative opinion of the legality of the law. If they answered yes, they were dismissed. This would seem to be a bias against the defendants. The issue came to a boiling point during the trial of Jeremiah Brown on November 10, 1841. Brown had not hired a defense attorney and so spoke for himself. After the evidence was presented, the jury went to deliberate and returned four hours later saying they were deadlocked. The foreman of the jury, B.F. Gould, stated that one of the jurors doubted the constitutionality of the law and they asked advice of the judge. This led to a discussion between the county attorney, Samuel Parker, the defendant and the judge concerning whether the jury could decide such an issue. Eventually, the judge convinced the jury that they could not write laws themselves. After another 10 minute deliberation, the jury found Brown guilty of two counts but could not agree on two others. Brown was fined $120 and that would seem to have ended the case.[31]

However, John C. Park, defense attorney for many of the license case defendants, asked if he could make a motion before the jury. Parker objected to this unexpected intrusion by a lawyer who was in no way connected with the case. Thatcher suggested Park put his motion in writing and it would be considered but Park said it was important that it be heard in court because it depended on a question he had to ask the Judge. Thatcher then dismissed the jury but Park commented that the judge had already done so but the jury was still there because they wanted to know the answer as well. He went on to state that he was representing 18 defendants in the license cases and, after watching the impaneling of jurors in the present case, he felt he could not get a fair trial for his clients.

Not unexpectedly, Parker interrupted Park, asking if it was the right of any attorney, not connected to the case, to be heard without asking permission of the prosecuting officer? Park was asking if the Judge had said that any potential juror who had doubts about the constitutionality of the law would be dismissed. Judge Thatcher denied that was what he said but rather that he was talking about those who had already formed the opinion that the law was unconstitutional. The foreman of the jury spoke up and agreed that the judge had not used the words that Park inquired about. Park was satisfied with the judge's answer and that his clients would receive a fair trial.

Parker then objected to Park's making a public speech to influence public opinion. He pointed out Benjamin Hallett, another defense attorney, and accused him of reporting to the press in order to get jurors to disagree. Hallett denied this and stated that Parker had personally paid two papers to print his own speeches in order to influence the public. At this point all three lawyers began speaking at the same time and the courtroom became a raucous debating society. The Judge adjourned the court and told the lawyers they could argue on their own time. The troubles between the lawyers reflected the tension that these cases were fostering in Boston. A correspondent wrote to a paper in New Hampshire:

Judge Thatcher and the public attorney, Mr. Parker, are trying hard to convict a list of liquor dealers for selling without license. But the juries seem to have grown obstinate, and either will not agree, or return verdicts of acquittal. These prosecutions are becoming very unfashionable.[32]

Public opinion took a more direct approach after the verdict in the Brown case. It was reported that several bottles filled "with offensive and filthy matter" were thrown through the windows of Benjamin Gould's house, seriously damaging the carpets. Gould had been the foreman of the jury and it was his question to the judge that led to the conviction of Brown. There was great outrage in the press that a juror, doing his duty under oath, was attacked. About a month later, a similar attack was made on the house of Henry Loring—it was thought, however, that the perpetrators actually wanted to attack the house of Ira Gibbs, deputy marshal, who was involved with the liquor license cases. The Board of Aldermen were petitioned to offer a reward for the conviction of the persons responsible for the outrages. The mayor was authorized to offer $1000 as a reward.[33]

While these trials were proceeding, Tukey could not stay out of trouble. On August 3, 1841, it was reported that Tukey assaulted a man named Jonathan B. Lewis. The report stated that Tukey ran a "restorator" on Commercial St. where a disturbance among some sailors occurred. The ruckus caused a crowd to gather at the front door and Tukey noticed Lewis in the crowd. He told him to go away, called him a loafer and, reportedly tried to hit him with a bottle. There is no reason given for Tukey's animosity but Lewis may have been one of the paid informers involved in the licensing trials. Later the same day, Lewis came back to Tukey's place and, when again ordered to go away, stayed where he was. Tukey then hit him and they began to grapple with each other. It was reported that Tukey hit Lewis a number of times with a slungshot. This was a short rope with a "monkeyfist" knot at the end which enclosed a lead weight. The reporter said that Lewis's left eye looked "as if a Rhode Island horse, with all four shoes on one foot, had kicked it."

The use of a potentially lethal weapon in the assault could have had serious consequences for Tukey. However, he had a witness who swore that there was no weapon. Conveniently, this was his brother-in-law, Charles E. Gay, who testified that he pulled Tukey off Lewis and if there had been a weapon, he would have seen it.

Despite this, the judge ordered a trial in the Municipal Court and J. C. Park was listed as the attorney for the defense. On the day of the trial, Tukey paid Lewis $50 and the costs of the court and was discharged.[34]

As the assault case went out with a whimper, the license violation cases did as well. Samuel Parker, the district attorney, had already publicly stated that he regretted having to prosecute these cases. The start date was postponed a number of times through the end of 1841 and into early 1842. He was about to start the prosecutions in May of 1842 when a compromise was reached. Parker stated that he was approached by four of those indicted who wished to avoid the cost of government witnesses being called. They proposed to come into court, admit to one violation, and pay the fine of $20. Parker accepted this and offered the same to all those indicted. There were not more of these trials.[35]

Francis Tukey's first ten years in Boston did not go well. He lost several businesses and went bankrupt at one point. He was on the wrong side of the law a number of times. He took direct action when he thought someone had offended him. The tar and feathering incident and the assault on Jonathan B. Lewis were both likely the result of those men testifying against him. His involvement in the licensing controversies of the 1830s and early 1840s had again brought him in contact with the court system and had cost him a great deal of money. At the age of 27, in 1842, he seems to have reached a crossroads in his life. The path he took from here would determine his place in history.

2

"But is he capable, assiduous, fearless in the discharge of his duty?"

After acquiring a less than stellar reputation in the previous decade, Francis Tukey set out to change his life in an unexpected way. He applied to and was accepted at the Harvard Law School. This must have seemed an abrupt change to both his friends and his enemies. A later newspaper article suggested that in defending himself over the past few years, he developed "a passion for the law." Whatever his reasons, he faced a daunting task. Tukey had been on his own since he was 15 and his education was elementary at best. The law school did not require any previous studies but 75 percent of the entering students had graduated from college. Succeeding in this environment would require great perseverance. Tukey moved the family from Boston to Cambridge and entered the school in 1841, only three weeks after his settlement in the Jonathan Lewis assault case. In addition to tuition of $100 per year, students were required to post a $200 bond with the university steward. An important requirement for admission was that the student present testimonials "of a good moral character" and no student would be matriculated without such references. It would be interesting to know from whom Tukey solicited these testimonials.[1]

Harvard Law School was a departure from the usual way men became lawyers in the 19th century. Normally, a man would apprentice with an experienced lawyer and learn by both reading and observing actual practice. There were no classes or lectures. The apprentice's exposure to the law would be restricted to the cases in which his teacher was involved. This led to a narrow focus for the student based on what his preceptor was involved with. He was expected to read privately to increase his knowledge. This system often led to lawyers who were inexperienced with the law in cases they were hired to prosecute.

The concept of a law school was that it exposed students to the broad expanse of the law in a structured way. Under Supreme Court Justice Joseph Story, who came to the school in 1829, the study of law was conducted as a science. While the school had been established in 1817, it was under Story that it became the leading law school in the country. Charles Sumner, in recalling this time, commented on the affection between Story and the students. He is quoted as saying, "He treats them all as gentlemen. ... The good scholars like him for the knowledge he distributes; the poor (if any there be) for the amenity with which he treats them and their faults."

The other professor at the school, who was in charge of the daily activities, was Simon Greenleaf. He was born in Massachusetts, but grew up in Maine. He practiced law in Portland from 1818 until he was appointed a professor at the law school in 1833. It is unknown if Greenleaf knew Tukey or his family in Portland but it remains a possibility. Greenleaf commented on the difference between studying in a law office or in the law school. He stated that studying the law as a science meant that the law was, "mastered with a facility and readiness, and in a spirit of sound philosophy, to which the student in his private clerkship is almost totally a stranger." Relations between the two professors and their students were extremely close and different from that of the average undergraduate student, who reportedly looked on the faculty as their "natural enemies."[2]

At Harvard, law students were expected to complete at least three terms of 20 weeks each and would then be recommended for the degree of bachelor of law (LLB). There were no specific classes but the professors would lecture on a book and comment on it. Students were expected to be ready to debate the various points expounded by the professor. In the catalogue, there is a long list of books which were used in various aspects of the course. There are 20 marked with an asterisk which were required for the regular course of instruction. After completing all the requirements, a student would still not be a lawyer. They would have to become familiar with the practice of law in their state and then pass the bar. The school stated, "No public instruction is given in the local or peculiar municipal jurisprudence of any particular state; but the Students are assisted by the Professors, as occasion may require, in their private study of the law and practice peculiar to their own States."[3]

In the catalogue of all the students, they are listed by name, where they are from and where they are staying. Many of the students are renting rooms from the University and their listing is by a letter, designating which Hall they are in and then the room number. The rent of a room varied from 75 cents to $1.25 per week. Those students who chose not to stay at the University are listed by the name of their hotel or the name of the boarding house keeper with whom they are staying, such as Mr. Thurston's or Mrs. Sawyer's. Tukey is listed as being from Boston and has his own residence identified as "Mr. Tukey's." In addition, two other students, Benjamin F. Cook and Sedgwick L. Plummer, are also listed with rooms at Mr. Tukey's. Both of these students list their residence as Gardiner, Maine. It is likely that Tukey took in these students to help make expenses meet. That Tukey was not living in a dorm is not surprising as he had a wife and three children at the time. He either owned or rented a house in Cambridge. This is an unusual arrangement as there are only two other students who appear to be staying on their own out of over a hundred.[4]

Tukey was at the Harvard Law School from 1841 to 1843. The Greenleaf papers list students by term and class. Tukey was first listed as a student in the August term of 1841 and is listed through the terms of 1842. On January 3, 1843, Tukey took the part of the defense in a moot court case, which Greenleaf recorded. In the March term of 1843, he was listed but his name was crossed out. At the end of the two years, as suggested by the school's catalogue, he was awarded a bachelor of law degree. He was examined before the Supreme Judicial Court of Massachusetts on March 7, 1844, and was admitted to practice law in all courts in the Commonwealth. Perhaps the significance of his experience at the college is demonstrated by another event in late March of the same year. Tukey and his wife welcomed their second son on March 29, 1844, and named him Greenleaf Story Tukey. Naming his son after his two college professors must have been important to him. That this was after both graduating from the law school and passing the bar, when he was under no further obligation, shows the depth of feeling his college experience had on him.[5]

Within a short time, Tukey was practicing law with a partner named George D. Wilmot in Boston. Wilmot was from Western Massachusetts, most recently from Lenox, and had been a Harvard Law School contemporary with Tukey. Their ad, published in the *Trumpet & Universalist Magazine*, first appeared in September 1844. This is an interesting choice of where to advertise. They do not seem to have advertised in any of the Boston newspapers, despite their office being located in the city. The choice of a religious periodical seems odd for a pair of lawyers.[6]

They shared an office at 20 Court St. in Boston, otherwise known as Tudor's Building. Frederic Tudor, later known as the "Ice King" for his business of shipping New England ice all over the world, built a granite, three-story structure at the corner of Court Street and Court Square in the early 19th century. This was directly adjacent to the courthouse and was a favorite location for lawyer's offices. To prove their professionalism as lawyers, their ad listed a number of prominent lawyers and politicians as references. Two of the references, Joseph Story and Simon Greenleaf, were their professors at the Harvard Law School and could have recommended either of them. The other four were H.W. Bishop, Charles A. Dewey, George N. Briggs and Julius Rockwell.

These were all men that Wilmot was acquainted with from western Massachusetts. Bishop, was a lawyer with whom Wilmot had read law and he wrote a letter of recommendation to the Harvard Law School for Wilmot. Dewey had served as District Attorney for the Western District and was currently a justice of the Massachusetts Supreme Court. Briggs was another lawyer active in the western part of the state and had, in 1844, become governor of Massachusetts. Rockwell had practiced law in Pittsfield and was then in the U.S. House of Representatives. This was quite an impressive list of references but most of them were for Wilmot and not Tukey.[7]

It is difficult to assess the extent of Tukey's law practice. Only the most sensational or topical cases were reported in the newspapers in enough detail to list the lawyers involved. The first trial we know he was involved with involved a dispute of pilotage fees. As the

British-owned brig *Zephyr* approached Boston Harbor, Elbridge G. Martin, a Boston licensed pilot, hailed the master of the brig asking, "Will you take a pilot?" and the master, John Hilton answered "Yes— if you will take me where I am bound–Weymouth." Martin told him he would guide him through Boston waters and then he could get a river pilot. Hilton tried to negotiate with him but Martin said he would charge him for pilotage whether he took him or not. Hilton replied, "I'll see about that." The brig continued on its way to Weymouth, traversing Boston harbor and Martin brought a suit against Hilton for not paying his fees.

Massachusetts, like most states, had laws that required a foreign vessel to pay an experienced pilot to guide them into the harbor. The law stated that any foreign vessel that was met by a pilot outside the lighthouse, at the harbor entrance, was subject to pilotage fees whether they took on the pilot or not. Tukey filed the suit in the Court of Common Pleas as an action of assumpsit, essentially a breach of contract. He contended that the brig came into and through the port of Boston and Martin was entitled to his fees. Further he alleged that it had been the custom for over 40 years for pilots to escort vessels though Boston waters even if that was not the destination of the vessel. The defendant's lawyer, Peter S. Wheelock, objected to the use of custom as the duty and rights of pilots were fixed by law. He further made the point that the brig was not bound for Boston but for Weymouth. Judge Merrick agreed with the defense and excluded the evidence of custom. Further he agreed that the ship was not heading for Boston but Weymouth, so the pilot was not entitled to his fees. Tukey raised objections to the ruling and the case was passed to the Massachusetts Supreme Judicial Court. On March 23, 1846, the Supreme Court decided that Tukey's exceptions were warranted and granted a new trial.[8]

Two of his other cases ended up in higher courts, one in the U.S. District Court and the other in the Massachusetts Supreme Court, and were reported in the newspapers. The first involved wages owed to a sailor from the ship *Sophia Walker* and the second was a divorce petition on the grounds of desertion. In both cases, the courts agreed with Tukey and granted his claims. It is unknown what other cases he might have been involved with but he seems to have been successful in his new profession. Given that he spent a good portion of the

1830s in the North End by the waterfront, it is interesting that two of the three cases involved his representing sailors against their ships. It may be that he was remembered there when a lawyer was needed.[9]

Soon after these cases, the partnership of Tukey and Wilmot seems to have been dissolved. George D. Wilmot appears to have left Boston sometime after October 1845. Early in the next year, Tukey began an extensive advertising campaign in the Boston newspapers touting his solo practice. The advertisement began, "Francis Tukey, Attorney and Counsellor at Law." It lists his office at 20 Court Street (Room No. 18). This advertisement first appears in the *Boston Daily Atlas* in March 1846 and continues into June of the same year. It is also found, during the same period, in at least three other Boston newspapers. It seems that Tukey was making a serious effort to boost his legal career through advertising until the middle of 1846. The advertisements stop in June of that year when Tukey's life took another unexpected turn.[10]

On June 22, Mayor Josiah Quincy, Jr., nominated Francis Tukey to be city marshal of Boston and the Alderman confirmed his nomination. Given the amount of money Tukey had been pouring into advertising his law practice, this nomination seems an abrupt change. Tukey's nomination was a surprise to many in Boston as well. The Boston newspapers had reserved but generally positive reports on his new position. The *Boston Post* said that he was "a member of the Suffolk bar, who has educated himself by his own industry, and we congratulate him on his appointment, in the expectation that he will make an efficient and judicious officer." The *Boston Mail* reported that "the inquiry in everybody's mouth is 'Who is Francis Tukey?'" The *Boston Eagle* replied that he was a Court Street lawyer and commented on the fact that he was appointed by a Whig mayor and aldermen despite his being one of the "unterrified democracy." Tukey was a Democrat and it was unusual for the other party to make such an appointment. The *Boston Bee* agreed that the inquiry should not be what his politics might be but rather "is he capable, assiduous, fearless in the discharge of his duty." From the reaction of the Boston press, it is clear that Tukey was a surprise choice for the office of city marshal.[11]

The fact that Tukey and Quincy were of different parties was odd enough but how did two men from such different backgrounds meet?

As we have seen, Tukey's background was with the working class of Boston. His experience was running a bar in the seediest neighborhood of Boston. Quincy was the son of a family whose roots in Boston were as old as any and was clearly part of the upper class. A tax list, from 1845, showed that Josiah Quincy, Jr., had property valued at $191,000. Prior to becoming mayor, he had served as president of the Boston Common Council from 1834 to 1837 and he was president of the Massachusetts Senate in 1842. While it is possible they met earlier, the most likely time they came in contact was when Tukey was attending the Harvard Law School. During that time, Josiah Quincy, Sr., was the president of Harvard University and his son, the future mayor, was often on campus. It is reported that Tukey was a "personal friend" of Mayor Quincy.[12]

Tukey had the qualifications to be city marshal, based on the men who had previously held that office. Of the five men who held this position before Tukey, all but one were lawyers. Four were from Boston's elite families and three of them went to college at Harvard. The other two did not go to college. One, who did not go to college, was a graduate of Harvard Law School. It seems that a knowledge of the law was important for the job but no specialized law enforcement training was necessary. No matter how they met or his background, Tukey seemed to be the type of man Quincy needed to reshape law enforcement in Boston.[13]

That Josiah Quincy, Jr., was concerned about the police in Boston was evident in his inaugural address on January 5, 1846. After general introductory remarks, Quincy began to mention his priorities as mayor. The first was widening and straightening the streets. Then he discussed revising the City Ordinances relating to the police:

> Since many of these were framed, the population has nearly trebled, and the mode of doing business with the country, owing to the establishment of railways, has entirely changed. The police regulations of a large City must differ from those of a small one. They should in no case restrain individual liberty, except where it is necessary for the greatest good, of the greatest number. But they should be clear and simple, the officer should have a single and defined duty, and be held strictly responsible for its performance. ... I would recommend the subject to your earliest attention.[14]

Fortunately, Mayor Quincy left a description of what qualities he thought the city marshal should have. This was after Tukey had been in the job for a year. The mayor began by stating that all police-men, because of what they had to contend with, needed to be of "high character" and to attract such men, the job had to compensate them adequately. This was particularly true of the head of the department. That individual, "should unite a strong intellect, the power of influ-encing and directing men, and great physical and moral courage. In addition to this, his labors are more varied and arduous than almost any officer of the government." As he had nominated Tukey for the position the year before and continued to do so throughout his three years as mayor, we have to believe that Josiah Quincy believed that Francis Tukey was just such a man.[15]

While Mayor Quincy, in his inaugural address, did recommend a review and updating of the police ordinances, his focus was not what we might think of as law enforcement. In his address, he did not mention things like gambling, vice or the heated controversies over alcohol. His specific focus was on the ordinances "that relate to the removal of obstructions in the streets, and on the sidewalks." This was in keeping with the original purpose of the city marshal. In the ordinance authorizing the establishment of this office, the marshal was "to enforce the by-laws and ordinances." But in the two decades since the office was established the nature of police work in Boston had changed. In 1823, when Benjamin Pollard became the first city marshal, the structure of law enforcement was based on the long established Colonial pattern. At the time, the police functions were carried out by two distinct but related groups, the constables and the watch. The constables were appointed by the city council and received a salary. Originally they served for a year but by the 1820s, constables were serving for multiple years and were becoming more professional. Much of their work involved carrying out orders of the court and serving notices.

The watch was drawn from the general body of citizens and were forced to serve for a specified period. They were paid in fees as wit-nesses and for attendance at court. They worked at night, patrolling the streets, looking for fires, drunks and other potential disturbers of the peace. Neither of these groups had any investigative ability. Both the constables and the watch had the power of arrest with-out warrant, that is if they saw a crime, they could make an arrest. However, that power was very limited. They could only exercise it in public places, on the highways and at night. When the office of city marshal was created, it was specifically focused on seeing that the ordinances passed by the city were enforced. How ineffectual this was can be seen by the requirements of the job. He was to "receive complaints during stated hours and to walk the streets, at least once a week, in order to uncover violations."[16]

There were a number of events over the years that showed the inadequacy of this police structure in a rapidly growing city, but none was more serious than the Broad Street Riot of 1837. On June 11, a company of volunteer firemen were returning from fighting a fire

Josiah Quincy, Jr.

Josiah Quincy, Jr., Mayor of Boston 1846–1848. Quincy and Tukey probably met when Tukey was a student at Harvard Law School. Quincy appointed Tukey City Marshal in 1846 and charged him with developing an "active" police force.

and stopped at a tavern to refresh themselves. Boston's firemen were all organized in volunteer companies, which were more like social clubs, and had no relation to the city government. The firemen were drawn from the working class and were consistently native-born and Protestant. The refreshed firemen left the tavern "in a more or less bellicose mood" and were returning to their station house. They ran into a group of about 100 Irishmen who were heading to a funeral procession.

Most of the firemen had passed through the crowd of Irishmen without incident until a scuffle broke out. The firemen, greatly outnumbered and beaten, retreated to their station house. Licking their wounds, the firemen sent out runners to ring the church bells, which would call out all of Boston's fire companies. A company responding to what they thought was a real fire alarm accidently ran its horses and wagon into the funeral procession. The Irish, knowing of the earlier altercation, immediately thought this was an intentional assault and the fight was on.

Irishmen came out of their houses in the area to help their relatives. As more and more fire companies arrived and Protestant workmen from all over Boston joined to help the firemen, the battle turned against the Irish. The Protestant crowd swelled to as many as 12,000 and they rampaged through the Irish neighborhood, breaking windows, smashing down doors, beating, looting and destroying. One paper reported that the street "was covered ankle deep with feathers and straw from the beds of houses that had been sacked, and the furniture destroyed and thrown from the windows."[17]

There was no police response to this riot. There were only 24 constables and none were on duty during the day on a Sunday. The watch was composed of many of the same people who were rioting and, even if they were not, there was no way to call them out or organize them. The riot was only quelled when Mayor Samuel A. Elliot, called out the militia. At the head of a column of cavalry and 800 bayonet wielding infantry, Elliot finally dispersed the crowd after about three hours. This event led to major developments in both the fire and police departments. The volunteer fire companies were dismissed and replaced with a professional force paid by the city.

Mayor Elliot proposed a new class of police officers who would "actively seek it out on their own before trouble had time to reach serious proportions." These would be full-time, professionals who worked during the day and were the responsibility of the city marshal. Their main purpose was to keep riots from developing but they were more active. While the city marshal was required to walk around the city at least once a week to look for violations of the ordinances, these men would do so every day. The act authorizing the City of Boston to hire "police officers" was short and simple. In one paragraph it authorized the mayor and alderman to hire officers as they saw fit and gave them all the powers of constables without that of serving civil process. They were to be employed at the pleasure of the mayor and aldermen. The Massachusetts legislature authorized the hiring of the police offices in 1838 and by July there were nine men so employed by the city.[18]

The new men patrolled the city, as they were intended, but did not materially change the nature of policing in Boston. They were successful in that no major riots occurred in Boston over the next few years but little else changed. By 1845, the force had risen to 12 men. Generally the politicians and the public were satisfied with their efforts and little notice was taken of them. The newspapers that reported on the activities of the police did so in a factual manner without any fanfare. With the election of Josiah Quincy, Jr., as mayor in 1845, that was about to change. While his first inaugural address may have simply suggested enforcing the city ordinances, he saw the police as a way of reforming society and his new city marshal agreed with him. Francis Tukey was sworn in as city marshal on July 1, 1846, by Mayor Quincy. The regular force was more than doubled at this time as 18 new men were hired, bringing the total to 30. Up to this point, the new force had patrolled only during the day but eight of the men were now detailed as a special night force.[19]

A traditional way of reforming the social fabric of the community was by the restriction of certain activities, either by outright prohibition or by licensing how and when those actions could take place. This would be Mayor Quincy's tool for changing the city. The power to license was granted by the legislature to the city of Boston. The city government would pass ordinances for the licensing and it would be the city marshal's responsibility to see that they were carried out. The first test of this system was already in the process of being set up when Tukey became marshal.

For a long time, young boys and girls had been making a nuisance of themselves in selling various goods on the streets, including newspapers. One of the first actions required of the police, under Tukey, was the regulation of the newsboys who roamed the streets of Boston. These were young, poor boys who were able to make some money by selling newspapers to passersby. In this competitive environment, they sometimes got boisterous and out of hand, often fighting with each other. They also fought with other groups who tried to prey on them, most notably the Irish apple girls. In 1843, ten newsboys were indicted for being a nuisance in State Street and complaints continued to be made about them over the next several years.

In April 1846, the legislature passed an act regulating hawkers and peddlers, making special provisions for minors who sold things. The act did not specifically regulate the sale of newspapers, giving that authority to the individual cities and towns. The Common Council of Boston, on June 26, sent an order to the mayor and aldermen directing them to restrict the sale of articles by minors, as specified in the act passed in April. The mayor and aldermen, on June 30, promulgated regulations for the sale of items, including newspapers, by anyone under 21 years of age. They were to be licensed and to have a set stand from which to sell. They also had to have attended at least three months of school in the previous twelve months. They were to wear a brass badge on their caps to show they were licensed. The act of the legislature took effect on July 1, 1846, and Boston immediately began the licensing of newsboys.[20]

On July 7, there were 18 newsboys granted licenses by the city. They were required to pay 75 cents for the license and were to wear a badge on their cap which read "licensed." One paper complimented the new arrangement saying that it eliminated a nuisance they had long complained about and made State Street much quieter. They described it as, "Eighteen in all, are now licensed, and they stand in different situations, and are not allowed to cry their papers." The fee of 75 cents was quite a large amount to the newsboys. One description of the business stated that the newspaper sold a dozen copies to the newsboy at 15 cents. They would then sell them at 2 cents each, earning 9 cents per dozen. They would have to sell more than eight dozen just to make the money for the fee.[21]

Those who were licensed were a small proportion of those who had been selling newspapers. Not surprisingly, there was considerable opposition from those who were not licensed. This may have led to some violence against those who did have licenses. One report stated that there was to be a meeting of the non-licensed newsboys on the steps of the State House and that one of them would display "a handful of hair which he has extracted from the head of one of the monopolists." Whether this was true or not, it reflected the strong feeling against those who had gained licenses. The *Brooklyn Eagle* took the licensing of newsboys in Boston as an opportunity to poke fun at a rival. They decried the restraint of free competition and suggested that Boston was religious but not necessarily moral. Before the month was out, the police were to use this ordinance against the rowdiness of some of the boys. The marshal found four boys were guilty of "fighting, being noisy and leaving their stands." All four boys had their licenses revoked and four other boys were then licensed.[22]

The regulation of the newsboys by licensing might seem like a minor thing but it serves to point out a larger truth. The mayor and his marshal would use this same power to make major changes in the social life of Boston. In this particular case, it not only restricted the number of sellers but the way they could sell, eliminating a recurring nuisance that people had been complaining about. But it went beyond simply regulating commerce. By requiring all licensed newsboys to have attended at least three months of school, it also addressed the problem of truancy which was a problem in the growing city. Controlling a powerless group of poor boys was easy enough but Tukey was soon brought into conflict with some of the most powerful politicians in the city.

Nineteenth-century Boston was heir to a street system derived from when it was a small, colonial town. It was notorious for its crooked and narrow streets. The process of straightening and widening them was only beginning in the 1840s. Because of the road congestion, the city had always been concerned with keeping the streets clear. As early as 1809, the Massachusetts legislature had given the city the right to regulate carriages and wagons on its streets. While the city had a long-standing ordinance against leaving carriages in the streets, it had lacked both the force and the will to deal with the problem. In his inaugural address, the previous January, Mayor Quincy stated that the ordinances should be enforced and pointed to clearing the streets as an example.

With a new police force patrolling the streets and a city marshal willing to use it, this was bound to be one of the first things they tackled. Because the law had not been enforced before, the marshal had his men place notices in any vehicle which was standing too long in the street. These quoted the relevant portion of the ordinance and what the fine would be. Such a change met with opposition from many but the marshal directed them to read the laws. However, one case prompted him to question the range of his authority. On July 7, 1846, Marshal Tukey sent a letter to the mayor and alderman, requesting direction:

> To the Hon Mayor and Aldermen of the City of Boston: The undersigned respectfully represents that he has received an appointment at your hands, for which he begs leave to thank you. He also begs leave to represent to your Honors, that he has received directions from your honorable body to

put the city ordinances (in relation to carriages standing in the streets,) into force; and in so doing he has found some difficulty, objections being made to the same by some officers of the State and city; but in such cases he has recommended to them to examine the laws. He also begs leave to state that a serious case has occurred, in which he find it difficult to know how to proceed. One of your honorable body (Col. Pope) left his carriage standing, directly in front of City Hall, over three hours this day, and when we requested others to remove their carriages, they asked if the law did not apply to the City Fathers? Your direction in this matter is earnestly solicited.[23]

In this letter, Tukey is very hesitant about using his power to censure one of his bosses. He was well aware that Colonel William Pope was both a distinguished member of the Board of Aldermen and an incredibly wealthy man. He was representative of the class of men who ran the city. He, and his family, had become wealthy in the lumber business in Maine, where he also served as a colonel in the militia. Pope had moved to Boston in 1841 and almost immediately was elected to the Common Council. In 1845, he was elected to be an alderman, and he would serve for the next four years before moving on to the legislature. In his first week in the job, Tukey was faced with a most delicate situation. If Mayor Quincy wanted the ordinances enforced, would that apply not only to the vegetable truckmen in the North End or to all citizens of Boston? There is no record of what the reaction to this letter was but we have to believe that Quincy backed him up on this issue. In the future, Tukey was not reticent to cite law breakers, no matter their wealth or social position.[24]

Because the police were now to be active in the community, it was important for them to be identified as such. Up to this point, there was no uniforms or even a badge to distinguish law enforcement officers. Because they were to be on the streets daily and their job was not only to arrest criminals but to repress crime, the police had to be visible. As the first step in this process, the mayor ordered them to display a badge on their hat. The first of these were issued on July 7 and the only description published was that the "word 'Police' was conspicuous." It was reported that Tukey wore a badge that had "City Marshal" on it. The use of badges to identify the police and their reorganization was remarkably foreshadowed by a letter to the *Boston Daily Atlas* about a month earlier, the writer being identified only as "A Bostonian." He wrote:

These things need a remedy, and we can easily have it if our city authorities will only appoint a sufficient body of police, compel them when on duty always to wear a certain dress and badge, and give also to each policeman a certain beat or walk.

Who wrote the letter is unknown but it clearly stated how the new police would be deployed under Quincy and Marshal Tukey. The size of the force was more than doubled and each man was given a set route to patrol. The addition of the hat badge made them visible to the public and achieved two important goals. To those thinking of committing a crime, they acted as a deterrent. To those who wanted to report a crime, they were available on the street and not at the office, blocks away, as they had been. This was part of the active policing that both Quincy and Tukey were instituting.[25]

Much of the reorganization of the police department was based on developments on-going in London. The use of identifying badges and the establishment of regular patrols for the police were part of this system. Another aspect of the London system was a separate detective force, which had been established in London in 1842. Tukey created a detective bureau, based in the marshal's office, whose job it was to seek out the perpetrators of crime and recover stolen goods. Originally there were three men in this branch but it soon increased to five. This completed the reorganization of the police and while the number of officers would increase over the years, the basic system would last through the 19th century.[26]

Soon after taking office, Tukey was involved in an incident that tested both the reason for the reorganized police force and his own personal commitment to law enforcement. On July 19, he was walking near the head of Hamilton Street in the Irish Fort Hill neighborhood, close to where the Broad Street Riot began about a decade before. About 7 o'clock, he found a man, Daniel Sweeney, by all accounts drunk and yelling loudly, threatening vengeance on the man that had struck his child. There was a large group of onlookers who urged Sweeney to take his revenge. Tukey walked up to him and advised that he "not whip him now but go away—and come tomorrow and whip him as much as you please." Sweeney refused to leave, swore that he would fight, stripping off his coat and vest and rolling up his sleeves. Tukey called for the police and three of his men, Dexter, Henry and Borden were soon there. They were ordered to arrest Sweeney and to keep him until he was no longer drunk. George Dexter began to handcuff Sweeney, attaching one cuff to his hand. The crowd which had gathered around, perhaps in sympathy with Sweeney or disappointed there would be no fight, decided on a rescue attempt. They swarmed the police officers and knocked them down. Sweeney was repeatedly hitting Dexter, one of the downed officers with his own handcuffs. At this, Tukey waded into the crowd and grabbed Sweeney, who then hit the marshal. The crowd greatly outnumbered the officers, who were taking quite a beating. One of the downed officers suggested that they let Sweeney go. Marshal Tukey reportedly said, "Don't let him go. Every man of you die first." This sentiment attracted the notice of Garrett Fleming, one of the rioters, who replied, "Well, die it is," and struck the marshal below his left eye, knocking him down. In the space of a minute, he was knocked down two more times. Several in the crowd were heard to yell "kill the city marshal." The affray was ended only when police reinforcements arrived and a number of concerned citizens helped out. Sweeny, Fleming and two others were conveyed to jail for rioting.[27]

This was exactly the kind of mob action that the new police organization was designed to stop and it did so with only minor injuries. Tukey gained quite a reputation for his fierceness, one of the bystanders saying, "he fought like one of the b'hoys." A reporter stated, "Great credit is due to the city marshal for his prompt and efficient action in this affair." The men arrested went before the Police Court the next day. Daniel Sweeney was charged with assault on the two police officers, Dexter and Henry. He was ordered to find bail of $400 for each of the two charges or be sent to jail prior to his trial in Municipal Court. There was no way he could come up with the money and so was ordered to the Leverett Street jail. Before he was taken away, Sweeney told the court that he had two children and that his wife had run away and abandoned them. He was worried about what would happen to them. Remarkably, Marshal Tukey offered to take them in until Sweeney's fate was decided. One reporter stated that this was, "A commendable case of consideration and kind feeling in an officer of the criminal law." On August 16, Sweeney and the other three men was found guilty of rioting in Hamilton Street and were each sentenced to one year imprisonment in the House of

Correction. How long Sweeney's children stayed in the marshal's house is unrecorded.[28]

However, even if he had intended to keep them longer, events were happening that would make that impossible. Three weeks later, on September 4, Mary Tukey, his wife of 11 years, died of consumption in Cambridge. This was the older name for what we now know as tuberculosis and was a leading cause of death in the 19th century. She was buried at Mount Auburn Cemetery on September 14. This left Francis Tukey with four small children, ages 2 to 10, to care for by himself. Undoubtedly, he hired servants to help with the children. Given the debilitating nature of the disease from which Mary Tukey died, it is likely that the servants were already running the household before she died.

One of the many ordinances passed by the city council was against smoking in the streets. In early 1845, one newspaper, in commenting on the fact that Baltimore was contemplating a similar ordinance, hoped that Boston would begin enforcing its own ordinance. As part of the "active policing" under Tukey, a number of people were arrested for violating the non-smoking ordinance. The most sensational case was that of John Diamond, who intentionally walked up to two ladies on Hanover St. and blew a large cloud of cigar smoke in the face of one of them. While he was laughing about what he had done, he was arrested by two officers. Diamond was convicted of an "insulting" assault on the woman and of breaking the non-smoking ordinance. For his little joke, he was fined a total of $15. The concept of an active police force patrolling the streets was one Boston was having some trouble adjusting to and, like the controversy over Alderman Pope's carriage, the public waited to see if the laws would be applied equally. By the end of September, they got that question answered. Officer Lysander Ripley was coming out of a house while helping a sick family into the alms house cart. In coming out to the street, he forgot to extinguish his cigar. A passerby noticed and informed the marshal of the infraction. The officer was cited and paid the $2 fine and costs, amounting to a total of $5.78. One newspaper reported that this was the first time a city officer had been punished for violating the non-smoking ordinance, not because they did not smoke but because no one would make the complaint. Their conclusion was "Go ahead, Mr. Tukey."[29]

The business of regulating the city continued through the rest of the year. In September, the City Council passed ordinances for the licensing and control of vehicles in Boston. All such vehicles for hire had to get a license and to display a badge, not less than one and a half inches in height. They were to have specific stands where they could pick up passengers. Out of town lines could ask for a stand but the City Council would prescribe their routes. All of this would take effect in November and the police would monitor the practice. Another initiative of the City Council was to require that anyone who had a "coal hole" in a public street had to make sure that the cover was non-slippery to avoid pedestrians falling. This also was to begin in November. Finally in October, the City Council got around to the street obstructions that Mayor Quincy had mentioned in his inaugural address. The new ordinance applied to "Bay windows, shutters, steps, cellar door or arch ways, cases, fruit stands or merchandise of any kind" which was blocking the streets. If they were not removed after thirty days from time of notice, the owners would be fined. The city could pass these regulations and expect them to be followed because of their new patrolling police force.[30]

While regulating traffic and keeping the streets clear were things expected of the new force, Mayor Quincy saw the police as a way of reforming the morals of the city and fighting vice. One of the first steps in this campaign was the reform of the theaters. Traditionally, theaters were places where liquor was sold illegally and prostitutes openly practiced their profession. The "third tier" of seats was their domain and often theaters had divided the seats into semi-private spaces, or "slips," so they could meet their customers. Theaters had hired their own security to keep the crowds under control. On September 15, again using licensing as a way of forcing change, the City Council passed a new ordinance concerning theaters. It first stated that no liquor of any kind was to be sold in a theater, that there be no divisions in the third tier but that the seats be open on all sides and that no woman be admitted to the theater without an accompanying male. Security at the theaters was to be provided by regular policemen, under the direction of the city marshal. Any violations of the ordinance would result in the loss of the theater's license. The fight for the soul of Boston was on.[31]

Perhaps while seeing that this new ordinance was enforced,

on November 9, Tukey was forced to take a more active role in law enforcement. The Marshal was standing outside the Boston Theater when he saw a man jostling various people as he passed them on the street. He followed the man up Franklin Street to Washington Street where he observed him lift an ivory fan from a man's pocket. As he seized the thief, the man passed the fan to an accomplice. When the marshal seized the accomplice, he passed the fan back to the original thief and both began to run. Tukey caught the thief, whose name was John Hall, and had him charged as a pickpocket. This tendency for direct action, which we have seen earlier in his life, would continue to characterize Tukey's approach to law enforcement.[32]

Another aspect of the reform movement which had been gaining strength was the temperance movement. The number of citations for selling alcohol without a license increased dramatically toward the end of 1846 and these cases often resulted in convictions. Perhaps Tukey's own experience with the license law enabled him to enforce it better. Tukey also took a personal hand in dealing with some of these cases. On a Sunday in October he set out to find those who were selling liquor illegally on the Sabbath. As he arrived at Jefferson House, on Ann Street, he saw a sign which read, "This establishment is closed until Monday. P. S.—Those whom we agreed to supply with water will be served at the pump at the back door." He went around back and was directed to where he could get his "water." Arresting the seller, he closed the place down. On the same day, he arrested two other proprietors for violating the Sunday law. Taking "active policing" to heart, Tukey was out patrolling on his own for violators and enforcing the ordinances.[33]

Near the end of November, Boston got its first significant snow of the year. Keeping the sidewalks clear of snow and safe for pedestrians had long been a concern of the city government. Landowners were required to clear their sidewalks within six hours of the end of the snowfall or sprinkle ashes, sand or gravel on them. Like most ordinances, this one was not actively enforced in the past. After the snow of November 27, Tukey and his officers brought 28 people to the police court for not clearing their sidewalks. Those so cited were not your average landowners. They included two aldermen, the city solicitor and a number of prominent merchants. One newspaper commented, "Quite an array of 'our first men' were before the police court on Saturday morning." This was very different from the timid letter Tukey submitted to the mayor and alderman in July about enforcing the carriage ordinance. He must have been given permission to enforce the ordinances no matter who the offender might be.

The first person charged before the Police Court was Charles P. Curtis, prominent lawyer, and former U.S. Representative. He pleaded "nolo contendere" to the charge and said he was glad that Mr. Marshal Tukey was doing his duty. He further stated that "In former years he had done all that he could to induce Mr. Tukey's predecessor to enforce the law in regard to cleaning sidewalks of snow and ice, but under the present Marshal there was no necessity of urging, as the duty was performed before there was an opportunity." While that may have been a backhanded way of complaining about Tukey's swiftness to cite violators, it demonstrated the difference between the previous way of enforcing the law and the use of the new police force. Each of those cited paid a fine of one dollar and were released.[34]

After just half a year as city marshal, Francis Tukey had already made his mark on the city. The police force had been reorganized and became professional. It provided the city with a way of actively enforcing the laws without having to wait for the citizens to complain. Through the use of the licensing function, various nuisances were controlled or eliminated. In the prosecution of the liquor laws and the elimination of prostitution from the theaters, we see the first inkling that this new police could also be used to regulate the morals of the community. While his men were patrolling the streets, Tukey did not simply sit behind a desk but rather took an active part in ensuring the well-being of the city he was charged with protecting.

3

"A gang of daring villains broke and entered the store on the corner of Washington and Milk streets"

In late November 1846, the Whig Party again nominated Josiah Quincy, Jr., for mayor. His opponents were Charles B. Goodrich for the "loco focos"—Democrats—and Ninian C. Betton for the Native American Party. Quincy handily beat his opponents in the election held on December 14 and all eight Whig candidates for alderman were elected. This assured there would be no major political change in the city for the coming year. This would include keeping Francis Tukey as city marshal. In a New Year's Day editorial, the editor of the *Boston Daily Bee* extolled what had been accomplished in the last year by the city and listed all the major public works then in progress. He also said, "and as for our industrious city marshal, there is no end to his labors." A week later, the same editor, in commenting on Mayor Quincy's second inaugural address, said, "Thus far, the new city marshal, Mr. Tukey, has been indefatigably industrious and entirely independent in the discharge of his difficult office." Tukey had certainly impressed the editor of the *Boston Daily Bee* and his coverage in other available newspapers was generally favorable as well.[1]

On January 4, 1847, the mayor and city council met to take their oaths and organize the government. Mayor Quincy then gave his second inaugural address which outlined a number of ambitious city projects including the introduction of clean water, a city gas works, land filling, street widening and a number of other improvements. In describing the police, Quincy gives a view of their use to change the city, "Public and private good requires that vice, where it exists

49

should be checked and kept under control, and that the paths that lead to destruction should be closed against the entrance of the innocent, as far as it can possibly be done." While this, to modern ears, may sound normal, the idea of a police force actively engaged in combating vice was a novel idea. This was far from the idea, expressed in his first address, that the police were to enforce the ordinances about clearing the streets. Quincy goes on to point out, "the police officer who, from necessity is obliged to descend into the haunts of vice, should possess a high character. To secure such men an adequate compensation must be paid." He said that this was particularly true of the person who leads the police. This request for a higher salary for the city marshal was the first rumbling of what, later in the year, would prove a great embarrassment to Tukey.[2]

A new kind of problem was presented to Tukey on the morning of January 28 when the father of a 16-year-old girl from Milford asked him for help in finding her. As the story unfolded, a man named Joseph Woodman had been an occasional visitor to the man's home and had developed an attachment to the girl. Woodman was a widower with four small children and was 40 years old. He promised to marry the girl if she came away with him. Her father tracked the couple to Boston and now he needed help finding them in the city. This was not Woodman's first brush with the law. It was reported that he had spent some time at the Thomaston State Prison in Maine and had twice been before the Municipal Court in Boston on a charge of counterfeiting. Tukey sent officers to check and they traced the couple during the day without finding them. They heard that Woodman had said he concealed the girl where she could not be found.

As evening approached, the officers returned to the marshal to report their lack of success. Tukey believed that something remained to be done and he, accompanied by the officers, returned to the boarding house where Woodman was known to live at 22 Oneida Street in the Back Bay. He was told, as his officers had been earlier, that Woodman was not home. Observing a light in the front room, he demanded entrance but no answer was given. He procured a key in the entryway and they opened the door. There they found Woodman and the girl. She stated that she had been deceived and was eager to return home. There was no report that Woodman was arrested or charged with any crime.[3]

As Tukey was relaxing after successfully finding the missing girl, a robbery was being planned that would be the first real test of his new detectives. Richard Currier and Peter Trott, jewelers, watchmakers, and silversmiths, had been doing business in Boston as Currier & Trott since 1823. Their shop was located in a three-story building at the corner of Washington and Milk streets and was across Milk from the Old South Church. They shared this space with Widdifield & Co., opticians who also sold telescopes, barometers and other scientific instruments. Both of these businesses handled large amounts of gold and silver. It appeared that the robbers entered a cellar window on Saturday, hid themselves until the stores closed, and then spent all of Sunday opening the basement safe and collecting loot from the stores. Most of the silver vessels they left, probably being too heavy to easily transport. At one point, they had lunch, a remnant of which was found in the store. After dark on Sunday, they left with the stolen goods. The robbery was discovered Monday morning, the first of February.[4]

The iron safe, in the basement, held the most valuable items from both stores. It was a recent addition having been built in New York. It had originally used by John B. Jones of the firm Jones, Low & Ball in Boston. Like Currier & Trott, they were silversmiths, jewelers and watchmakers. The robbers spent considerable time forcing this safe open. It was described as an "iron safe with three doors." and was said to have five locks. The complexity of the safe did not deter the robbers. They, "bored into it in all directions; drew the bolts with wrenches (one of which was broken and left behind) and finally after defacing the entire front, succeeded in prying off the locks, and opening it." From the way the safe was opened, it was obvious that this was no amateur job.[5]

By all accounts, this was one of the biggest robberies in Boston history, with the total take between $10,000 and $15,000 (roughly $360,000 to $540,000 in 2022). Included in the list of stolen items were 64 gold watches belonging to the store and 12 belonging to customers, 38 silver watches and six others belonging to customers, gold chains to the value of $1000, 300 ounces of silver spoons, $400 in gold pins, $200 in gold pencils and $1000 in gold eye glasses. The robbers also took $350 in cash and a note of exchange for 50 pounds sterling. Getting this amount of heavy metal out of the store unobserved must have been quite a chore.

How would one solve a crime such as this in the 19th century? There was no thought of fingerprints as a means of identification. In fact, there was very little knowledge of forensic evidence at all. The best hope was to catch the thieves in the act but that had not happened. Alternatively, the police frequently used informants. Tukey undoubtedly did three things almost immediately. First, a reward was offered for information that would lead to the thieves and the recovery of the property. Originally the reward was $500 but was soon raised to $1000 or ten percent of the value of recovered goods. Secondly, he most likely sent his detectives around to every pawn shop and shady dealer in Boston to see if any of the loot had been converted to cash. Finally, his detectives probably sought out criminal informants and offered leniency on lesser crimes for information on the big one. There is no specific evidence that any of these led to useful information.[6]

An apparent break in the case came on February 7 when John Hall, the pickpocket arrested by Tukey in November, was being released from jail. A group of three men came to meet Hall and take him away. Tukey recognized one of the men as the accomplice who had gotten away. He had the detectives follow the men who ended up at the Suffolk House where one of them lodged. They were found in a room on the fourth floor, smoking cigars and drinking. The men were identified as Charles Morton, George Bell and William Brown. Tukey came and talked to them and decided to arrest them for committing the robbery. No specific reason was given for the arrest and none of the stolen property was found with them. It was reported that "some curious circumstances have come to light, which will be made public in due time." The suspects were to be brought to the Police Court on February 8 but the examination was postponed until the 10th because the marshal did not have sufficient time to collect all his witnesses. Each of the men was given bail at $15,000 but, not being able to raise the money, all were remanded to jail.[7]

The *National Police Gazette*, on hearing the tale of the arrest, was extremely skeptical of the action. It suggested that pickpockets were not capable of pulling off a crime like the robbery and that men who were capable of doing so did not act this foolishly. In conclusion, it pointed out, "False arrests are great checks to the detection of real thieves, and we hope therefore, that the Boston authorities will commence and end the examination of Bill Brown and his troop as soon as possible." However, its opinion changed dramatically the next week, when, "some private information having been put in our possession, we are satisfied that the three rogues now in custody on the charge of the above burglary are the real perpetrators." It went on to identify Charles Morton as the "notorious Charley Cooper" and William Brown as "Bill Henderson, alias 'Black Bill' both of whom were well known to the New York police as pickpockets. It seems that somewhere behind the pickpocket story, there was other evidence of their guilt."[8]

The examination in the Police Court to see if the case should be sent to the Municipal Court was begun on February 10. John C. Park, who had previously defended Tukey, was the attorney for the defendants. On this first day, there were 18 witnesses called, but most of their testimony was not reported. George Bell had been employed as a machinist at the mathematical instrument factory of Nathan Chamberlin and several of the workmen there were questioned. Numerous tools from the shop were produced and the witnesses all agreed these types of tools were probably used to open the safe. It was reported that "A skillful worker in iron and brass testified that he had little doubt that some of the incisions on the safe were made by the tools exhibited." Mr. Leman, a shoemaker, testified that on Saturday night, about 9 o'clock, he saw three men standing near the store and he knew one of them was Bell. He could not see the faces of the other two. He heard one of them say they "would have the place clear before daylight Monday morning." Two other witnesses, including Charles Starkweather, one of the detectives, testified to seeing Morton in the vicinity of the store several times on Sunday.

Testimony continued the next day with witnesses testifying that the kind of meat and bread found at the store had been delivered to the Suffolk House. Mr. Gault, a baker, testified that the French bread found in the store was of his making and that he sold it to the proprietor of the Suffolk House on Saturday. Other witnesses again placed Bell in the vicinity of the store on both Saturday and Sunday. A Mr. Cooley said he had known Morton for a while and met him at a public house in Tremont Row, the Friday after the robbery. Morton, who was intoxicated, told Cooley that he had a friend "who could get through anything in the shape of iron or a safe."

The examination concluded the next day when a Colonel Shattuck of Pepperell testified that he was coming up Milk Street on Sunday about noon when he heard a loud noise from the store. When he stopped to look, a man came up behind him and forced him off the sidewalk. He identified Bell as the man who pushed him. Park, the lawyer for the three defendants, offered no witnesses or evidence but consented to have the case forwarded to the grand jury. It was reported that Park intended to provide an alibi for his clients.[9]

While the lawyers were preparing for the trial, scheduled for March 6, a couple of incidents were reported. First, two men, named Marks and Gore, were arrested in New York on suspicion of being involved in the robbery. They were sent to Boston and, in the Police Court on February 20, they were examined and jailed on a $15,000 bond. A few days later, on February 25, they were again in the Police Court where Samuel D. Parker, the district attorney, said he had looked at the evidence and found nothing to implicate them. They were immediately discharged. It is likely that someone in New York was looking to collect the reward for information and had some slim evidence to connect these two with the robbery.

Secondly, information on George Bell was sent to the *National Police Gazette* which, it claimed, allowed it to identify him as Bill Hoppy, a noted safecracker. Hoppy had recently been released from Sing-Sing Prison after serving a four-year term for robbing a jewelry store in New York City. He was a British citizen and had escaped from the penal colony at Botany Bay. Coming to America, he used a number of aliases but was known to be "a general mechanic, and is rated among his professional brethren to be a 'screwsman' or lock fitter of the highest order."[10]

On March 3, the grand jury met in the Municipal Court and presented 64 indictments for the March term. This included six charges against "William Brown, George Bell and William Morton, alias Charles Cooper" with three for breaking and entering and three for larceny. The trial, which was supposed to begin on the 16th, was postponed until the 30th due to the absence of an important government witness. It was reported that John C. Park would defend William Morton, while Tolman Wiley would defend Brown. George Bell did not have a lawyer. However, when the 30th came around, the judge, who lived in Salem, sent a note saying that he was ill and that the trial would need to be postponed again.[11]

The trial began on April 19 with the selection of a jury and examination of 19 witnesses. Most of the testimony was reported to be the same as given in the Police Court and so was not detailed in the newspapers. Detailed coverage began when the prosecution brought out their surprise witness on the next day. The witness was Charles Johnson, who had recently been convicted for breaking and entering a store in Watertown but had not yet been sentenced. The attorney for Morton, J.C. Park, objected and asked for a delay so he could review the record of the trial. Judge Cushing, who was presiding, said there was no need as he, Cushing, had been the judge and could provide the information.

Charles Johnson was a remarkable witness and everything the prosecution could have hoped he would be. He testified that he knew all three men but knew Bell the best. He reported several conversations with Bell. In one, Bell told him that the store of Currier & Trott was ripe for being broken into and, later when he saw Bell with a bag of tools, Bell told him they were for breaking into the store. Finally, Bell had said that he had already looked over the goods. Johnson claimed that he was to participate and have a full share and had already helped the group in December, when they broke into the store but did not rob it because the tools were insufficient to open the safe. During this attempt, Johnson claimed to be on Milk Street as a lookout. Johnson did not participate in the actual robbery as he was in the Leverett Street jail at the time. He was present when Bell was brought to the jail and they talked about the crime. Bell told him that "there were certain instruments left behind which would be the means of fetching him out." Johnson then examined some tools and testified that they had been in the possession of Bell. Under cross examination, Johnson said that he had been told that it would go better for him on his upcoming sentencing if he made "a clean breast." He admitted that he had read the testimony reported in the newspapers from the hearing in the Police Court.

Among other witnesses, the defense called Nathan Chamberlin, the man who employed Bell. He testified that to his knowledge, the tools which had been exhibited had not been out of his shop until Marshal Tukey took custody of them. Further, the crowbar that Johnson claimed to have seen in Bell's possession had been covered in dust when delivered to Tukey and Chamberlin was confident that it had not been used for some time. A number of witnesses were called to prove alibis for the defendants which showed they were elsewhere when the crime was committed. It must have seemed strange to Tukey that the same lawyers and the same defense, that of being elsewhere, was used in this trial as in his trial for tar and feathering.

Perhaps the most interesting testimony came when the Court asked Bell if he had anything to say. He stated that he had come to Boston a year ago from Springfield. He denied ever being arrested in New York and serving a term at Sing-Sing. He reported that he had met Johnson at the Suffolk House but had never had any conversations with him about the robbery and denied all of Johnson's allegations. Tolman Wiley gave a three-hour closing argument for the defense. The jury came back with a verdict of not guilty.[12]

This trial points out many of the difficulties the police had in solving crimes in the 19th century. Although Tukey tried to use the tool marks on the safe to match the tools in Chamberlin's shop, the effort was flawed and without a scientific basis. The evidence presented was clearly circumstantial. Johnson's testimony was not credible to the jury and was obviously self-serving. There was no compelling evidence of guilt and none that could overcome the alibi testimony.

After the not guilty verdict, the robbery continued to be talked about. Currier & Trott once again advertised a $1000 reward for any information on the robbery. Early in May, a man named Joseph Brown was arrested in Providence on suspicion but it turned out to be another false lead. In July a report was published that some boys in Cincinnati were playing in a canal when they found the remains of over 50 watches. The watches had been stripped of their gold and silver cases. The newspapers speculated that they were part of the Currier & Trott loot but none were ever identified. Still, with time, certain things became clear. In December 1847, acting on a tip of a planned robbery, Tukey and three officers hid themselves in the basement of the Essex Manufacturing Company in Lawrence and waited. About midnight a window was forced open, two men entered and began working on the safe. The officers surprised the men who tried to flee but were caught. One of those arrested was Charles Morton, one of the defendants in the robbery trial. In April 1848, Morton was sentenced to three years of hard labor at the state prison.[13]

However, the only real evidence related to the Currier & Trott robbery soon came from New York. In November 1847, about $300 worth of stolen merchandise was recovered from various shops in New York City. Mr. Trott came to New York and personally identified the items. In February 1848, William Brown, otherwise known as "Black Bill" Henderson, another of the defendants, was arrested in New York and was found to have in his possession a considerable amount of jewelry. The New York Police had used a time-tested method, later made famous by the Pinkerton Detective Agency, of introducing the suspect to a "stool pigeon" who would get close to him and inform the police of any relevant criminal activities. When examined, one of the items in Brown's possession was a gold thimble which Currier & Trott identified as having been stolen in the robbery. They thought several of the other items were theirs but they were too defaced to be identified.

On February 24, the Boston newspapers reported that Brown was being indicted on "constructive grand larceny" for conveying stolen goods across state lines. This was not the case; however, the actual charge was grand larceny for stealing the goods in the first place. On May 25, "William Henderson, alias Robinson, alias Black Bill, indicted for having robbed Messrs. Currier & Brott's [sic] jewelry store, at Boston, was discharged, he having been previously tried and acquitted in Boston for the offence." How could the New York prosecutor not be aware of the concept of double jeopardy? Bill Henderson walked free and continued his criminal ways for many years.[14]

While the Currier & Trott case was playing out in February and March, more mundane things were also going on in Boston. On March 8, Tukey began to publish in the newspapers a section of the ordinance about licensing dogs that the city had passed in 1825. It required all dogs to be licensed, at a cost of $2 per year, and that such animals had to have a collar with a tag listing the name of the owner. Dogs found wandering the streets without such a collar and tag would be destroyed. He noted at the bottom of the notice that violators would be prosecuted. This ordinance had been on the books for over 20 years but apparently was not enforced. Now with an active police force, the marshal began to enforce it.

At the same time, Marshal Tukey was sued by William Wright for trespass. This was another case that had been in and out of the courts since the 1820s. Wright, of South Boston, claimed that the City had not properly laid out or improved the roads in South Boston, as had been promised when the area was annexed in 1805. Wright claimed that the land used for a road that passed over his property was his, not the City's. He gave notice to the City that he was going to build fences across Broadway and G streets. The City directed the Marshal to be on the spot. When Wright erected the fences, Tukey and his men tore them down. The case was heard before the Court of Common Pleas with George Minot arguing for Wright and P.W. Chandler, the City Solicitor representing Tukey. After the introduction of a large amount of background evidence and legal arguing, the City won the case and absolving Tukey of trespass.[15]

During this period, Tukey's name was associated with two major charitable drives. The first was associated with the Temporary Home for the Destitute. On February 13, the *Christian Register* published the appeal for this charity. Their purpose was primarily to set up an orphanage and school for children in need. They had already secured a building and begun developing it. Their appeal was for money to finish the building. They made the very practical point that a little money spent taken care of the children would prevent them from being a bigger problem later on. The advertisement began, "To the benevolent, and all those who wish to prevent Pauperism and Crime." Some of the most prominent men and women in Boston were on the organizing committee. At the end of the appeal was a list of six men, who "recommend it to the attention and support of those to whom it is addressed." Francis Tukey was one of the six who gave their support. Of the other five, four were clergymen and one was a prominent businessman. The inclusion of Tukey in this list reflects what the Boston elite thought of him at the time.

Throughout 1845 and 1846, newspapers were full of the horrors descending on Ireland as a result of the Potato Famine. These events would soon swamp Boston and change it forever. However, in early 1847, it was still a far-off humanitarian crisis and Bostonians responded by organizing aid for the victims. A group of Boston businessmen petitioned Congress to allow use of a warship to send collected supplies to Ireland. Eventually, President Polk approved the use of the sloop of war USS *Jamestown* and money was raised from all segments of the Boston community. As part of this effort, Tukey organized a relief committee and the Day Police contributed $100 to the famine relief. This represented two days of pay for each of the officers.[16]

Taking part in these charitable drives must have seemed ironic to Tukey who was having financial troubles of his own. Mayor Quincy hinted at the problems when he specifically mentioned, in his inaugural address of 1847, that the head of the police should be paid better. Tukey was already struggling at that point. It became overwhelming by March 4, 1847, when he declared himself insolvent for the second time. He submitted a petition to Bradford Sumner, a master of chancery, who directed the sheriff of Suffolk County to seize Tukey's assets by March 15. Sumner appointed Marcus Morton, Jr., son of the governor, to be the clerk in the case and Daniel J. Coburn, deputy sheriff, to be the messenger. The first meeting of the creditors was set for March 15.[17]

Unlike the first time he declared himself insolvent, the list of creditors was attached to the case this time. His total debt listed was $295.09 owing to four creditors. Some of the debts were owed for a long time. There were three notes to Jeffery R. Brackett. One was dated February 1845 and was for $30 while the other two were dated to September 1845 and each was for $10. Brackett was a jeweler on Washington Street in Boston. All of these debts were due by the end of 1845 yet none were paid. Two other creditors were owed money on account. The company of Munroe & Cook was owed $76.51. It was a firm of grocers in Cambridgeport, where Tukey lived. The other was Samuel Beal, a furniture merchant on Washington Street in Boston. Tukey owed him three dollars on account.

The largest creditor, however, was Sarah D. Butman, a resident of Salem. On January 19, 1847, Tukey gave her a note for $160 to be paid in February. It was now March and it had not been paid. Sarah D. Butman was an unmarried woman, living with her sister, Elizabeth Butman, also unmarried, at their house on Essex Street in Salem. At the time of Tukey's note, she was 37 years old. Tukey must have gotten to know the Butman sisters during his stay in Salem in the early 1830s. Their house was close to the location of his bakery. The exact connection between Tukey and the Butmans is unknown but they and their brother, Asa O. Butman, would play a recurring role in his life over the next decade. That Sarah D. Butman was willing and able to lend him $160 is a sign of the closeness of the families. And, despite his inability to fully pay it back, the families stayed close.

The first meeting was held in Sumner's office on March 15, where Tukey handed in a list of his creditors. The creditors then elected George A. Smith to be the assignee of Tukey's estate. Smith was a lawyer practicing in Boston. Why the creditors chose him is unknown. A second meeting was held on June 2 where Tukey appeared and took the oath that he had truthfully produced the list of creditors and had delivered to the messenger all of his estate, his books, deeds and all papers relating to the estate. The final meeting was held on September 6 at which Tukey was given a certificate discharging him of his debts.

That the man serving as city marshal of Boston and head of the police declared himself insolvent would seem to be an important event. Yet. as far as the surviving newspapers are concerned, it was not worth of a notice. The only notice of these events was the legal notice required by the process. Mayor Quincy had implied that Tukey was having problems in January but it took till March for the city to do something. It was reported on March 29 that the Common Council had raised the salary of the city marshal from $1100 to $1800. As a result, Tukey said that he would dispense with the service of one of his deputies.[18]

Despite the stress in his personal life, Tukey continued to do his job. Mayor Quincy, in his inaugural address the previous January, had stated that "Public and private good requires that vice, where it exists, should be checked and kept under control." Tukey now began to carry out this instruction in a way never seen before in Boston. On the night of March 20, around 9 o'clock, Marshal Tukey, accompanied by 40 policemen, raided the Terrapin Coffee House in Post Office Avenue. In the upper rooms, they found a number of people gambling, including playing a game of props. Little known today, this game was very popular, in Boston particularly, in the mid–19th century. It involved four small, white cowrie shells whose hollows were filled with red sealing wax. The betting was on the number of red or white sides showing when cast on the table. They arrested 49 people for illegal gambling and one man got away by jumping out a second story window. On the way to the jail, two more ran away while hand-cuffed together.[19]

While the police planned on visiting other places that night, the word had gone out. They visited four other places but found no one gambling. At the Café-à-la-mode, in Sudbury St., they seized a number of decks of cards and several instruments used in the faro bank game. They also arrested Samuel Knight, owner of the cafe. On Monday morning, J.W. Pierce, one of Tukey's detectives, raided an establishment in Flagg Alley, seizing gambling equipment and arresting the owner, William Tenney. On that morning, 45 of the prisoners were brought before the Police Court and fined $2 plus costs. The other two prisoners, Samuel. K. Head and George Blaisdell, owners of the coffee house, were held to be tried in the Municipal Court, along with Samuel Knight and William Tenney.

The Boston press was very enthusiastic about this raid. The editor of the *Boston Evening Transcript* said, "The public feeling is animated in admiration of the vigilance of Marshal Tukey in ferreting out the lurking places of gamblers." The editor of the *Boston Daily Bee* was even more laudatory, saying, "The efforts of Marshal Tukey to break up the infamous gambling hells to which we have alluded will be sustained by every good citizen, … Thus far, he is the best City Marshal we have ever had, and we trust he will always deserve this praise."[20]

In an unusual twist to this story, the handcuffs which were lost when two of the prisoners escaped were returned to the jail office a week later. With them was a note addressed to J.W. Pierce which read:

> Boston March 24, 1847, Mr. Pierce—Not being partial to ornaments, I have taken this opportunity to return your bracelets, hoping they will do you more good than they have done me. Yours, very suddenly Titus A. Peep

It was reported that the handcuffs bore the marks of a cold chisel used in their removal. While "Titus A. Peep" was a false name, the papers suggested that the police knew the real name of the person involved. In fact, when Tukey and the police made a raid on Montezuma Hall in April, they found gambling equipment but did not see any gambling going on. The twenty people found there were allowed to go free, including one lad identified as the returner of the handcuffs.[21]

While Tukey received praise for his raid on the gamblers, he was about to experience the down side of "active" policing. During last year's raid on those selling liquor on Sunday, Tukey arrested Michael Tubbs at the North American House on a warrant issued by the Police Court. Although the warrant was issued on Wednesday, the arrest was not made until Sunday. On that day, Tubbs was put in jail and held till his appearance before a judge on Monday. When brought before the Court, he was given bail until his case was heard. This would seem to be no different from any of the other cases. However, when it came to trial, Michael Tubbs claimed that he was not the owner of the bar in question but that his son, Hiram Tubbs, owned it. The judge found Michael Tubbs not guilty and released him.[22]

Michael Tubbs then sued Tukey and the constable who served the warrant for trespass and illegal imprisonment. He claimed he had been held without the possibility of bail, because it was Sunday, and claimed damages of $1000. The trial was held in the Court of Common Pleas on May 7, 1847, with John C. Park defending Tukey. The plaintiff contended that the warrant commanded that he be brought before the Police Court, not put in jail to wait until the Court was in session. The jury agreed with him and found Tukey guilty. They assessed damages of $304.58 but the defendant's lawyer alleged exceptions to the ruling and the case was finally determined in the March term of 1849 in the Massachusetts Supreme Court, which also found for the plaintiff.

Some of the flavor of justice in Boston at the time may be seen in accusations made by a newspaper called the *Chronotype* which questioned the makeup of the jury. It pointed out that one of the jurors was a distiller and that another, Moses Clark, held a $500 mortgage on gambling equipment that Tukey had recently seized. They went further and claimed that Clark had played checkers with another juror to decide the amount of damages the plaintiff should receive. Elizur Wright, editor of the *Chronotype*, was sued for libel over the last accusation. However, no one seems to have objected to the original complaints about bias on the jury.[23]

Given his recent financial difficulties, fighting this suit must have put a lot of pressure on Tukey. Eventually as it was clear that he would lose the case, he applied to the City to reimburse him for the fine and court costs. In 1849, after the decision of the Supreme Court, the City granted him $491 to cover the cost of the judgment and his counsel fees. It was an expensive lesson for both Tukey and the City.[24]

The new police force was changing how people viewed law enforcement but perhaps was confusing to many of Boston's citizens. They were uncertain of how or when to report crimes. Because of this, the mayor and aldermen authorized the publication of an extensive "Special Police Notice" in several Boston newspapers beginning in May and extending into September. It first stated that the Police Office was located in City Hall and was open all hours of the day and night. It informed the public that records were kept in the office of all stolen goods, robberies, larcenies or other crimes. It encouraged people to turn in lost or recovered items and promised to attempt to obtain a reward for the finder. It further stated that no police officer was entitled to such rewards. Another part of the notice informed the public that they could get information on cabs, hacks and other licensed vehicles by reporting their license number to the office. The notice also mentioned that the police were monitoring beggars and giving cards to those who truly deserved charity. It reminded people who were vacating their houses for the summer to inform the police. Finally, it informed other police departments that there was a telegraph office nearby in case they had need of contacting the Boston police.[25]

On October 4, 1847, Marshal Tukey presented a report to the mayor and aldermen detailing the state and condition of the Police Department. This was a subject which he was very concerned about. In July, he had gathered his officers together and "addressed them on their duties and the high opinion which the public have been led to entertain of their efficiency." Now he echoed this praise to the city authorities. He commended "the general good order, promptness and fidelity of the members of the department 'as is manifest by the quiet and peace of their respective districts.'" Tukey reported that there were 25 day police and 10 night police. He recommended that the night force be expanded to 20 men for the rest of the year.[26]

In his report, Marshal Tukey gave detailed information on the types and number of crimes the police had dealt with over the six months prior to October 1 and this gives us a good view of what policing was like at this time. The biggest source of crime in Boston had to do with alcohol. There were 514 arrests for drunkenness, 94 violators of the license law, and two violators of the Sunday law. This was, by far, the most frequent crime in the city. Not surprisingly, given the mayor's emphasis on the ordinances and Tukey's enthusiastic enforcement of the same, the second most common offense was a violation of the ordinances. There were 178 arrests for this cause. This was followed closely by the crime of larceny, or the taking of property without force which accounted for 148 arrests. There were 22 other crimes mostly resulting in one or two arrests. Tukey spend some time talking about the recovery of property by the police. Taken together there were 185 incidents of robberies and larcenies, resulting in the loss of $33,667. Through the efforts of the police, $24,805 was recovered.

Marshal Tukey stated that within the last three months, there were 95 minors arrested, principally for larceny. He concluded his report with a call for the city to deal with this issue:

> I earnestly call the attention of the city government, and through them the benevolent of the city, to the great and increasing amount of crime, among the young of both sexes. I am satisfied that prisons will not prevent it, but that schools and employment may.

One of the crimes listed in the report was the passing of counterfeit money, for which eight people had been arrested. While the number of people arrested was small, the impact of this crime was much greater. Prior to 1861, there was no standard Federal paper money issued but states granted charters to banks to issue their own notes, which were backed by government bonds kept at the bank. Needless to say, these banknotes were easily forged and this lead to a blizzard of counterfeit notes. Acting on a tip about the passing of counterfeit bills, Marshal Tukey and his detectives raided a bowling saloon on Merrimac St. on the night of October 15. There they arrested a man named Joshua Silsby, who fought the arrest desperately. When they searched Silsby, they found 136 forged banknotes totaling over $400. These notes were supposed to be from eight different banks, located in Boston, Worcester, North Adams, and Marblehead, Massachusetts, as well as Nashua, New Hampshire, and three banks in Maine. In addition to the counterfeit bills, Silsby had four trunks full of stolen clothes, shoes, silks, vests and other articles which still bore the shop marks on them. He was brought before the Police Court and held on a bail of $6000 to appear in the Municipal Court.[27]

One of the most famous of Tukey's cases began at the end of October 1847 with the robbery of the jewelry stone of Abraham Hews & Co. on Washington Street. The robbery occurred either on Saturday or Sunday, when the shop was closed, and was probably discovered on Monday morning. This was an unusual robbery and very different than the Currier & Trott case. The only thing taken from the store was about $1150 in cash, despite the presence of $10,000 in watches and jewelry. The cash was taken out of the safe, without breaking the door, suggesting that the robber had access to a key. Of the cash taken, $1000 had been deposited with the firm by a neighbor who was looking for an investment and the other $150 belonged to the business.

By Tuesday morning, Tukey had already arrested George H. Herbert for the crime. He was a watchmaker by trade and had worked for Hews for about a year. A search of Herbert and his room did not uncover the money. Shortly thereafter it was reported that a man came to the marshal's office and told him that he had seen someone digging in the Public Garden two weeks earlier. In a most extraordinary statement, the man claimed that he thought the person digging was burying a child and so took no more notice. How many children are buried in the Public Garden? The man was taken to the jail but could not identify Herbert as the person he saw digging. That evening, a Saturday, Tukey and three others went to the indicated spot and dug for some time but found nothing. The next morning, he returned and, after further digging, found a glass jar containing the stolen money. This mysterious digging and the discovery of the money made an impression at the time and was frequently recalled in stories about Tukey's time as city marshal. After the money was found, the story of its owner was published, adding to the pathos of the story. The cash belonged to a "hard working seamstress" named Miss Brackett, who had saved it for 15 years. She had withdrawn it from the bank and was going to invest it the following Monday. The recovery of her money gave a major boost to the reputation of

Marshal Tukey and his police force. Surprisingly, on November 20, Herbert was discharged of the complaint of stealing the money from the safe but was still under indictment for taking a silver watch from the store. He was given bail and then went to New York. There this mysterious story ends for the time being.[28]

Throughout the fall of 1847, Tukey continued to be personally engaged in police work. In addition to helping to dig up the money from the Hews robbery, he helped put down a disturbance in Faneuil Hall. The noted temperance speaker, John B. Gough, had been giving lectures in Boston at the Tremont Temple. When the Boston Total Abstinence Society decided to hold a mass meeting at Faneuil Hall on October 21, they asked him to address the crowd. As the meeting was called to order, a group in opposition to temperance began to create a disturbance. The two sides hurled chairs and tables at each other and then the rioters made a rush for the platform. The temperance advocates were driven from the platform and the keeper of the hall was about to extinguish the lights to try to quell the disturbance. At this point, Marshal Tukey arrived with a strong force of the night police and order was restored. Faneuil Hall, site of so many protests in the past, would continue to be a flash point for the various causes that riled Boston in the 1840s and Tukey would repeatedly be required to restore the peace.[29]

He also continued to make patrols on the city streets. On November 20, while walking along Washington Street, Tukey noticed a man in a very large overcoat apparently trying to store things in it. Under his coat he found "60 yards of silk, a pair of pants, two rolls of ribbon and a pair of hose," all of which the man had just stolen from the store of H. Huston. The value of the goods hidden under his overcoat was $125. The marshal arrested the man whose name was given as John Burns, alias O'Brien. This was the kind of "hands on" police work that Tukey was famous for.[30]

The system of policing set up by Mayor Quincy and Marshal Tukey had never been seen in New England before. While there were many successes, there was also growing resistance to the active form of patrol. Some was fairly gentle and humorous. The *Boston Post* published a short piece claiming to be from an old woman who was afraid of the new police. She said, "they are frights sure enough; only to see 'em going round town all marked and labelled like big potecary bottles ... a poor woman like me is afeared to throw even a little ashes into the street; but neighbor Tripe, the butcher man, can fill his sidewalk with boxes with perfect impunity." Actions which were in violation of city ordinances used to be ignored but with an active police, people began to complain that they were now being enforced. An editorial in the *Boston Daily Bee* went further and stated that the police needed to be more moral than anyone else, stating, "the principal of which we believe to be the unpopularity of our present police system. ... The police of a city are set for its moral protection, and moral men alone have any right to exercise its offices." It went on to complain about police officers swearing and visiting "dram shops."[31]

When the Whig party met to nominate a candidate for mayor, Josiah Quincy, Jr., received 40 out of 71 votes. Because of the opposition, Quincy submitted a letter stating that he would withdraw and let them select someone else. After long discussion, the party leaders finally convinced him to accept the nomination. The opposition to Quincy was partly due to his veto of the license law during the previous year. The Council had been evenly split and the mayor used his vote to defeat the liquor interest. Those who objected to Quincy's actions held a separate meeting on December 7 at Chapman Hall and nominated their own Whig candidate for mayor. Their choice was William Parker, who was termed the "independent Whig nominee." They did not directly address the license vote but stated that their opposition was due to "injustice to mechanics," or to concerns about "private speculation," and finally, an "obnoxious police."[32]

Normally, the municipal election was a fairly quiet, sedate process and the Whig party had a solid hold on the offices. With the party split and the opposition from Democrats and the Native American party, it looked like Quincy's experiment with the police was about to end. The election was scheduled for December 13 and result was anything but certain.

4

"His articles have appeared too *savage* and *fiendish*, too much like the ravings of a man stark mad"

In the election for mayor held on December 13, 1847, Josiah Quincy, Jr., won re-election by a wide margin. He garnered 4752 votes while the next highest total was for the Democratic candidate Charles Goodrich, who received only 1656 votes. They were followed by the Independent Whig, William Parker, with 1535 and the Native American candidate, Ninian C. Betton, with 868. The strength of Quincy's victory is evident by the fact that he received 573 more votes than all the other candidates together. It was a resounding victory for Quincy and for the policies he had put in place.[1]

Mayor Quincy gave his third Inaugural address on January 3, 1848. It covered a wide range of plans for the future and discussion of past events. He did not spend as much time on the police in this address as in the last two years, stating that he believed the police to be "in a satisfactory state." He reported that in the last year, a permanent, full-time police office was established at City Hall, where assistance could be obtained at all hours of the day. The force now consisted of 24 day men and 10 night men, all under the control of the city marshal.[2]

He was proud to report that the police had made major improvements in the areas of the theaters and public transportation. By having paid police officers in the theaters, they had eliminated both alcohol sales and prostitution, which had been rampant during shows. By licensing cabs, hack and other public conveyances, they had made companies and drivers responsible to the public. He claimed that it had "given greater respectability to the employment, and security and convenience to the citizens."

Because of innuendos made during the last election and printed by some of the newspapers, the mayor took pains to point out that the police were well paid, $2 a day, and that they were not permitted to receive witness fees, rewards or gratuities. Violation of that rule would lead to termination. Further, he went on to briefly explain how the police used rewards to recover stolen property. The police made every effort to find and return lost or stolen property but many times they lacked the evidence necessary. In such cases, they contacted their informants and tried to negotiate for the return of the goods. The mayor stated that the marshal had been given $330 by owners of lost or stolen property to negotiate its return from whomever held it. Except for $5 of that amount, the owners had made Tukey their special agent in the transaction. Quincy had reviewed all of these cases and said, "I feel it is my duty to him to state that I am satisfied that all the money was used for the purpose intended." Over the previous nine months, there was a total of $49,110 reported to the police office as lost or stolen. The amount recovered by the police was $35,430.

The $5 that Mayor Quincy referred to in his address may have been related to a case which was soon in the newspapers. A man named Joseph Fisher, a baggage master on the Old Colony Railroad, went to the Police Office and reported that a number of silver spoons had been stolen from his house on Hudson Street. The police began to make inquiries and after some time, they sent to inform Mr. Fisher that his spoons were found and he could pick them up by calling at the marshal's office. His wife went there and was told that she could have the spoons if she paid the $5, about a quarter of the value of the spoons. She paid the money and was given the spoons. Mr. Fisher, on the other hand, was incensed that he had to pay to get his spoons back and filed a petition with Common Council to get his $5 refunded. His petition accused Tukey of either being the thief himself or colluding with the thief to collect the money. It further indicted Mayor Quincy for conniving with the marshal.[3]

This seemingly innocuous case over $20 in spoons may have

been the beginning of a larger attempt to remove both Tukey and Quincy from office. The problem of how to recover stolen goods was a vexing one in the 19th century. The police had a full-time officer whose job it was to visit pawn shops and secondhand stores looking for stolen goods. If they recognized something as stolen, they could seize it and no money was exchanged. However, many stolen items could not be readily identified, most had no serial numbers to check, and if they were to be recovered, some compromise had to be used. This was outlined in the "Special Police Notice" published in May 1847, as discussed in the last chapter. One of the paragraphs of that notice said, "all persons finding goods are informed that by leaving the same, or a description of them, efforts will always be made to obtain a reward for the finder." To the modern eye, paying someone for returning things they had stolen is a dubious moral choice. At the time however, most people were willing to pay a fraction of the value to get back goods they would not otherwise have.

Fisher's petition raised some eyebrows in the Common Council. The language was very disrespectful to both Tukey and Quincy. Rather than do anything with it, the Council voted 47 to nothing to give Fisher the opportunity to withdraw his petition. Apparently he did not and a committee was set up to hold a hearing on the matter. Tukey was questioned and stated that the $5 was given to a person who had "obtained the stolen articles and delivered them into his hands." After hearing from a number of other witnesses, the Council decided that no action was necessary and stated they found the Marshal,

> entirely free from the charge of receiving unlawful compensation as an officer, and of extortion of those calling for his services; but on the contrary, they think his conduct worthy of commendation, as being directed and controlled by a paramount regard to the public good.[4]

Fisher's lawyer in this case was also the lawyer for Samuel K. Head, publisher of the *Boston Herald*. This may be significant in light of the almost fanatical feud between Tukey and the *Herald* that was remembered in the Boston newspaper community for several generations. Head was mentioned in the last chapter as one of the owners of the Terrapin Coffee House raided by Tukey and the police in their sweep of gambling halls in March 1847. Later in October of that year, he was again in court and fined $10 for keeping a brothel. Perhaps as a way of venting his frustration, Samuel K. Head purchased the *Boston Herald* in May of 1847.

It is hard to assess the nature of this newspaper before Head bought it. Although the *Boston Herald* began publishing in 1846, the earliest copies that are preserved date to May 1848. However, the well-known habit of 19th-century newspapers to repeat news items from other papers makes it possible to see, at least a little, of the editorial policy of the *Herald*. In January 1847, the *National Police Gazette* castigated the *Herald* for defending the Boston police against charges that they knew of pickpockets but refused to arrest them. The editor of the *Gazette* commented that "The Herald of that city, which evidently receives its information direct from the officers concerned, ... takes up the cudgels for them in downright earnest."[5]

The new attitude of the *Herald* was noticeable in the mayoral election of 1847. The newspaper campaigned heavily against Josiah Quincy, Jr., and his reforms. On the Saturday before the election, they brought out a special edition with "stirring appeals to voters to oppose him at the polls." It is unknown if they supported a particular candidate or were just in opposition to Quincy. When Quincy won overwhelmingly, the *Herald* was still defiant, "We came pretty near winning it, though, we deprived Mayor Quincy of twelve hundred votes, at least." Their claim of almost winning is debunked by the final vote total, discussed above. In the same editorial, they claimed to be the largest circulating newspaper in Boston and said they would apply to the mayor and alderman for the city's public advertising. While they did apply, not surprisingly, they got turned down.

One of the important changes that Head made, early on, at the newspaper was to hire William J. Snelling as the new editor on June 10, 1847. He would become Tukey's nemesis over the next year. Snelling was a gifted writer who had a tendency to be sarcastic and offensive, which got him into trouble frequently. He was born in 1804 to Josiah Snelling and Elizabeth Bell. His father was a lieutenant in the army and away most of the time. When his mother died in 1810, he was shuffled around to various relatives and boarding schools. At age 14, he received an appointment to West Point. He did not do well under the discipline there and, after two years, resigned his position. Going west, he became a fur trader and spent most of the 1820s on the frontier. These adventures became the basis for a number of short stories he published under the title "Tales of the Northwest; or, Sketches of Indian Life and Character" in 1830.

Returning to Boston, Snelling became part of the literary scene and began writing for various publications. In 1832, he wrote a scathing review, in the *New England Magazine*, of two pamphlets advocating the settlement of Oregon and called into question the character of the author of those pamphlets. Hall J. Kelley, the author, replied that Snelling "evinces an unusual degree of depravity." Kelley claimed that of the 161 sentences in Snelling's six-page review, 70 were falsehoods and that an additional 39 were of "doubtful import." While the facts of this controversy are uncertain, it is clear that Snelling was willing to use his pen to damage others and, perhaps, was somewhat loose with the truth.[6]

His various writings soon gained him the position of editor of the *New England Galaxy*. Instead of sticking to the literary genre, as it had been, Snelling used the newspaper to start crusading against vice and corruption. One of his major thrusts, which he pursued fanatically, was against gamblers and gaming halls. He began to publish the names of the owners of gambling houses and took a more active role. In April 1833, Snelling personally charged a man in the Police Court with being a vagabond and gambler but no positive evidence was produced and he was dismissed. Next, Snelling convinced a man to go into the hall and gamble just to gain evidence. That man, George Amerige, testified against Otis Spurr, the owner of the establishment, and Spurr was convicted. However, Spurr turned around and charged Amerige with gambling. This charge was later dismissed because the judge believed that Amerige only gambled to get evidence of illegal activity. As part of this campaign, Snelling was assaulted and threatened with death. The *Lowell Mercury*, while applauding Snelling's zeal against gamblers, stated, "We confess, however, that to us, his articles have appeared too *savage* and *fiendish*, too much like the ravings of a man stark mad."[7]

This continued for a while but Snelling became increasingly frustrated with the judge of the Police Court, Benjamin Whitman, who was more lenient than Snelling thought he should be. He began to assail Whitman in the pages of the *New England Galaxy*. Whitman took offense at this and charged Snelling with libel. At the same time, two other cases of libel were begun against Snelling. Dabney

O. Harrison and Amos S. Allen, Jr., sued Snelling for printing that they were gamblers and cheats. Finally, the daughter of Mrs. Susan E. Munroe claimed that Snelling had intimated that her mother, now deceased, was a woman of ill-fame. All three cases were tried in the Municipal Court in July 1833 and Snelling was found guilty in each case. For each count, Snelling was fined $50 plus costs and sentenced to 60 days in the common jail. He immediately appealed to the Massachusetts Supreme Court. The case dragged on until June of 1834 when Snelling was again found guilty and sentenced to three months in prison.[8]

His troubles with the law caused him to be removed as editor of the *Galaxy* and after his stint in prison, he tried to make his living by writing articles and being a reporter. This latter attempt did not go well and the *Boston Post* reported: "He attempted reporting, but carrying into that profession his private feelings and animosities, it became necessary to qualify his reports, and he was too proud of his talents, and confident in his own judgement, to submit to critical mutilation." Apparently, Snelling had a serious problem with alcohol and by 1837, he was brought before the Police Court on a charge of being a common drunkard. At his trial, he asked the judge to sentence him to six months in jail to help him dry out. The judge reduced this to four months and Snelling went back to jail.[9]

When released, Snelling went to New York where he continued to write and embroil himself in controversy. In 1841, he founded the *Sunday Flash*, the first of a series of lascivious, obscene and satirical newspapers which appeared in New York in the early 1840s. One contemporary of Snelling called him the "father of the smutty papers." On the masthead, the paper was edited by "Scorpion, Sly and Startle," which were the pseudonyms of Snelling and his partners George B. Wooldridge and George Wilkes. The *Flash*, like newspapers which followed it, was described as "salacious and sex-oriented, humorous and ribald, in league with the brothel world and also in varying degrees attuned to the saloon culture." The trends which stand out from this type of journalism are the use of sexual innuendo to smear one's opponents and a strong disbelief in anything resembling piety, both of which Snelling would deploy against Tukey. The *Sunday Flash* lasted less than a year before Snelling was arrested for libel and obscenity. George B. Wooldridge turned against his partners and gave evidence against them. Snelling and Wilkes were found guilty of libel but the jury could not agree on the obscenity charge. In a second trial on obscenity charges, Snelling was convicted and probably served a month in jail.[10]

After Samuel K. Head bought the *Boston Herald* and was looking for an editor who would take on Mayor Quincy and City Marshal Tukey, he knew Snelling would be the man. Beginning in June 1847, the *Herald* became increasingly critical of Tukey and his Police Department, often engaging in vituperative personal attacks on Tukey's character. In one of the earliest copies of the *Boston Herald* that has survived, May 3, 1848, the editor wrote, "The dishonored name and infamous conduct of this craven, sneaking dog, and deep dyed villain, are ... daily entailing increased disgrace upon the authorities who employ him." Even by the loose standards of 19th-century journalism, this was very harsh. From May 1848, when the first issues of the *Boston Herald*, are found to the end of the year, Boston newspapers mentioned Tukey 230 times. Of those, 136 were in the *Herald*. They mentioned Tukey even if there was no specific news to report but rather used every opportunity to say something derogatory. The *Herald* began calling him "Mayor Tukey," implying that he was usurping the authority of Josiah Quincy, the elected mayor. They also began calling him Hassarac Tukey, a reference to the Captain of Thieves in *Ali Baba and the Forty Thieves*.[11]

However, none of that was as outrageous as the pamphlet that was published by the *Herald* in 1848, entitled "A Narrative of the Life and Adventures of Francis Tukey, Esq., City Marshal of Boston." The author of this pamphlet is only identified as "One Who Knows Him" and the publisher is simply listed as "Boston Herald Office." Snelling, remembering his last brush with libel in Boston, made sure that his name was nowhere evident even if it was clearly from his pen. The pamphlet was available from the *Herald* office for six and a quarter cents each. It was first printed in 1848 but exactly when is uncertain. The latest item included in the narrative appears to be a reference to Joseph Fisher and his spoons which was decided in late January. The first issue of the *Herald* to be preserved, May 1, 1848, advertises the second edition of the pamphlet. Two days later, it advertises the third edition and would list this until mid–October when it was no longer advertised.

The pamphlet itself is an amazing mixture of half-truths, outright lies and salacious stories about Tukey. Because of the nature of the writing, it is hard to assess any of what is included in the document. The story begins with a description of Tukey's childhood in Portland. In describing his youth, the author commented that he was a "pest of his teacher, the plague of his parents and the terror of every school boy smaller than himself ... a dirty, troublesome, brutish little whelp, whom no kindness could effect, no correction reclaim."

The comments on Tukey's life in Portland provided the only contemporary response to the pamphlet. A man named Daniel C. Colesworthy, an editor and religious hymn writer in Portland, read some of the extracts about Tukey and was incensed. In May, he sent a small notice to the *Olive Branch*, a religious publication in Boston, which complained about what he saw as lies. Colesworthy reported that several months earlier a man came to Portland asking questions about Tukey. He told the man "that Mr. T. sustained a good character in Portland when he left, and that we never knew of a mean or dishonorable act of his." He further stated that "We knew Mr. Tukey when he was a boy, and his character was then as good as any youth of his age." This notice was reprinted in the *Boston Journal* and the *Herald* felt compelled to respond. It investigated who Colesworthy was and was informed that he was "a bookseller in Portland and a professor of religion, which is strong presumption that he is a hypocrite and a knave, and his volunteer defense of Hassarac Tukey makes this fact certain." This says more about the *Herald's* editor than it does about Colesworthy.[12]

Throughout the rest of the document, Tukey is portrayed as a sexual predator and pervert. In discussing his time in Chelsea in the early 1830s, the author reports that Tukey fell in love with another man's wife. When she died, according to the author, Tukey offered to stay by the corpse all night with the intention of having sex with the dead body. In episode after episode, Tukey is said to have lusted after and corrupted many females, married or otherwise. Even when it might be thought his motives less sexual, the author imputes such things to him. Tukey's superintendence of the Sunday school in Cambridge was, according to the pamphlet, to allow him access to young, unmarried females. Much of this innuendo was the result of Snelling's recent association with the *Sunday Flash* in New York. In the end, nothing in the pamphlet can be believed because the bias is so evident throughout the document.

There is no indication of Tukey's reaction to this infamous publication. Nor was there any outcry in other Boston newspapers. Whether it was because Tukey was a public official or was due to the lack of knowledge about the author of the pamphlet, no suit for libel was begun. Newspapers outside of Boston, unaware of the *Herald's* vendetta against Tukey, reprinted parts of the document, further tarnishing the marshal's reputation. In New York, the *National Police Gazette*, whose editor, George Wilkes, was a good friend and former business partner of William J. Snelling, was highly critical of Tukey and the Boston Police, parroting much of what was published in the *Herald*. In December 1848, William J. Snelling unexpectedly died of apoplexy or congestion of the brain. This was followed shortly by the withdrawal of Samuel K. Head from ownership of the *Herald*. While the newspaper continued to be critical of Tukey, it lost much of its sarcastic, vituperative tone.[13]

Marshal Tukey, despite the opposition from the *Herald*, continued to develop his police and detectives. A serious problem for the police, as seen in the Currier & Trott robbery, was that there had developed a mobile, professional, criminal class that went from city to city under assumed names and then fled the scene. At the time there was no way to identify these people. Photography was still in its infancy and very expensive. Written descriptions only went so far. In April 1848, two pickpockets from New York, who were known to one of the detectives, were nabbed and taken to the police office. Tukey called together his officers and asked them to take a good look at the offenders and watch their movements. The two men thanked the marshal for their not being arrested and agreed that they should leave town as soon as possible. Today, such actions would not be remotely legal but at the time the police had no choice. This was the first of many "show up of rogues" which Tukey conducted. While it began with a few criminals and just the police, later these would develop into major roundups and the public would be involved. These show ups served to familiarize the police with known criminals.[14]

Early in March, Tukey risked his life in saving an individual in distress. On the night of March 10, the printing establishment of Damrell & Moore, on Washington Street, went up in flames. This was a massive fire, burning two granite-front buildings and damaging several others. The loss of property was estimated at $200,000. Tukey was on scene, with the police, to control the crowds. The police arrested three people who were found having stolen goods that were being thrown out of the building to save them. A young man, who was a foreman in the printing company, got on a ladder and entered the second floor. Tukey followed him up the ladder, into the burning building and dragged him out. The man was covered in lead spatter from the melting type.[15]

More mundane issues began to occupy the time of the police force. Despite the ordinance passed in 1847 to license and regulate hacks, cabs and omnibuses, Boston's streets continued to be obstructed. On April 26, Marshal Tukey was making his rounds of the city when he came across an omnibus standing in Court Street near Brattle Street. There was no driver present and the carriage was blocking the street. Tukey looked in a couple of shops for the driver but did not find him. Taking direct action, he jumped up on the omnibus and drove it to the stand where it belonged at Haymarket. Later, Charles P. Philbrick, a policeman in charge of supervising carriages, complained to the Police Court against the driver, Nathan Lewis, for leaving his vehicle unattended. Unfortunately, the warrant charging Lewis stated that the omnibus was found in Brattle street while the witnesses stated that it was in Court Street. Because of this mistake, the driver was excused. In a strange twist, Mr. Giddings, the operator of the East Boston omnibus line, then charged Tukey with driving too fast, over six miles per hour, as he took the carriage to the stand in Haymarket. Tukey did not deny the charge and was fined $3 and costs by the court which he paid "with the best possible grace." This was the opening shot of what the newspapers began to refer to as the "Omnibus War."[16]

The strongest opposition to the licensing law for carriages came from Horace King, proprietor of the omnibus line running from Norfolk House in Roxbury, along Washington Street to the Old State House. King began running coaches from Roxbury to Boston in 1825. Starting with one coach, by the 1840s, he had 16 omnibuses, drawn by four horses and holding more than 14 passengers each. They left Boston every seven minutes. While the fare to Roxbury was 12 and a half cents, rides on the line within Boston were 6 and a half cents, like other omnibus lines. When the City passed the ordinance regulating coaches in 1847, they set routes for each of the omnibus lines. The lucrative Washington Street route in downtown was given to King's rivals, Hobbs & Prescott. The Roxbury line was required to drive on Tremont Street, which one contemporary newspaper described as "an uninhabited street, which in bad weather is very bleak, and uncomfortable" and seriously cut into King's profit from casual riders. His exclusion from the profitable Washington Street route may have been due to the size of King's omnibuses but, when he offered to change to much smaller two-horse carriages, the City Council was not moved.[17]

The Mayor and Aldermen of Boston insisted that King's drivers be licensed and stick to their assigned route. They instructed Tukey to force compliance with the 1847 ordinance. On May 19, 1848, Tukey took one of the drivers off his omnibus on Washington street and hauled him before the Police Court for not being licensed. This driver asked for a postponement until the next day so he could consult with Mr. King. Just as the postponement was granted, Tukey brought in another driver on the same charge. He was convicted, fined $5 and costs, which he refused to pay and was confined in the Leverett Street jail. The omnibus this driver had been taken from remained in Washington Street for half an hour before anyone came to clear it from the street. One newspaper called this an example of "hurrying up the cakes" but it caused King to take notice.

King's lawyer, H. Weld Fuller, said that the ordinance was illegal and he intended to take these cases as far as the Massachusetts Supreme Court. Fuller claimed that it could not be enforced against coaches running from any other town into Boston. On Monday, May 22, three more of King's drivers were brought to court. Fuller went to see Marshal Tukey to complain and Tukey reportedly told him that he had eighteen complaints ready and, "as fast as the drivers came into the city, they shall be taken from their boxes and arrested." Clearly the City Government was not backing down. However, the town of Roxbury now got involved in the dispute saying that night soil carts, which crossed from Boston to Roxbury to dispose of their contents, would be stopped at the border.[18]

Tukey carried out his threat the next week, arresting six of King's drivers in a row. They were brought to court and all asked for a continuance, which was granted. When the drivers left the court, there was a crowd of men and boys who cheered them. One of the newspapers ended their report with the phrase, "Straws show etc.," which was a shortening of the phrase "Straws show which way the wind is blowing." The tide of public opinion was against the City. Tukey called a temporary halt to the arrests until these cases were decided. As often happens, the hearing of these cases were delayed for some months until, in July, they were fined $5 each and allowed to appeal their convictions. In August, Tukey arrested 12 more of King's drivers and the "war" was renewed. Eventually, District Attorney Samuel Parker reached an agreement with King's lawyers to try one of the cases and then wait until a higher court decided the legality of the ordinance.[19]

The test case was heard before the Massachusetts Supreme Court in the November term of 1848. The case revolved around three basic questions. The first was whether, under the act passed by the legislature for the regulation of hackney carriages, the City of Boston had the right to restrict travel through the streets of the city by establishing specific routes for each omnibus line. Secondly, was it legal for the City to require residents of another town to pay for a license to run an omnibus from another town into Boston and back again. Finally, did the act grant Boston the right to require a license of nonresidents of Boston who set up such an omnibus line. The opinion of the court was delivered on March 12, 1849. Justice Charles A. Dewey wrote the opinion and the court split its decision. It very strongly supported the right of Boston to regulate how omnibuses used their streets and supported the right to establish specific routes for all omnibus lines. However, on the other two questions, it just as strongly denied the right of Boston to either collect a license fee from non-residents or even to license such operators. The case was sent back to the Municipal Court but it was likely not pursued. Based on the decision, King's omnibuses did not have to be licensed but were still restricted from the downtown part of Washington Street.[20]

While the "omnibus war" was raging in May and June of 1848, two events demonstrated how the citizens of Boston felt about their Marshal and his police force. On May 15, it was reported that a petition was presented to the mayor and aldermen requesting the use

of Faneuil Hall for a meeting on May 18 to consider the purity of
the Police Department. The petition was presented by Stephen A.
Pierce, a well-known auctioneer in Boston. Pierce belonged to the
same faction that tried to unseat Mayor Quincy in the previous election and was heavily involved with the agitation for the free licensing
of alcohol by the City. In March 1847, he applied for and was denied
a license to sell spirituous liquors. At that time he was opposed by
Moses Grant, the leader of the Boston Total Abstinence Society. In
May of the same year, Grant held a temperance meeting in Faneuil
Hall which was disrupted and hijacked by the liquor interests. Pierce
was elected secretary of that meeting where he read a series of resolutions calling on the mayor and aldermen to "grant licenses immediately to those who have applied for them, and thereby secure their
just rights." The Mayor and Aldermen took their time considering
Pierce's request such that the meeting had to be postponed.

The meeting on the "purity of the Police Department" was
held in Faneuil Hall on May 25 and the *Boston Herald* trumpeted
the importance of the meeting: "...let all who think with us be on
hand to-night, at Faneuil Hall, to raise their voices against the man-
ifold abuses of our city government." Pierce, and the other organizers, should not have been surprised that their own tactics were used
against them. The hall was packed with temperance people who
were not going to be denied their voice. They seized the podium and
enacted their own set of resolutions. According to the *Boston Evening Transcript*, they resolved that the city government was "entitled
to 'confidence and support'; that the charges against Marshal Tukey
by 'obscure individuals' have not been sustained, and that his conduct in the discharge of his duty entitles him to the favorable consideration of the 'good citizens of Boston.'"[21]

The following month, Tukey was able to directly earn the favorable consideration of the "good citizens of Boston" by his actions
during the collapse of a building in downtown Boston. The Dearborn Block was a five-story granite building at 27–31 Federal Street.
In the basement, the structure was supported by seven brick piers,
16 inches thick, on top of which were granite caps, eight inches
thick. It was later suggested that the building had been built on top
of an old sewer and that the filling of that sewer was not as well
done as it could have been. In any case, about 10 a.m. on a Saturday

morning, a portion of the building pancaked into the cellar, taking with it a large amount of goods and bales of material. There were thirty clerks and customers in the building when it collapsed but they made it out safely, including one boy who went out on a narrow ledge on the fourth floor and walked to a standing part of the building. Marshal Tukey responded to the scene and immediately sealed off the street to both protect the public from falling debris and to keep looters from stealing the scattered goods. The standing walls were propped up and the business of removing the goods began. About 4 p.m., one of the walls gave way and more of the building collapsed into the cellar. Several of the people who were removing goods were injured but none were killed. In accounting for people after the second collapse, it was realized that Carlos Pierce, a clerk of Dutton, Richardson & Company, one of the stores damaged, was missing.

Isaac Brooks, a handcart man, heard a groan from inside the building. Tukey asked for and led 18 volunteers up a ladder to the third floor where they began removing bales in the area where the groan was heard. Pierce was able to poke a stick up to show where he was. The *Boston Evening Transcript* described the perilous situation they faced, "A portion of the west wall remained standing, but so loosely that it vibrated at the least jar. On the east side a portion of the flooring and partitions hung suspended over the confused mass of flooring, beams, laths, and ceiling below." By 6 p.m., a portion of the collapsed floor was visible and the men set to it with axes and saws. They managed to free the man at 8:15 that night. While he had no broken bones, a doctor who examined him stated that he was so exhausted that he could not have lived another hour.[22]

Tukey was universally praised by the newspapers for his actions in the crisis. Even the *Boston Herald*, his fiercest critic, stated "too much credit cannot be paid to our City Marshal, and his police, who were the means of preventing the crowd encroaching to a dangerous position, and who exerted their strength where it was needed." The actions of Tukey, and others, on that day so impressed the merchants of Boston that they collected $500 to reward the rescuers. The majority of that sum, $300, was distributed to the many laborers who helped release Carlos Pierce. Isaac Brooks and Capt. Caleb Page were given gold watches. Tukey was given a silver pitcher, described as "massive and beautiful" and made by the firm of Jones, Ball & Poor. It bore the legend, "Presented by the Dry Goods Merchants of Boston to Francis Tukey, Esq., for his noble and humane assistance in rescuing Carlos Pierce from the ruins of the Dearborn Block, in Federal Street, June 24, 1848." Not surprisingly, Tukey was unanimously reappointed as city marshal on June 27, 1848.[23]

Whether it was his involvement in recent events or his known skill at organization, Tukey was soon called on to take a larger role in the symbolic life of the City of Boston. The first instance of this was the celebration of the Fourth of July, which the city organized each year. Tukey was named chief marshal of the celebration. His first duty was to lead the Children's Floral procession in the early morning. This consisted of groups of children carrying floral displays. It ended at the Public Garden where they sold their displays to the public. Later Tukey was to lead the civic procession. In the listing of the order of the procession, he came second after the military escort and before the mayor. The day concluded with a banquet at Faneuil Hall and a fireworks display on the Common. Tukey was a major force in organizing all of the celebration.

While the Fourth of July was always celebrated in Boston, there was another, bigger celebration in 1848 and Tukey was also selected to be the chief marshal and organizer. The centerpiece of Mayor Quincy's program, from the very beginning, was to bring clean water to Boston. The water was to come from Long Pond, renamed Lake Cochituate, about 22 miles west of Boston. Work began late in 1846 and took two years and two months to complete the first part of the project. Originally estimated to cost 1.6 million dollars, by the time of the celebration, the total was already over $3 million. The system was said to be able to deliver three million gallons of water a day. At a time when most of Boston got its water from wells, cisterns, and natural springs, the thought of having clean, running water was a cause for joy which the City expressed eagerly.[24]

The organization of this celebration was very complex as everyone wanted to participate. It was estimated that on the day, 40,000 people marched in the procession, which was estimated to be five miles long. Planning seems to have begun as early as August 1848 and was kept under wraps until October. Tukey had a preliminary program printed and distributed only to the marshals who would organize the procession. The *Boston Herald* obtained a copy of this secret program and published it on October 9. It consisted of a Cavalcade, consisting of a large number of citizens riding horses, followed by the Military Escort and then the Main Procession, divided into nine divisions for all the government departments, societies, organizations, etc.—and this was where the trouble started.

The Fire Companies were assigned to the seventh division and they took this to be a slight against them. They felt they should come right after the City Government. Further, they objected to being behind a "O'Shamaria" society. While the companies had been reorganized, they clearly had not forgotten their conflict with the Irish during the Broad Street Riot of 1837. As a sign of how many more Irish were now living in Boston as a result of the Great Famine, most of the charitable organizations in Division Four represented Irish Catholic groups. Within a week most of the fire companies had voted unanimously not to participate. Their demands included not only a better place in the procession but having their own officers appointed as marshals to direct them.[25]

In addition to the firemen, the Boston military companies objected to the plans. While they also complained about their place, their main objection was that the City had not voted them any appropriation to entertain military companies from other cities coming to participate in the celebration. When the Bunker Hill Monument was dedicated in 1843, the military companies were voted an appropriation of $3000 to entertain guests. Now, with even more visitors expected, they did not feel they could properly welcome other military companies. They, like the firemen voted to sit out the procession and celebrations.

Negotiations with both the firemen and the military continued through October, coming close to the deadline. The celebration was scheduled for October 25 and the differences were not resolved until October 21. There was no report that the military were given any money but they were given first position in the parade. The firemen were placed after the military and before the Cavalcade. Both were in advance of the Main procession. Apparently, they were satisfied with the concessions as both groups voted to fully participate in the celebration.[26]

On October 25, at sunrise, the celebration began with the firing of 50 guns and all the bells in Boston were rung for a full hour. The procession was organized by 10 o'clock and began to move at noon. The procession was so long that it was measured to take two hours and ten minutes to pass a single point. As stated above, the military companies led the ensemble, followed by the firemen and the Cavalcade. Francis Tukey, the chief marshal, led the main procession. Immediately after the chief marshal and his aides, was a platform, drawn by seven black horses, carrying two of the large iron pipes, with diameters of 36 inches. The Boston Common Council later described the parade by saying, "The procession, which was arranged with great judgement and conducted with admirable order and regularity, was under the direction of Francis Tukey, Esq., as Chief Marshal for the day."

Not everything went according to plan. The National Lancers, leading the military escort, got to Court Street and had to wait ten minutes for the rest to catch up. A more serious problem was in the sixth division where an actual sloop-of-war was mounted on a platform and dragged by horses. When it reached Cambridge Street, it got caught in a tree overhanging the road and caused a delay of fifteen minutes. The part of the procession before the ship kept going and the two sections never did join up again. On Commercial Street, the ship again ran afoul of a tree causing further delays. Because of all the delays, the mayor and members of the city government left the procession and cut through School Street so that they could be on time for the functions on the Common.

The program on the Common was centered around the Frog Pond. Prior to the event, the pond was drained, pipes laid and then the pond was lined with clean stones and gravel. At one end was the fountain where the water would be introduced. When all was ready, the mayor addressed the crowd, "Citizens of Boston, it has been proposed that pure water be introduced into the city. All who are in favor of the proposition will please say 'aye.'" Naturally the crowd roared their approval. But the beginning of Boston's new water system does not seem to have begun so well:

> All eyes were instantly turned towards the fountain. A moment's pause, and there was a gush of rusty-looking water, small and doubtful at first, then spreading and gathering strength, then rising with beautiful gradations higher and higher, until it towered up a strong, magnificent column

The major achievement of Mayor Quincy's administration was the completion of the water system bringing fresh water into the City. Tukey organized the celebration on the Boston Common shown in this print and led a procession of 40,000 people through the streets (Library of Congress).

of at least seventy feet in height, flashing and foaming in the last crimson waves of the setting sun!

Once the water was flowing well, the operators switched between five different pipes, producing different effects from the fountain. While the fountain was still playing through its various functions, fireworks began to be set off in another part of the Common. At sunset, 50 more guns were fired and the bells of Boston were again rung for an hour.[27]

The Water Celebration represented Mayor Quincy's major achievement and the completion of his promise to bring clean water to Boston certainly boded well for his reelection. However, Quincy, for his own reasons, decided that three years as mayor were enough and, in early November, at a meeting of the Whig county and Ward committees, he declined to be nominated again for the office. In his place, the Whigs chose John P. Bigelow to run for mayor. Bigelow was an experienced politician who had served in the Massachusetts House of Representatives, was chairman of the Common Council of Boston, and a member of the Governor's Executive Council.[28]

While the decision to not run was Quincy's, the major effect was on Tukey. He had been appointed by Quincy and the mayor had consistently supported him. Now that Quincy's protection was to be removed, the many enemies that Tukey had made were ready to have him removed. The day after Bigelow had been nominated, the *Boston Herald* published an editorial stating their support. Not unexpectedly, they conditioned their support on his removing and replacing the city marshal. Later, the *Herald* was happy to report that a committee of Tukey's friends called on Bigelow to state whether he would keep Tukey as city marshal. He declined to give an answer. While Bigelow was being noncommittal, the *Herald* subtly claimed to have inside knowledge. "We know, then,—mark, we say we *know*, no matter how, that, if John P. Bigelow go in, Hassarac Tukey goes out." When the opposition posted placards all over the city suggesting that Bigelow would reappoint Tukey, the *Herald* assured its readers that only the day before Bigelow had reiterated his position to make no decision on the issue until after the election. Despite this assurance, the editor persisted in saying that Tukey would be replaced.[29]

Bigelow faced a field of four other candidates. The Democrats nominated John W. James, the Native Party supported Dr. J.V.C. Smith and the new Free Soil Party nominated Bradford Sumner. The election was held on December 11, 1848, and Bigelow won by a landslide. He received 5064 votes which was 2551 more votes than all of his challengers combined. The Whig candidates for Aldermen were also swept into office by a similar margin. Naturally, the *Boston Herald* was delighted by the result. In describing a crowd which congratulated Bigelow after the election, it reported he said,

> that the people had invested him with power without receiving any pledges, either one way or the other, upon this or that measure; and he therefore felt at liberty to follow that line of conduct which seemed to him best for the happiness, peace and security of our citizens.[30]

The result of the election left Tukey uncertain of his position. His position as city marshal would run until July 1849. After that there was no indication of whether he would still have a job. Bigelow's ploy of being uncommitted loomed large over the next few months.

5

"Who are truly in a pitiable condition, being stowed into garrets and cellars"

While the administration had changed, many citizens of Boston were still grateful to Josiah Quincy, Jr., for his three years as mayor. The Council of the Massachusetts Temperance Society and "other friends of Temperance" presented Quincy with a silver pitcher and salver, said to be worth five hundred dollars, for his efforts on behalf of the cause. This presentation was widely covered in the Boston newspapers, including the *Herald*, which used the occasion to bash its old enemy, "While the Ex-Mayor is receiving presents for the good he has *not* done, the new Mayor has laid down a plan of operation which cannot fail of ultimate success." The *Herald* brought it up again the next day, using it as a way to assail Tukey and the police. It claimed that the silver was only worth about $200 and that the police had donated about $140 of the total. It listed each police officer, taking the opportunity to say something derogatory about each one. Had this been true, certainly one of the other newspapers would have at least mentioned it. This is most likely an example of the unreliability of the *Boston Herald*.[1]

In addition to the temperance presentation, John A. Whipple, the famous daguerreotypist, assembled all of the aldermen of 1848 along with Quincy, Tukey and Samuel F. McCleary, the city clerk, and had them sit for a portrait. This picture is described as being about a foot square. Whipple said that he was planning on doing this every year thereafter but does not seem to have done so.

The final piece of business left over from 1848 was the printing of a pamphlet by the city describing the Water Celebration. This had been authorized by the Common Council on November 2. The pamphlet was entitled *"Celebration of the Introduction of the Water of Cochituate Lake into the City of Boston, October 25, 1848"* and was printed by J.H. Eastburn, the City Printer. It was 48 pages long with soft covers. Generally, the pamphlet is thought to have been printed in 1848, partly because there is no date except that in the title. However, at the end of January and into the beginning of February, Marshal Tukey was tasked with distributing copies to the various newspapers in Boston. At least four of these acknowledged the delivery of the pamphlet.[2]

Boston's new City Government was organized on January 1, 1849. Mayor Bigelow was sworn in by Lemuel Shaw, chief justice of the Massachusetts Supreme Judicial Court. Bigelow, in turn, swore in the aldermen and the members of the Common Council. After the ceremonies, Mayor Bigelow gave his first inaugural address and it was immediately apparent that things would be very different than under Mayor Quincy.

John P. Bigelow

John P. Bigelow, Mayor of Boston 1849–1851, who was initially opposed to Tukey. They developed a close working relationship during the cholera epidemic of 1849. He told the assembled police force late in 1849 that "Your chief, the City Marshal, possesses the full confidence and support" of both the mayor and the Board of Aldermen.

He began by assuring the citizens that he would work for the public good and not be swayed by any "considerations or influence, other than my convictions of right." This was essentially what he told the crowd outside his house the night he won the election. He admitted that this might bring him in "collision with the interests, the prejudices, the passions of a greater or less number of my constituents." This did not deter him from his own principles and, if necessary, he would be happy to return to private life. While this sounds like a noble stand, he never bothered to say what those principles were. In his time as mayor, Bigelow would be reluctant to make any decisions for which he could be blamed or could not shift the burden onto others. His vision for Boston was narrow and bland. This thread runs through his entire address.

The first subject he presented was the value of having a good school system. He made the point that Boston's position was due, in part, to the excellent system of public schools that the city had set up. However, he went on to complain about the cost of the last two school buildings. Next he launched into a discussion of the new jail being planned to be built on Charles Street and again complained about the cost. He expressed the opinion that the old jail might be expanded at less cost. Next he mentions the Fire Department and praises its efficient organization. With the introduction of water from Lake Cochituate, he suggested they might lower their appropriation. In considering the extensive public lands owned by the city, he proposed that the city could sell off parts of it to reduce its debt. Throughout the address he called for program cutbacks and spending less money. Near the end of his address, he was very specific about his vision for the city, "Cut off every expense which is not absolutely necessary for the honor and interest of Boston. Commence no expensive projects, however alluring or desirable, ... consider not what we would like, but what we can afford!"[3]

Nowhere is this more evident than in his discussion of the program of widening and straightening the streets. Over his three years as mayor, Josiah Quincy, each year, argued for the need to upgrade the streets, often referring to the "crowded nature of our narrow thoroughfares." Bigelow, in his address mentions that Boston had spent over a million and half dollars in widening and straightening streets since it changed status from Town of Boston to City of Boston in 1822, with "two-fifths of this great sum ... expended within the last three years." He argued that the streets were wide enough as long as the police kept obstructions from blocking them.[4]

During the election, the regulation of the police and the question of Marshal Tukey's reappointment was an important issue. Candidate Bigelow refused to say what he would do about the city marshal. In his inaugural address, Bigelow continued to avoid the issue. When he mentioned the police, he stated that they needed to be under the "constant and vigilant" supervision of the mayor. He admitted that the nature of the work often brought complaints and vowed to investigate thoroughly all such issues. He then moved on to the next issue without actually saying anything other than he would look into it.

Bigelow used the issue of the police to address the subject that many of his supporters thought was most important, the liquor licensing law. He referred to the city's refusal, since 1847, to grant licenses but still prosecuting for the offense of selling liquors as an experiment which failed. Admitting this, he stated, "The refusal to license has practically resulted in a *general* license." Like many in Boston, he professed to favor total abstinence but recognized that that would not work. Instead he favored the old licensing system, saying it was better than the current situation.[5]

The address argued for a much narrower vision of Boston's potential and made few definite proposals for the future. The only thing clear from his statement was that he favored granting liquor licenses and cutting public debt. As to the position of Tukey and his police, the mayor was still keeping his own opinion.

While he complained about the cost of new schools, Mayor Bigelow was justly proud of the reputation that public education had acquired in Boston. He, like the mayors before him, indeed like most of the native-born population, believed that public education was the cornerstone of city improvement. They shared a widely held belief that by educating the individual, they were making a better society. There was an almost universal belief in school attendance. That opinion was not shared however, by most of the recent immigrants in Boston. The Irish who came to Boston in the 1840s had practical reasons for not sending their children to Boston's public schools. One reason was that, often, the meager money the children made by working odd jobs, was needed to support their poverty stricken families. Perhaps a more important reason was that public schools were seen as Protestant institutions which threatened their children's souls. For these and other reasons, many Irish children did not attend school.

The increasing number of youths wandering the streets at all hours, inevitably getting into trouble, caught the attention of the city government. As in 1846, one of the first tasks assigned to the new police was the regulation of newsboys. In addition to getting a license, they were required to have attended school for three months prior to applying. This was a first step in getting young people to go to school. It did not solve the problem and complaints were constantly being made to both the police and the mayor over the nuisance of idle young people. In 1846, two constables were ordered to search out boys who did not show up at school. When they found them, they would bring them to the school and exhibit them as delinquents before giving them over to their teachers. In this way, 600 boys were taken from the streets. This was done despite the fact that there was no compulsory attendance law. While applauding the efforts of the constables, one editor was less sanguine about the results.

> The truth is the constabulary force can do nothing but frighten the boys, and they are not long in finding it out, after which a reaction necessarily takes place, and they become worse than ever. Our laws are excessively deficient on this point, and many parents are all too willing to allow children to be absent from school on trivial excuses.[6]

The responsibility for truants was switched from the constables to the police in 1847 and a record of names was kept at Police Headquarters. Late in 1848, Mayor Quincy and several Aldermen were formed as a committee to see what could be done to check truancy. At that time, the list the police maintained had 500 names on it. Under the direction of Mayor Quincy, the city marshal was instructed to compile a report on the problem. That report was published in March 1849 and detailed the statistics of the problem. Tukey reported that there were 1,066 "vagrant and truant" children between the ages of 6 and 16 years old, with 882 of these being male. He pointed out that 103 of them were children of "Americans" while 963 were of foreign parents. The marshal acknowledged that his statistics were based only on the children his men had found. In his estimation, if the total number could be determined, it would be closer to 1,500.

The increase in crime associated with these youths was also detailed. The Marshal said, "There is evidently a great increase of crime among minors. The police books show that the number arrested and brought in, is more than one hundred each quarter." The newly opened State Reform School at Westborough was praised for what it was doing. However, Tukey had several problems with it. He argued that the law was defective in that the police had to wait until a boy was convicted of a crime to send him there. Further, he stated, "I am satisfied that it will cost the State and the city, more for police courts and prisons if they are suffered to go at large, than it would to take them now, maintain them, and make them useful citizens."

Further, he pointed out that there was no similar place to send female minors, so they had to go to the House of Correction or the House of Industry with more hardened criminals. Various editors decried the lack of any way of forcing vagrant children to go to school but little was accomplished. A bill was introduced in the legislature that would make school attendance compulsory. It was hotly debated but eventually was tabled permanently. The authority to force children to attend school would not become law in Massachusetts until 1852.[7]

At the beginning of 1849, a serious epidemic was sweeping through parts of the United States and Bostonians was terrified that it would soon be amongst them. Mayor Bigelow, in his inaugural address, mentioned that cholera had, so far, spared Boston but that precautions needed to be taken. During the past year, cholera had arrived in the American South and was already in New York City. While the exact cause of cholera was not known, it was known that the disease was always worst in places of poor sanitation. Marshal Tukey, in December 1848, presented a detailed report which surveyed properties in the city and listed nuisances such as stagnant water, animal or vegetable waste, lack of vaults, lack of proper drains and the keepers of swine. The mayor and aldermen ordered that all licenses for keeping swine be revoked and that the city marshal inform all property owners where nuisances were noted to correct these under penalty of being brought before the Police Court.[8]

One of Mayor Bigelow's first actions was to form a Board of Health, consisting of himself and all of the aldermen, which divided the city into districts, each under the management of a board member. They were authorized to "obtain from the Police and Internal Health Departments as large a force as should be necessary for the effective and thorough cleansing of his district." Police officers, detailed by the city marshal were to "carefully inspect, from garret to cellar, every building in the City; to order and see to the removal of every offensive substance which could readily be removed." It was reported that they performed this duty "in the most quiet and gentlemanly" manner. Gangs of workmen were hired to "purify" all streets, alleys and lanes in the city. Further the city was authorized to use any public building or to procure other buildings for the use of cholera hospitals should the need arise. The City had done all in its power to prevent the coming of this contagion.[9]

Despite the preparations, people knew the worst was coming. Throughout May 1849, there were numerous cases reported that were thought to be cholera but turned out not to be. The uncertainty about which deaths were cholera related and which were not makes it impossible to determine when the disease actually reached Boston. A typical case was that of William H. Mason, of 1 Barry Place, who suffered from diarrhea and vomiting for a few days before dying. When the death was reported to the marshal's office, officers Clapp and Starkweather went to view the body and report. Such viewing was part of the job assigned to the police by the Board of Health. Although Mason had symptoms consistent with cholera, no one was certain about it.[10]

The first acknowledged case of cholera in Boston occurred on June 3, 1849. David Edwards, a Scotch carpenter from the brig *Argyle*, died of "spasmodic cholera" at 11 Hamilton Street. Reports say that he had been feeling sick on board for several days. The *Argyle* had sailed from the Cove of Cork with 246 Irish steerage passengers. Cholera was already epidemic in Ireland and it is likely that many on the *Argyle* had been exposed to it. Shortly after Edward's death, two other people from the *Argyle* died of cholera as well. This was particularly distressing because the *Argyle* had already passed through quarantine, which was supposed to stop such exposure. Still, given that those who were sick were all associated with the ship, one editor was not worried. He commented, "There is no ground for serious alarm. All the disease is traceable to a filthy emigrant vessel" and that it should not be surprising that the disease was found on an "Irish passenger vessel."[11]

The city government could not be as sure as the newspaper editor. The mayor and alderman passed an order to employ an additional policeman in each ward whose specific duty would be to inspect all yards and lanes and report unsanitary properties to headquarters. It was reported that the marshal's office had several hogsheads of chloride of lime, a disinfectant, that it was distributing freely to people who could not afford it and that they had sent large quantities into Ann and Broad streets, representing the poorest neighborhoods and those most likely to be affected by cholera. As the number of cases began to climb, the city appropriated a building on Fort Hill, known as the Gun House, to be used as a hospital. This was a large, brick building which had been used for meetings. To get the building ready, the entire structure was cleansed and then whitewashed, inside and out. A kitchen was built on one end and a room on the other end was converted into an office for the medical staff. Stoves were added to the rooms, ventilators installed and bathing facilities created. Initially 20 beds were set up but that could be expanded to 30 if necessary.[12]

As the epidemic was getting started, Boston was shocked to hear that City Marshal Tukey was showing symptoms of the disease. He was at his office on the morning of June 8 when he began to have stomach cramps and cold sweats. His officers took him to see Dr. J.W. Warren and then to his house. Dr. Warren later stated that this was not cholera but was brought on by "over-exertion and irregularity at meals and sleep." A newspaper editor, reflecting on this, said, "We are prepared to vouch that since the primary rumors of the cholera, the City Marshal has exerted himself with extreme assiduity in fortifying the city against the unwholesome visitor." Another editor commented that "He has been up late and early, and in person visited all sorts of lanes, alleys, yards, and cellars, the stench of which alone would prostrate any but an extraordinary constitution." He also reported that other police officers, detailed as "inspectors" were also sick. While the illness afflicting Tukey may not have been cholera, it was serious enough for the doctor to confine him to bed. Within two days, Tukey was said to be recovering rapidly.[13]

While cholera was striking the city and Tukey was suffering his own malady, politics in Boston continued as usual. In early May, a petition was presented to the Board of Aldermen by N.H. Moulton and 16 others which remonstrated against the reappointment of Francis Tukey as city marshal. This petition rehashed many of the same items that the *Boston Herald* had been claiming against the marshal for several years. At the same time, James H. Blake, who had been city marshal from 1840 to 1845 submitted a petition to replace Tukey. As always, the *Boston Herald* was leading the way. While other newspapers merely mentioned that such petitions were submitted, the *Herald* took pains to point out that those who submitted the document, "were citizens of influence and high-standing." Over the next couple of days, the *Herald* went to war with other newspapers that did not give the petition the respect it was thought entitled to. The *Boston Mail* had commented that "For some time past a clique has been formed, ... of certain persons interested, whose measures have been dictated solely against Marshal Tukey." The *Herald* replied that this was "a lie in the most repugnant sense of the term, and a base and atrocious slander upon a majority of the citizens of Boston."

The *Boston Traveler* had the nerve to ignore the petition against Tukey and only mention that James H. Blake had applied to be Marshal. The *Herald* published a letter from someone named "C.H." who castigated the editor of the *Traveler* in very harsh terms. In response to the above petitions, D.K. Wardwell submitted a petition that supported the reappointment of Tukey as city marshal. The petition was accompanied by 150 signatures. The petition states "that the duties of the office have been faithfully performed by the present incumbent, and that the interest of the city demand his continuance in office."[14]

The mayor and aldermen met on June 25, 1849, and one of the items on their agenda was a consideration of the position of city marshal. Mayor Bigelow, who had refused to state his opinion on the question of the reappointment of Tukey, was now on the spot. When the vote was taken, there were eight ballots and one Alderman declined to vote. Of the eight ballots, seven were in favor of Tukey and one was discovered to be blank. The blank vote was attributed to Mayor Bigelow who still refused to make a decision. The mayor's indecision raised an issue with the entire proceedings. One editor pointed out that the City Charter reserved the "nominative process" to the mayor and that the aldermen only had the power to vote on the nomination. According to the paper, one of the Aldermen moved that they vote and there was no objection from the mayor. Naturally, the *Boston Herald* had much to say about Tukey's reappointment. They blasted the aldermen for their choice and said "Is it any marvel that Boston is regarded as the most hypocritical city in the United States?" While the *Herald* was virulent in its criticism of the Board of Aldermen and individual members, it was strangely silent on Mayor Bigelow. Not a word about his blank vote.[15]

The same day that Tukey was reappointed as city marshal, he suffered a severe relapse of the disease that befell him in early June. This was said to be worse than the original episode.

However, he continued to work through this. Recently, there had been a number of news stories about some philanthropists in New York City raising money to provide public bath houses for the poor. Since Boston now had an abundant water supply and unsanitary personal hygiene was thought to be partially responsible for cholera, it seemed like a good idea to do the same here. Marshal Tukey began a subscription to provide a free bathhouse to the poor of Boston and by early July he had raised $1,200. He was present to be sworn in as city marshal on July 3 and led the city government in the parade on the 4th of July. However, on July 5, he was again sick and at home. All the work did not help and he did not seem to be getting better.[16]

To aid his recuperation, on July 10, Tukey joined many Bostonians and went to Gloucester and Rockport for his health. He left from T wharf on the steamer *Jacob Bell*. The steamer had recently been purchased in New York and brought to Boston as a tow boat. However, by early July, she had a regular route carrying as many as 200 passengers to Gloucester for recreation. In a satirical article, one of the Boston newspapers referred to the *Jacob Bell* and her captain, "Now if you, or any of your friends, get the Choleaphobia, my advice to you is to take a prescription from Capt. Cummiskey ... and aboard his little steamer he'll give you the best antiseptic air." The trip took a little over two hours and left passengers at the wharf by the new Cape Ann Pavilion, run by Albert Morgan. The Cape Ann Pavilion was a large, new hotel located right on the sea shore.

It is not known where Tukey stayed in Gloucester, the *Herald* only said that he was at the "private residence of a boy that was now doing business in Boston." Later, Tukey was reported to be at Mt. Pleasant House in Rockport. This was also a new hotel, opening in 1848, which catered to the tourist trade from Boston. It was said that "The Mount Pleasant House, kept by Messrs. Giles & Tarr, is just such a home as quiet people, in search of real enjoyment, pure sea air, and rational recreation, would desire at such a place." A slightly later ad mentions that it is a "delightfully situated sea shore house.... Most excellent bathing, fishing boats and tackle, and bowling."[17]

Tukey returned from Rockport on August 4 but was reportedly still weak. No matter his condition, he would not have time to fully recover. During his absence, the cholera epidemic became much worse. In July, the average number of cholera deaths per week was only 10 but in August, that number would rise to 83 deaths per week. The very height of the cholera epidemic in Boston was the week ending August 18, barely two weeks after he returned to the city, when the number of cholera deaths was 111. The city marshal was given the additional responsibility of overseeing the Cholera Hospital on Fort Hill. Strange as it seems, the Cholera Hospital was an attraction for a large number of people, some relatives of the inmates but most curious strangers.

New regulations were put forth that restricted access to the hospital at specific times. A police officer, Lysander Ripley, was assigned to bring patients to the hospital and oversee visitors. Officer Ripley was widely praised for his actions and one report gives an idea of the horror of his job: "His labors on Friday, when there were so many new cases, were extremely severe. One little girl, whom he was conveying from Burgess's Alley, died in his arms on the street." Soon afterward, Ripley was confined to his house with bowel complaints which were thought to be cholera. However, he soon recovered and was back at work.[18]

While there were some cases of cholera outside the Irish slum areas, it was clear that the disease was concentrated in the areas where people were poor and living standards were low. The city government began to take notice of these areas. Perhaps one of the good outcomes from this epidemic is that the mayor and aldermen, who never visited these places before, were confronted with the appalling conditions under which many of the Irish were forced to live. In particular, they were disgusted by the use of cellars for dwellings. The Committee on Internal Health described what they saw in their visits,

Most of these cellars are entirely underground with no outlet for air or light.... They are dark, small, low, and, of course, wholly unsuited for any purpose except for storage ... most of them are crowded with human beings, men, women and children.

> Two, three, four, and five families, numbering in all from ten to twenty persons, are found in a single cellar, some fifteen feet square, which they make their abode. In numerous instances, a part of the dwelling is a grog shop....
>
> In the opinion of this committee, such use of cellars, ... is inconvenient to passengers, contrary to law, perilous to the health and lives of the unfortunate beings who occupy them and propagate the epidemic now existing among us.

The mayor and alderman decided to take action and ordered the city marshal to stop the use of cellars as dwellings and to evict anyone currently living in such a place. Tukey reported that there were 586 cellars in Boston used as dwellings and he began clearing them. Several newspapers pointed out that while this seemed like a good idea, the question remained where would these people live? They ended up in the cellars because there was nowhere else they could afford. While proposals for affordable housing for the poor were suggested, there seems to have been no action taken.[19]

According to the report on the Boston cholera epidemic of 1849, there were 707 total cases, of which 96 recovered. In the end, 611 deaths were attributed to cholera. The majority of these were Irish immigrants crowded into the North End and Fort Hill neighborhoods. The 448 immigrants who died of cholera represented three-quarters of all the deaths. However, 163 "Americans" died of the disease, most of whom were sailors and other transients. Only 79 Bostonians were recorded as dying of the disease, or 12 percent of the total number. The final death was on September 30, 1849. The cholera hospital was finally closed on November 15 and the epidemic was over. Through it all, the city marshal and the police were responsible for seeing that the streets and alleys were cleaned and disinfected, for transporting patients to the hospital and keeping records of the epidemic. They were highly praised for their efforts.[20]

The more traditional work of the Police continued despite the cholera in Boston. The previous year, Tukey had the first of his "show ups" familiarizing his men with known criminals. That process continued to evolve over the year of 1849. In May, a man who gave his name as James Watson was taken to the Marshal's Office and exhibited to the officers as a noted hotel thief. The marshal summoned several hotel keepers to attend this so they would also know the young man. Watson was released without charges and disappeared. Several days later, Officer Starkweather arrested John McDonald, whom he saw trying to pick pockets at an auction house. McDonald was one of the class of thieves who traveled from city to city relying on anonymity to keep them out of serious trouble. The *National Police* Gazette followed his pickpocketing in both New York and Philadelphia. The prisoner was held at the Marshal's Office until the roll was called at 2 p.m. when almost all of the officers were present. Tukey then presented McDonald to the assembled men and said,

> This person, gentlemen, has been unfortunate. ... He has been in the State Prison. He has today been detected in examining the pockets of some five or six persons. He is a notorious pickpocket—one of the worst to be found in the country. I wish you all, gentlemen, to take particular notice of him; and, whenever you see him, watch him. If you see him in a crowd, follow him; and if should be at a time when you are off duty, you must consider yourselves on special duty to watch this man.

McDonald was convicted in the Municipal Court but his lawyer filed an exception on some point of law. The Judge reduced his bail to $300 and released him until the case could be tried. However, McDonald promptly skipped bail and left town.[21]

In July, the marshal had a "show up" of a culprit that led his police on a long chase over the city. The subject was identified as Chauncey Larkin but the *Boston Herald* nicknamed him "Dazzle" after a character in a recently produced play. The character of "Mr. Dazzle" has been described as "one of those men who dress handsomely, live well, and ride fine horses, without having any visible means of support for these expenses. The secret of their maintenance of their false position lies in the simple word appearance." This was clearly what Larkin did in his comet-like spree in Boston.

He arrived in Boston about July 3 and checked into the Tremont House under the name of Lt. J. Smith of the United States Navy. After a couple of days the owners came to realize he was a fraud but before the police could be called, he skipped out without paying his bill. He then was found at the Revere House where, after a few days, he left without paying another bill. He wore a naval uniform and gave various names as it suited him. He went to the store of Lane & Reed, giving his name as Lt. C. Hunter, of the *Princeton*. Here he used his main swindle, ordering a gun, a bowie knife and other items, valued at $60. To pay, he offered a check for $100 drawn on the North

Bank. Of course, the check was worthless but Larkin took the goods and $40 in change. Next he went to the store of H.D. Gray & Co. and negotiated the purchase of $1500 worth of goods for the mess-room of the *Princeton*. In the process, he tried to get them to cash a $50 check drawn on the Bunker Hill Bank but this was refused. He visited several other shops trying the same tricks.

All of this activity was reported to the police and they began looking for him. On July 22, the marshal received information that he was lodged at the United States Hotel. Three detectives, Clapp, Butman and Philbrick, were dispatched to bring him in. When showed into his room, he was lying in bed while a servant fanned him and bathed his temples. Clapp asked the servant what was wrong with him and she said he had cholera, which was then epidemic in Boston. Nevertheless, Clapp detailed the charges against him. When asked for the bowie knife, he pulled it out from under the sheets and handed it over. He pointed out other items in the room which he had swindled. The detectives, assuming he was too sick to escape, left the room, posting guards at the exits to the hotel, and called for a doctor to attend the patient. When the doctor arrived, Larkin was gone, dressed in a new suit he had swindled out of a tailor the previous evening.

Larkin then went to another hotel, Hanover House, where he stayed for several days. During that time, he visited a liquor dealer and ordered 40 casks of liquor for the Navy. Going to Long Wharf, he engaged a boat with fishing tackle, telling the owner that he was from the *Princeton* and that a party of officers wanted to go fishing. The owner conveyed him to the Charlestown Navy Yard, "avoiding the *Princeton* as much as possible." Once there, he told the boatman that he would be right back but instead went to a stable and rented a horse and chaise to go to Chelsea Beach. Taking this conveyance, he went to a stable in East Boston. The next morning, a Dr. Parcher, of East Boston, came to the stable to get his own horse. He noticed a "fine and apparently fast horse" in a stall next to his. Asking the stable owner who the horse belonged to, he was told it was owned by a rich North Carolina planter. Later, while talking to the planter, a deal was struck to exchange horses. Larkin got the other horse and $25 in cash. He left the chaise at the stable and took off on the horse.

Knowing the police were on his tail, and most Boston hotels were aware of his frauds, Larkin sought a place to go to ground. On July 26, he took a room in a boarding house on Columbia Street, representing himself as minister from North Carolina. He gave his name as Williamson. The next day, he went out and began another swindle at a wharf in Broad Street. Here he claimed to be a planter from North Carolina and began negotiating for 40 tons of coal. Not begin satisfied with the quality, as he said, he then inquired about renting part of the wharf to unload a large cargo of cotton which was supposedly on its way from his plantation. He left the wharf without actually swindling anything but had set them up for some kind of con. The wharf owner was not convinced and sent for the police. Detective Starkweather showed up and began trailing the suspect. He followed him to Milk Street where he confronted him. Larkin had a knife out and was ready to use it but Starkweather knocked it out of his hand. The suspect began to resist strenuously but Starkweather grabbed him by the throat and tripped him, subduing him on the pavement.

When brought to the police office, Larkin, who gave his name as J.W. Williams of Wilmington, North Carolina, asked why he was arrested. Detective Starkweather began a catalog of his transgressions whereupon the suspect, "laughed heartily at them and appeared to consider the whole affair a 'good joke.'" That afternoon, a "show up" was arranged at the city marshal's office where the prisoner was paraded before the police and various invited hotel keepers. An hour later he was brought up before the Police Court where he was held on two counts to be tried in the Municipal Court. At about this time, the proprietor of the Revere House received a letter from Anthony Morse, a conductor on the Hartford and New Haven Railroad, which said that he knew the swindler as Chauncey Larkin and that he had recently been released from Sing Sing Prison where he served a term for the same kinds of swindles. After his many exploits, Larkin was convicted of only one crime—larceny of a horse and chaise, and sentenced to three years in the State Prison.[22]

Perhaps the most famous of the criminals who did the "show up" was William Darlington, otherwise known as "Bristol Bill." Darlington was an experienced safecracker, burglar and counterfeiter. He began his career in England and according to a very romanticized account of his life, was convicted and sent to Botany Bay. There, he swam out to a New Bedford whaler and was carried to America.[23]

His brush with the police in Boston came as a result of his failed attempt to free his mistress from police custody. On July 30, Margaret O'Connor was brought before the Police Court on a charge of pass-ing altered $10 bills and her trial in the Munici-pal Court was on August 17. As she was being trans-ferred from the court back to jail, a man, wear-ing fake whiskers, took her arm and tried to get her away. This effort was observed by a detective and the man was followed back to a house in Essex Place. It was determined that this house was rented by James Edgerton and his wife, who were already wanted by the police on a number of charges. Get-ting a warrant, detec-tives and a contingent of the police arrived at the house on Saturday morn-ing about 5 a.m. when everyone was asleep. They arrested Edgerton and his wife and in another room found Bristol Bill. When they searched his trunk, they found "as complete an assortment of cracks-man's kit, as was ever manufactured."

The suspects were

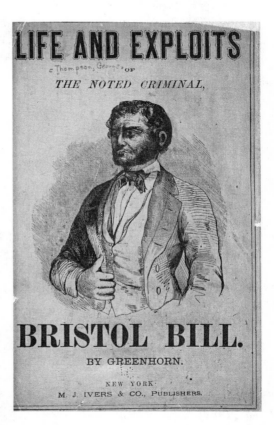

Bristol Bill Darlington was an internation-ally famous burglar and safecracker. Tukey believed he was one of three men responsi-ble for the robbery of the Currier & Trott jewelry store in Boston. However, with-out any evidence, he had to let them go. Later, two of the three were found with sto-len loot but Bristol Bill was never charged, even though he bragged about the robbery in his biographical pamphlet (Library of Congress).

taken to the Marshal's Office, Margaret O'Connor was brought from the jail and all four were exhibited to the police, press and interested citizens. While Bristol Bill was included, the marshal was intending to let him go, as no current crimes were alleged against him. However, a telegram was received from a jewelry store in Portland, Maine, saying that one of the watches seized in the house was stolen from them and three others were probably from the same robbery, so he was held for trial. At the show up, Tukey addressed the police saying,

> Gentlemen: The arrest made today is one of more importance than any that has been effected for the past six months, for the persons you see before you I have every reason to suppose are of the worst kind. ... I would say to you, gentlemen, in closing, to take a good look at these individuals. To follow them and hunt them out if you ever meet them in the street, and keep me informed of their whereabouts. ... Keep your eyes on them, but in no way molest them, if they choose to turn from their evil ways, and walk in the path which all honest men should follow.

After the "show up" Darlington claimed that when he was let go, he was heading out to the "California diggings." As it turned out, the stolen watches were found in James Edgerton's room and had no apparent connection with Darlington. Lacking any specific charge against Bristol Bill, the Marshal had to let him go.

The "show up" which started as a novelty the previous year, had now become an important part of identifying criminals. It was becoming a regular aspect of the work of the detective force. Later, in 1851, this was spelled out in a report Tukey presented to the City Council on the police force. In it he stated, "whenever a suspicious person is made out to be a rogue by information derived from other cities or from other sources he is taken to the Police Office, where he is 'shown up' at the roll-call, and thus made known to the whole of the police."

While the public reaction to these lineups was generally positive, there were some who doubted the legality of them. In the last case, the exhibition of Margaret O'Connor the day before her trial in the Municipal Court was thought to be prejudicial to her case.[24]

In early September, the mayor decided to have a "show up" of his own. He invited Marshal Tukey and the entire police force to a meeting of the Board of Aldermen. As they marched into the meeting room as a group, Mayor Bigelow rose to address them:

> As you have entered the police service voluntarily, and not under the odious system of impressment, you are particularly bound to perform your duties faithfully, cheerfully and courteously. You will find ... that firmness and energy in the discharge of your duty may be easily combined with gentleness and a proper regard to the feelings of the community.... It has not been the intention of the Board to appoint any man to the office of policeman whom they did not believe to possess the feelings and character of a gentleman. ... It is not necessary to address you in detail in relation to your duties. Your chief, the City Marshal, possesses the full confidence and support of the Board and its chairman.

After he addressed the assembled force, the members processed by the mayor's chair, where he shook each man's hand as they passed out of the room.

Quite a remarkable turnaround for a mayor who was so uncertain about the job Tukey did as marshal that, only two months before, he did not nominate him for reappointment and when the vote came, he cast a blank ballot. This was the period when Tukey was most popular in Boston. The newspapers regularly praised the job he was doing. One editor said of him, "He is a very energetic and efficient officer; doubtless the best we have ever had: and the police organization, which is in his hands, is most perfect." Another recognized the difficult job he had to do and praised him for converting his enemies to his friends:

> No other office in the gift of the city is so thankless, or so calculated to make a man enemies, as that of City Marshal. ... Marshal Tukey has been as unpopular as anyone who ever filled the office; but his administration has killed his opponents—many of his former enemies are now, by the Marshal's conduct, made the warmest friends: it would be a hard matter, indeed, to name a more popular officer—and no one could name a more able or energetic one. Marshal Tukey is one of those men who have "lived down his enemies"[25]

Late in November, one of his former enemies, James Blake, came to him with a problem. Just last year, Blake had petitioned the Board of Aldermen to have Tukey removed and to give him the job of city marshal. Now Blake, accompanied by his uncles, Robert Gould Shaw and the Rev. Francis Parkman, came to report that Dr. George B. Parkman, another uncle of Blake's was missing since the day before. Parkman had left his home Friday, November 23, for a 1:30 meeting with an unknown man. It was not like him to stay away from home overnight and on Saturday morning, his family was very worried. He was a very wealthy man and a member of one of Boston's most prominent families. Inquiries by the family had shown that he was last seen in the west end of the city. Immediate action was called for and the police were called into service.

Once Tukey heard about the disappearance, he informed the police who patrolled the west end to explore the houses, yards, and alleys of the area to see if he met with an accident and to interview people who may have seen Parkman. This was at first done quite discretely but as the day wore on and there was no sign of Parkman, all of the police were pressed into action. Tukey's detectives had the Charles River dredged, searched the woods surrounding Boston and visited many of the towns in eastern Massachusetts and on the Cape, inquiring about Parkman—all to no avail.

A notice was placed in the Saturday night papers asking for the public's help in finding Dr. Parkman. This was followed by others offering a $3000 reward for information on his whereabouts, a $100 reward for a watch that he was carrying and, finally, a $1000 reward for his body. Tukey had 28,000 handbills printed up and distributed throughout the city. There were numerous rumors of sightings, each of which had to be checked by the police. The newspapers reported that the "most active exertions have been made by the city police, and the friends of Dr. Parkman, for his recovery, but as yet to no purpose."[26]

As the detectives developed their information, it became apparent that the man Parkman was to meet at 1:30 p.m. was Dr. John Webster, a professor of chemistry at the Massachusetts Medical College on North Grove Street. When interviewed, Webster said that he had met with Dr. Parkman and had given him $483 to pay off a mortgage that he owed. According to Webster, Dr. Parkman told him he was going to go to the Registry of Deeds in East Cambridge and "relieve the mortgage." In support of this, the tollman on the nearby bridge across the Charles River leading to Cambridge told the police that he had seen Dr. Parkman as he went across the bridge. However, Mr. Hayden, the Register of Deeds, who knew Dr. Parkman well, said that he never came to the office that day. Despite this apparent lead, the police had some doubts. Just before Dr. Parkman went to the Medical College, he had stopped at a grocery store and left a package, saying he would be back "in five minutes." He never came back for the package.[27]

Tukey was suspicious of the Medical College from the beginning. Many people had either seen Dr. Parkman on his way to the College or heard that he was heading there. There were only isolated reports about him after the meeting. And the abandoned package was worrisome. The police searched the Medical College for the first time on Monday. Accompanied by the building's janitor, Ephraim Littlefield, officers searched all of the rooms from the attic to the basement. Dr. Webster let them into his lab but they found nothing. Still harboring suspicions, Marshal Tukey had an officer stationed to watch the building. Without any further leads, detectives went over the ground again, including on Tuesday, going back to the Medical College. Again they searched the building, including Dr. Webster's labs, but found nothing.[28]

Marshal Tukey was not the only one who was suspicious. The janitor, Ephraim Littlefield, out of curiosity or with an eye to the reward, began to suspect Dr. Webster had something to do with the disappearance. He noted that Webster had begun to lock his laboratory when he never had before. Webster started working odd hours and was firing the furnace in his lab so much the adjoining wall outside the lab was very hot to the touch. Littlefield conducted his own investigation, at one point peeking through the keyhole and even sneaking into the lab through an outside window. He decided to investigate the only place that had not yet been searched, the vault under Dr. Webster's privy. As he could not do it from inside the lab, he decided to break a hole though the brick side wall in the cellar under the building. He discussed this plan with Dr. Bigelow, the head of the Medical College, who gave him permission to proceed with the plan.[29]

When Littlefield managed to open a hole in the wall, he saw pieces of a disarticulated body. Knowing that such a thing should not be in the space, he assumed that it was Dr. Parkman and quickly went to Dr. Bigelow's house to inform him. Bigelow told him to go back to the College and he would bring Marshal Tukey there. When Tukey and his detectives arrived, along with other officers, there was already a crowd gathered. While the other police controlled the crowd, Tukey had Littlefield take him down to the cellar. Sticking a lamp through the hole in the brick wall, the Marshal surveyed the scene. He send Littlefield and an officer through the hole and had the remains carried out. There were three parts, a thigh, a portion of a body and part of a leg. As he was completing the investigation, there was a noise upstairs and it was thought Dr. Webster had returned. Tukey, Detective Clapp and Officer Trenholm searched the building but found no one. As they went into the laboratory, Detective Clapp looked in the ashes in the furnace and found pieces of bone and teeth mixed with the ashes. Perhaps the most important find from the furnace was a piece of a denture which Dr. Parkman's dentist reported making for him recently. Further investigation in the lab revealed a tea chest where, hidden under a layer of minerals and tan bark, officers found a section of torso and a piece of leg. The torso had evidence of a couple of stab wounds.[30]

With the discoveries below the privy and in the furnace, the marshal gave orders for three of his detectives to go to Dr. Webster's home in East Cambridge and arrest him. At the house, Detective Clapp told Dr. Webster that the police were again searching the Medical College and asked for him to come help. He later said that he did this to spare Webster's family the shock of the arrest. As they came across the bridge from Cambridge, Webster complained that the driver had missed the turn to the Medical College but Clapp assured him they were going the long way around. The farce was finished as the carriage arrived at the Leverett Street Jail. There Clapp told Webster that he was under arrest for the murder of Dr. Parkman. While waiting for the paperwork to be completed, Webster, although under observation, took a dose of strychnine which make him extremely weak but did not kill him. At the time, this weakness was attributed to emotional collapse but later he admitted trying to kill himself. The trial of Dr. Webster would provide sensational headlines for the newspapers in the next year but for now, he stayed in a jail cell.[31]

The arrest took place in the evening of November 30 and was published the next day in the Boston newspapers. The details of the finding of the body in pieces excited the populace and lead to threats against the Medical College. Its reputation was already tarnished in the minds of many Bostonians by the discovery, the previous year, that one of the cadavers used for medical studies had been the victim of a botched abortion. The mayor put the State Militia on alert and Tukey stationed men around the Medical College to prevent any rioting. However, things remained calm and there were no incidents.[32]

The coroner's inquest on the body found at the Medical College was convened on Saturday afternoon, December 1. Jabez Pratt, the coroner, decided to keep its activities private to spare Dr. Parkman's family. They heard testimony and deliberated until December 13. The jurors concluded that the body parts were the remnants of Dr. George Parkman and that, in their opinion, he met his death at the hand of Dr. John W. Webster. The jurors took the unusual step of voting thanks to the city marshal and the police "for the prompt and efficient services rendered by them to this Inquest, in procuring evidence and rendering such other assistance as was in their power."[33]

December was the month for the annual mayoral election but with all the excitement over Dr. Parkman's disappearance and the subsequent discovery of the body, little attention was given to the election. John P. Bigelow was again nominated by the Whig party. He faced Bradford Sumner of the Freesoil Party and James Hall of the Democratic party. Unlike previous elections, the question of the reappointment of Tukey as city marshal was not even mentioned. Apparently the truce between the mayor and the marshal was still in effect. The election was held on December 10 and Bigelow, as expected, was swept back into office by a wide margin.[34]

6

"There has probably never been a criminal trial ... which called for such an immense amount of varied learning"

After his overwhelming victory—he garnered more than 80 percent of the votes cast—Mayor Bigelow organized the city government on January 7, 1850. His inaugural address was primarily in the same spirit as the one he gave the previous year. The address began by thanking the voters of Boston for their "emphatic" support and repeating his promise to be swayed by no influence but his own conscience. Throughout the speech, he maintained the theme of fiscal responsibility. He discussed the construction of the new jail, which he opposed the previous year, suggesting that it would be the most expensive building ever built by the city. The sale of public lands to offset the city's debt is again an important topic. This included a parcel known as the "Public Garden," calling this name "a sort of misnomer." Fortunately, the city did not sell this property and today it is one of the jewels in the greenspaces of Boston.[1]

Naturally, the recent cholera epidemic formed an important part of his comments. Mayor Bigelow had been widely praised for his leadership during the crisis and this accounted for his great support in the election. He commented that the 5,080 deaths over the previous year were the most recorded in the city during a single year. More than one-fifth of those were attributed to the epidemic. He gave praise to the city physician and the Board of Health for their efforts and for their direction of the Cholera Hospital. He recommended that the city consider continuing this institution as a permanent hospital for the poor. In speaking of the epidemic, he again renewed his call for the city to establish a cemetery "beyond the boundaries of the City," because all of the in-town cemeteries were full.

In discussing the rise of crime and the police, Bigelow was much more complimentary in his speech. The previous year he had urged that the police needed to be under the "constant and vigilant" supervision of the mayor. This year he stated that the Police and Watch Departments "have been satisfactorily conducted" and that they are "entitled to great credit." He suggested that the only way they could get better would be the addition of more men, which, unfortunately would be very expensive. However, this could be achieved if the two separate departments were combined under one head. The mayor had come a long way since casting a blank vote in the reappointment of Marshal Tukey.

That the mayor had been listening to the city marshal was evident in his comments on the rise of crime in Boston. He attributed this to five factors: "...the increase of the intemperate use of intoxicating liquors; the unwillingness of juries to convict culprits, ... the leniency of judicial sentences; the facility of procuring pardons; and that morbid philanthropy, which practically prefers the escape of the offender to the security of the innocent." He uses the first of these factors to complain about the licensing law where no licenses are granted and the flouting of it thereby. The second, he said, made fear of the law obsolete and gave criminals freedom to do as they pleased. In regards to pardons, the influence of the Marshal is apparent, "it is well known to our police that many of the most atrocious offenses ... have been the work of pardoned criminals." Finally he inveighs against those who make celebrities out of criminals and do all in their power to see them released. In his indictment of the justice system, Mayor Bigelow reflected what Marshal Tukey was telling him.

Both the mayor and the marshal were responding to the general feeling that the rate of crime in Boston was increasing greatly. In late December 1849, Marshal Tukey, following the dictates of the Board of Aldermen, prepared the first annual report on crime in Boston which showed that the police had dealt with 3087 crimes. In 1847, his first year as city marshal, Tukey presented a report of crimes, totaling

1,052, dealt with by the police in the first six months of the new force. These statistics can be used to assess the extent and change in criminal activity in Boston. If the 1847 total is doubled, suggesting the total for the whole year not just the last six months, then during the three years that Tukey was marshal, crime rose 32 percent. However, this must be tempered by several factors.[2]

The first such factor is the great increase in the population of Boston over this period. From 1845 through 1850, there was a large influx of immigrants fleeing the Irish Potato Famine, as well as in-migration from other parts of New England. The population of Boston from 1845 to 1850, rose from about 110,000 to 136,000. This was an increase of 20 percent over the period. The second factor to be taken into account was the introduction and enlargement of an active police force in the city. Prior to 1847, crimes needed to be reported to the marshal or handled by the citizens. Once you regularly send officers into the streets to look for crime, they are going to find it more easily. Not only was there an active police force but it increased from 30 to more than 50 by 1849. These factors were guaranteed to show an increase in crime.[3]

Perhaps more importantly, the types of crime had not changed greatly between the two reports. In 1847, alcohol related crimes (drunkenness, license violations) accounted for 59 percent of all crimes. By 1849, these crimes represented 57 percent of the total. One of the types of crime to go down significantly was violation of the city ordinances. The active police force was, in part, created to deal with this problem. In the earlier report, violations of the ordinances made up 17 percent of the total but by 1849 they accounted for only 7 percent. Violent crimes (murder, rape, assault) did not increase significantly over this period. What did increase was the number of miscellaneous crimes for which people were arrested, including such things as attempting to extort money, obtaining goods on false premises, lewdness, obstructing a railroad, disturbing religious worship and "pipers and fiddlers," among others. An active police force can be used to enforce things which might not have been previously called a crime.

Larcenies and robberies were the crimes which actually showed a small increase between the two reports. In the last six months of 1847, there were 185 larcenies resulting in the loss of $33,667. Of that, the police recovered $24,805 or 73 percent of the total. The number of larcenies investigated in 1849 was 675 resulting in the loss of $45,724. The police recovered $36,423 of this total or 79 percent of the total. The increase in the recovery rate may be due to the continued development of Tukey's detective bureau.

Besides the recovery of stolen goods, the detectives could sometimes use their contacts to anticipate crimes. Probably in late December, they got a tip that three men were planning to rob a jewelry store on Quincy. While this was out of their jurisdiction, Marshal Tukey shared this information with the store's owner. As the New Year dawned, the owner and his men waited outside for the robbers. Two of the robbers broke into the store while a third stood watch outside. The owner's men subdued the lookout, locked the others in the stone and sent for the deputy sheriff. The arrest of the robbers in the act was a direct result of the Boston detectives' activity.[4]

Tukey's increasing approval and popularity in Boston brought him into contact with most of Boston's elite. It may have also led some others to capitalize on his fame. On January 5, 1850, Messrs. Whitney and White, owners of the Commercial Coffee House, a large establishment at the corner of Milk and Batterymarch streets, reportedly held an invitation-only dinner for "some of our most distinguished men." The proprietors reportedly asked Marshal Tukey to sit at the head of the table and to address the invitees. He is said to have "abounded with much felicity and wit." Other significant attendees were B. Perley Poore, the editor of the *American Sentinel*, and Thomas Gill, a reporter from the *Boston Post*. This was reported in the *Boston Daily Times* with a glowing recommendation of the food and establishment of the Commercial Coffee House. The *Boston Herald* also mentioned the dinner, regretting that it could not be there, without mentioning any of the attendees.

However, a couple of days later, the *Boston Daily Bee* took notice and claimed that neither Tukey, Poore nor Gill were present at the dinner. The editor said, "The publication of such statements, while they do no one any good, may be the means of doing those whose names are thus unceremoniously handled, much harm." Finally, the *Boston Daily Times* had to come out and admit that "it is also alleged" that none of the men were present at the dinner. Clearly the "puff piece" that was originally published was either given to the

Times by the proprietors of the restaurant and simply run as is or the editor thought he could get away with stretching the truth. That Tukey's name formed such an important part of the piece is reflective of his popularity and importance in Boston.[5]

Mayor Bigelow and Marshal Tukey took up the cause of judicial leniency by intervening in the case of Dennis Scanlan, an experienced pickpocket. The details of the current case were that on January 12, while at an auction store in Congress Street, he removed a purse from a lady's pocket. Realizing something was wrong, she followed him and had him arrested. He was taken to the marshal's office where he was searched and her property was found on him. Scanlan was brought before the Police Court on January 15 where both the lady and Officer Starkweather testified to the facts of the case. Judge Cushing was about to require Scanlan to come up with $300 for bail to ensure his appearance in the Municipal Court in February when Marshal Tukey addressed the Court, saying "May it please your honor; I am instructed by his honor the mayor, to appear here in behalf of public justice. I wish to say a word to the court in regard to pickpockets, and particularly respecting the one at the bar."[6]

Tukey went on to outline the fact that this was the fifth time Scanlan had appeared before the Police Court within the year. The first time, he was fined $15 and the second time he was sent to the House of Correction for four months. Barely two weeks after he was released, he was again arrested and sent for two months back to the same place. On his last arrest, in November, he stole a purse and was running away when caught. In his hands he had the purse and a five dollar bill. The arresting officer could not swear that the five dollar bill was from the purse and the purse's owner had not come forward at that point. The purse was held but the money was given to Scanlan, who then paid his fine with it. Finally, Tukey mentioned his current arrest. Having detailed Scanlan's history before the courts, the marshal then went on to offer his experience with this sort of criminals:

> I wish to say a word touching this sort of crime. There are no criminals so difficult to convict as pickpockets. This is in consequence of not being able to identify money, for not one man in a hundred can identify money which he has about his person. There are different kinds of pickpockets. One class rob the breast pocket, another the side pocket of the trowsers, another the coat pocket; and then there is another class who rob ladies—and this man is of the latter. He is one of the worst thieves in Boston. ... In various

disguises he visits auction rooms and there robs poor women of their last pittance.—He is void of that honor claimed among thieves, or he would not make woman [sic] his victim. He had not the courage to rob a man. But ... out of all those who have been arrested within two years past he is only the second one that has been sentenced.

Marshal Tukey then went on to describe various cases of pick-pockets who had been arrested during the previous year. Many were given bail and skipped town. Some were convicted but their law-yers filed exceptions and the suspects were then given bail, and left town. In one case, he claimed the wife of the man convicted joined a church attended by the sister of the wife of the lieutenant gover-nor, and through this influence was pardoned out of the State Prison in less than a year though his sentence was for two years and nine months. He compared the lenient sentences and low bail in Massa-chusetts to much stricter sentencing in New York and stated, "No wonder they come here."

In conclusion, Marshal Tukey referred to a section of Massa-chusetts state law which required a heavy sentence for stealing from the person. He understood that the Police Court had jurisdiction in such cases and normally gave much lighter sentences and lower bail. There was a case before the Supreme Judicial Court which would set-tle the issue of jurisdiction. He asked that the judge set the bail high enough to hold the prisoner for a month or so until this case was decided. Judge Cushing raised the bail to $500 for his appearance in February. Scanlan was eventually convicted and sentenced to a year in the House of Correction.[7]

The speech that Marshal Tukey made in the Police Court was well received and served to support his growing popularity. However, Lieutenant Governor John Reed objected to the implication that he was influenced by his wife or her sister when granting a pardon to John White. He denied that White's wife had joined the church where Reed's sister-in-law worshiped. He further suggested that the story was presented to further Mayor Bigelow's political aspirations. Tukey replied to the same editor two days later, saying that while Mayor Bigelow had asked him to speak to the court, the words were his own and the mayor did not know what he would say. Tukey claimed that his information on the church and the pardon came from John White himself and that he boasted about deceiving the Board and the lieutenant governor "in particular." He ended on a conciliatory note stating that he would never imply that the lieutenant governor did anything wrong and that he held his character in "deserved respect."[8]

This was not the end of the matter, however, as another letter was sent to the *Courier*. It was written by William W. Marjoram, a well-known advocate of many of the 19th-century reform movements that occupied Boston in the 1840s and 1850s. He was involved in the temperance movement, the abolition movement as well as what we would today call the prisoner's rights movement. Marjoram was the prime mover in having White released from prison, had been taking care of White's wife while he was in prison and believed that White would have practiced the trade he learned in prison except that the police continued to hound him. He was sure that Tukey had heard incorrect things about White after his release from a "person who ought not to be credited." As White was dead from sickness by this point, there would be no way to assess any of these points. For Mayor Bigelow, this was an example of the "morbid philanthropy" about which he complained in his recent inaugural address. Marshal Tukey made his point that White had served only 10 months of his 33 month sentence, underscoring Bigelow's other point about the ease of getting pardons.[9]

About mid–January, a ship arrived in Boston harbor from Maine on the way to California. The California Packet Company had been formed to build a ship and take a party of settlers from Maine to the gold fields in California. The ship was built under the direction of Capt. George Kimball and launched on December 29, 1849, in Cutler, Maine. For over a year, tales of gold in California had fired the imagination of many in New England. Capt. Kimball, with no money or credit, decided to build his own ship and sells shares to people who wanted to emigrate. This venture was looked on with pride by many who saw it as an example of the positive attitude of New Englanders. The ship and its passengers became folk heroes when they arrived in Boston. The editor of the *Congregationalist*, published in Boston, said, "It is a novel enterprise, and a little more hardy, democratic and Yankee, than pro-slavery disunionists will like to see fitting out for the golden territory."[10]

Unfortunately, while doing their last fitting out in Boston, they ran up a bill for supplies. To help them on their way, a number of

Boston men who were from Maine, decided to hold a "Complimentary Ball" in the hall over the Fitchburg Depot with tickets selling at a dollar a piece. City Marshal Tukey, a proud son of Maine, was the head of this committee. One editor said that the ball, "bids fair to be one of the most fashionable gatherings of the season." The *California Packet* left Boston on March 4 and arrived safely in San Francisco on August 24. The reports of gold in California made many New Englanders dream of such a voyage and this ship may have had an effect on Francis Tukey.[11]

While the dream of finding gold filled many an eye in New England, there was money of a different kind to be had in California. People were flocking into the state in such numbers that many things were in short supply. At the time, California had no industry to speak of and all manufactured items had to be shipped there. As did others, Tukey purchased items and shipped them to the newly developing settlements. Over the next two years, he shipped bricks, clapboards, shingles, stoves and pre-made house frames to Sacramento. This was his first real involvement with California which would become very important in his life in the next few years.[12]

Soon after the *California Packet* sailed out of Boston harbor, Marshal Tukey was getting ready for one of the most sensational events in the city's legal history. The trial of Professor John Webster for the murder of Dr. George Parkman would begin on March 19. Not only was this murder a sensation because of the gruesome details of the discovery of the body parts but it involved two members of the very top social strata in Boston. Public interest in the trial was intense. The *Boston Herald* informed its readers that it had two reporters who would attend the trial and accurately report the testimony. They intended to put out hourly editions so that the public could read the testimony almost as soon as it was given. The editor of the *Herald* was aware that this trial would be like no other. He suggested,

> There has probably never been a criminal trial in the United States which called for such an immense amount of varied learning as will be required in the present case. Anatomy, chemistry, and natural philosophy will claim a large share of the attention of the counsel for the accused and the government.[13]

The *Herald's* editor was reacting to the central issue in the case, the identification of body parts found under Professor Webster's privy and in his laboratory. People who knew Dr. Parkman intimately stated that certain features resembled the doctor but their testimony was only an opinion. If the government was to get a conviction, they had to find evidence that was not based on simple opinion. This case was not just a sensation in 1850 but would set standards for forensic evidence for many years to come.

The most important evidence for the identification were the teeth and bones discovered in the assay furnace in Webster's laboratory. Dr. Nathan C. Keep testified that he had been Dr. Parkman's dentist for 25 years and, that after the discoveries at the Medical College, he was shown a block of "mineral teeth" which he recognized as one he made for Parkman in 1846. He went on to explain that because of the peculiarity of the shape of Parkman's jaws, the fitting of the teeth was difficult and he had to grind down the inside edge of the teeth to make them comfortable. The dentist pointed out to the jury the grinding marks to which he was referring. Finally, Dr. Keep had made molds for forming the teeth and he fitted the discovered teeth into the molds that made them.[14]

The defense naturally brought in their own dentist, William Morton. He, in contrast to Keep, denied the peculiarity of Parkman's jaw although he had never studied it and said that the teeth found were not unusual. Also, he commented that it was standard practice to grind the inside edge of the teeth to make them more comfortable. However, on cross-examination, Morton admitted that he could identify teeth he had made and that any dentist who had spent considerable time on a difficult case could probably identify their own work.[15]

Another example of the early development of forensics used in this case were the letters written to Marshal Tukey purporting to give clues to what happened to Dr. Parkman. During the trial there were three letters presented by the prosecution, all addressed to Francis Tukey, which stated various causes for Dr. Parkman's disappearance. One suggested that he was murdered on Brooklyn Heights and another that he was shanghaied aboard the ship *Herculean*, which had just sailed from Boston. The prosecution brought in several handwriting experts who testified that the letters were written by Dr. Webster. One of the letters, the one reporting Dr. Parkman was shanghaied, was not written with a pen but some other object.

Testimony was taken about a twig with one end wrapped in cotton which was found in Webster's laboratory and it was suggested that this was used to write the letter. One of the letters was cut from a piece of white wrapping paper and the matching paper was found in the desk of Professor Webster.[16]

Marshal Tukey testified about the case on March 20, 1850. He recounted being informed of the disappearance and the subsequent search for Dr. Parkman. The most dramatic testimony was concerning the discovery of the body. Perhaps expecting trouble, Tukey put a revolver in his pocket before he left the office. It was during this part of the testimony that the prosecution presented to the court a detailed scale model of the Medical College along with a plan map of the ground floor. The model was made by James Hobbs, a well-known model and pattern maker in Boston. It was designed so each floor of the College could be removed separately. The use of courtroom exhibits was another innovation of this trial. Tukey used the exhibits to describe where the body pieces were found and how the search was conducted. Professor Webster was found guilty of murder and, before he was executed on August 30, he confessed to stabbing Dr. Parkman.[17]

The city marshal had one other tangential relation to the trail of Professor Webster. The day after the marshal testified, a fire broke out at the Tremont House on the corner of Tremont and Beacon streets. The attorney general, who was prosecuting the case, had a room there and the trial was delayed while he went to secure his baggage and papers. When the alarm was first sounded and before the firemen got there, Marshal Tukey and a force of police were in the lobby controlling the crowd and looking for thieves. As was his practice, Tukey responded to fire alarms both to clear the crowd so the firemen could do their job and to protect property removed from the building.[18]

While the Webster case fascinated Boston and the entire nation, Tukey, and his police force, were aware that crime was no longer just a local issue. This was evident when they dealt with criminals like Bristol Bill and others who made their home in New York City but travelled far and wide to complete their illegal jobs. In the previous year, the gang had worked in Boston, where Margaret O'Connor, Bristol Bill's lover, was arrested for passing counterfeit money. She and Bill were in one of Marshal Tukey's "show-ups" but no charges were filed against Bristol Bill. It was said that Bill contacted the head of the gang, Samuel Drury, to get bail money for O'Connor but was denied. Burning with anger, Bristol Bill went back to New York to act as "stool-pigeon" against Drury.[19]

At the same time, Drury and a lawyer, Thomas Warner, were engaged in their own affair. A bomb was sent to Warner's house but it failed to kill him. Who sent the bomb was never determined. George Wilkes, editor of the *National Police Gazette* and friend of Warner suspected Drury and set out to investigate by using his underworld contacts, specifically Bristol Bill and "One-eyed" William Thompson, to trap his suspect. Warner and Thompson travelled to Boston to get O'Connor to sign an affidavit that Drury was responsible for the bomb. If she did so, Warner would have her bailed and take her to New York to testify. She signed the document in the presence of Marshal Tukey and Officer Smith of New York. O'Connor was bailed and returned to New York where she changed her story, saying that Thompson built the bomb for Warner, in order to kill Warner's wife. Marshal Tukey was brought into this when "One-eyed" Thompson was arrested for counterfeiting and asked for a halt in the trial so that he could get Marshal Tukey to testify. While the trial did continue, there is no indication that Tukey did so.[20]

However other business brought Marshal Tukey to New York City near the end of the trial. In March, George Bulloch, cashier of the Rail-Road Bank in Savannah, Georgia, absconded with as much as $100,000 in negotiable securities. He fled Savannah in the British schooner *Abel*, headed for Fowey, Wales. Before his destination was known, the authorities in Georgia sent telegraphic messages all over the country alerting police forces to look for him. Marshal Tukey, put these pieces of information together and realized that a steamer from Boston could arrive earlier than the *Abel* under sail. He sent Officer Asa Butman over to England. Butman arrived ahead of Bulloch and was waiting on a pilot boat in the harbor of Fowey to arrest Bulloch. Butman and his prisoner came back across the ocean on the steamer *Cambria*. When the ship stopped in Halifax, Butman telegraphed the marshal to meet him New York. Tukey was on the pier when the *Cambria* docked on May 2, with the intention of escorting the prisoner to Savannah. Whether, before the arrival, he was in contact about the trial is unknown.[21]

Police business kept Tukey travelling quite a bit at this time. On May 16, Detective Starkweather arrested a man named Milo A. Taylor, who was wanted for passing counterfeit bills in western Massachusetts. When brought to the Marshal's office, a search revealed that he had 11 "false bills" on him as well as $730 in good money. The next day, Starkweather, in company with officers from Northampton, brought Taylor to the Hampshire County Jail. On the way to the jail, Taylor gave the Boston detective information which led him to a house in Chicopee where he recovered 25 more counterfeit bills. Believing that Taylor had useful information on a gang of counterfeiters in Springfield, Marshal Tukey made a quick trip to the western part of the state, visiting Holyoke, Springfield and Northampton, where he had an interview with Taylor in his cell. The *Springfield Republican*, in a piece that was widely repeated in the Boston newspapers, said that "No man is better fitted for the responsible post he holds, for he is intelligent, shrewd, active, penetrating and energetic. Boston may well be proud of her Chief of Police."[22]

In his inaugural address, Mayor Bigelow had raised the possibility of combining the police with the town watch. The watch was the original law enforcement in Boston, beginning in the Colonial era. Their job was to patrol at night, mainly watching for fires but that activity inevitably brought them in contact with criminals. When Josiah Quincy, Jr., founded the Boston Police, their patrols were in the daytime and the watch continued its usual activity. While Tukey's police did have a small, dedicated night force, they were mainly there to respond to disturbances. Mayor Bigelow had suggested that by combining the two departments, the city would be better served. In January, a committee was formed, consisting of two aldermen and three members of the common council, to consider how such changes might be made. They decided that it would be good to see what other major cities were doing and a trip along the Atlantic Coast was planned. Marshal Tukey, as head of the police, was asked to go along but there was no representative of the watch invited.

The committee left Boston on May 25 and travelled to Washington, D.C., where they stayed at the Willard Hotel. Their next stop was in Philadelphia. Neither of those cities took much notice of the delegation. The committee arrived in New York on June 5 where they checked into the Astor House. The Common Council of New

York City hosted a dinner for the committee on the night of June 6. The next day, they were taken on a tour of the prison on Blackwell's Island and the orphanage on Randall's Island. The committee returned to Boston the next day. Their report was submitted near the end of the year, recommending the union of the two forces but left it to the next City Council to consider the change.[23]

Tukey knew that if the two forces were united under one chief of police, he was likely to be that person. He had the support of the aldermen and now the mayor. When the watch force held a dinner for its members, they invited most of the city government, including the city marshal. The dinner was a large affair, held on June 26 at the United States Hotel, and there were over 300 guests present. It included the music of a brass band at the end. Tukey sat at the head table, next to Mayor Bigelow. As was usual at these kinds of affairs, there were a number of complimentary toasts given during dinner. One of the toasts saluted Tukey, proclaiming, "The city marshal—an industrious, faithful, fearless officer." As was expected, Tukey rose to reply and used this opportunity to both flatter the watchmen and to reiterate a point that both he and the mayor had been pushing. Tukey began by thanking them for the invitation, saying that he was glad to meet them all, and that he felt almost as if he were one of them. The main part of his speech was reported as follows:

> He mentioned the fact that 150 armed rioters had been subdued by 20 watchmen. Look at the records and see the cause why the cry had gone forth that Boston was becoming as iniquitous as other cities south and west of us. The cause was in the leniency of the judicial branch and the misplaced sympathy of public opinion. He claimed to be a watchman in some part, although he seldom put his hand on a man in the night, or a woman either. (Here the Mayor held up his finger and a general hurra burst from his guests.) He concluded by offering the following—The Watchmen of Boston: may they know their rights and knowing dare maintain them.[24]

Tukey's reference to rioters and the city's reputation for public disturbances both praised the watchmen and the establishment of his own force. There had been no major public disturbances since the police force had been established. His comments on the judiciary and "misplaced sympathy" echoed the mayor's inaugural address and his own speech to the Police Court in the case of the pickpockets. The toast at the end suggested that, with change in the air, Tukey stood with them.

Unlike the previous years, Tukey's reappointment as city marshal was smooth and well-received. At a meeting of the Board of Aldermen on July 1, Mayor Bigelow nominated Tukey to be city marshal and the vote in his favor was unanimous. He was then sworn into office by the mayor. The editor of the *Boston Evening Transcript* commented on this change, "The re-appointment of this faithful and energetic officer seems to give very general satisfaction. Marshal Tukey has quietly lived down all opposition by a steady persistence in well doing."[25]

Shortly after his reappointment, Tukey arranged a special treat for his men. They and their families went on an excursion to Lake Cochituate for a day-long picnic. The gathering included all 51 of the police and an estimated 189 family members. They enjoyed the country air, played sports and danced to a band. Tukey was the organizer and it was reported that he was "issuing orders and making himself agreeable and useful, as every captain of such an excursion ought to do at such a gathering." About 2 p.m., the mayor and many of the aldermen arrived and were welcomed. Marshal Tukey rang a bell to bring everyone to the tables for the meal. After this, Tukey introduced Mayor Bigelow, who spoke for 20 minutes. The main thrust of his speech was that it used to be money that distinguished the worth of men is society but that due to them, "mind, energy and enterprise characterized the man and his standing in society."[26]

In August, Marshal Tukey had the opportunity to repay the kindness shown to him and the committee on police reform while they were in New York. President Zachary Taylor died in Washington in July and, like many major cities, Boston planned a funeral procession and memorial. A large delegation from New York, including a number of aldermen, came to Boston to represent their city. While they were here, Tukey led them on tours of the public institutions on Deer Island and in South Boston. They were particularly impressed by the city's water works.

The otherwise splendid tour ended on an unfortunate but humorous note. On Friday night, August 16, a group of eight people were celebrating the end of the tour. They had imbibed quite a bit of rum and were found on the streets, early Saturday morning, loudly calling "fire" and singing bawdy songs. They were confronted by members of the watch who told them to be quiet and go home.

There was some resistance to this suggestion and the watchmen called for reinforcements. At this point, four of the company escaped while the other four were arrested and taken to the watch house. There it was determined that the four were representatives of the New York city government, including three aldermen. The unknown four who escaped were said to be Bostonians. Captain Barry, the head of the watch, met them and, with their promise to be quiet and go home, sent them back to their hotel. The delegation left for New York that afternoon. In commenting on this incident, the *New York Times* was less concerned with the Aldermen being drunk than with their letting down the city by not evading the watchmen as did the Bostonians.[27]

On September 9, 1850, California was admitted to the Union, with its senators and two representatives in Congress. With its admission, the appointment of federal officers was a topic debated in Congress. One of the offices to be filled was that of U.S. Marshal and Tukey was said to be a candidate for that office. There is no direct evidence of this rumor, however Tukey did make a trip to Washington on September 16, again checking into the Willard Hotel. While in Washington, Tukey was reported as a witness to the demonstration of an "electromagnetic" engine. He is listed directly after the "Hon. Mr. Wright" who was George W. Wright, newly elected U.S. representative from California. Tukey did not get the office of U.S. marshal but his interest in California was likely spurred by this trip.[28]

Later that month, Tukey and his police force were tested by what the newspapers called "Lind mania." In 1849, P.T. Barnum arranged to have noted opera singer Jenny Lind make a tour of America. In his usual way, Barnum hyped the tour long before she arrived and the level of excitement was beyond anything that had been seen before. Lind was in New York in September and Boston was to be her second stop. She was to give two performances in Boston although demand was high and she ended up giving five concerts. The nominal ticket price was set at $3. However, Barnum held an auction for the right to choose specific seats in the theater. As the auction of tickets for the first performance proceeded, the bids for the first choice rose rapidly to a winning bid of $625 (roughly $22,630 in 2022). While the prices fell rapidly, the second ticket sold for $24, they were still well above the nominal price.[29]

Marshal Tukey realized that the crowds were going to be both large and unruly and plans were made on how to handle them. The police, under Tukey, had experience in handling large crowds as they often dealt with them at fires and events like the water celebration. One technique they often used was to erect rope barriers behind which the police stood to keep an area clear and this was their plan now. Long before Lind arrived, it was reported that the police were planning to "take every precaution to insure order."[30]

From her first moment in Boston, Lind attracted large crowds and the police were there to handle them. She arrived in Boston on the morning of September 26 and was greeted by a large crowd at the railroad depot. From there, she was whisked by carriage to her quarters at the Revere House in Bowdoin Square, where another large crowd was waiting for her. Police were permanently stationed outside the hotel to keep the crowds out.

The first concert was held on the night of September 27, and the papers described the arrangements outside the Tremont Temple, where the show was held. It was reported that the crowd began to assemble as early as 5 p.m. in hopes of catching a glimpse of the famous singer. The police roped off a section of Tremont Street, in front of the venue, so that carriages could arrive. They also excluded anyone who could not show a ticket. One editor commented "great credit is due to the police for their firm and, at the same time, courteous discharge of their duties." The crowd was said to be well behaved although some outside were chanting and yelling loud enough to be heard in the venue.

On the following night, the City planned a musical and fireworks tribute to the singer to be held in Bowdoin Square, in front of her hotel. Again the crowds assembled early. There were an estimated 10,000–20,000 people awaiting the appearance of Jenny Lind at her hotel window. A brass band began playing but was drowned out by shouts from the crowd for the famous singer. Shortly thereafter, the fireworks began. The band, not being heard over the shouts or the fireworks, concluded its performance and gave up the space. An orchestra from the Music Fund Society was supposed to perform and the police were required to clear a space for it, which they did, though not to its satisfaction. After playing one piece, it also gave up and the crowd continued to shout.

One report concluded that "Much credit is due to Marshal Tukey and his Police force for their efficient services, and by midnight Bowdoin Square resumed its usual quiet."[31]

Not everyone was so complimentary of the police. In a letter to the editor of the *Boston Evening Transcript*, an unnamed correspondent complained of the treatment of the Musical Fund Society. He stated that the mayor had given its members assurances that they would be protected and given sufficient space for them and their instruments. He said they had waited an hour in the cellar of the Revere House and then were confined to the sidewalk in front, not nearly sufficient space. The only thing separating them from the crowd was a thin rope which was pushed inward by the crowd. According to the correspondent, there were only six policemen present and they were standing by the front of the Revere House and not between the musicians and the crowd. After the musicians gave up, they were not permitted into the Revere House and were forced back into the cellar. The dinner, which the letter-writer stated they were promised by the proprietor of the Revere House, never materialized. The editor responded in defense of the Revere House, saying, "we do not think that its neat and commodious basement is fairly entitled to the name of a 'cellar.'" He further suggested that if there were problems it was because of the unexpectedly large crowds.

Marshal Tukey was not one to let such a slander on his men go unrefuted. He wrote his own letter to the editor of the *Transcript* and stated that he had orders from the mayor that the entire police force was to be deployed to Bowdoin Square that night. He said there were 45 men in total and that 10 of them, "with stakes and ropes" were detailed to close off the streets leading to the square to carriages. There were four men who were assigned to the doors of the Revere House to keep out the crowds. The remaining 31 men formed a square and held it for the brass band, as was requested. When the band decided to leave, Tukey had his men "drop the chains." Nearly an hour later, he was requested to clear a space for the Musical Fund Society and his men cleared the sidewalk in front of the Revere House and held it until 10 o'clock. He concluded by saying, "I cannot think that you, or the public, would expect any more to be done by *forty-five* individuals, than was done against the pressure of a crowd of 'ten thousand persons.'"[32]

With Jenny Lind's sweet voice fading in Boston, a new crisis was brewing in the City, the State and the Nation. About the same time that Tukey had been in Washington, D.C., perhaps to seek the U.S. Marshal position, Congress passed what became known as the Compromise of 1850. These were a series of five bills designed to settle disputes between the North and the South over slavery. Of the five bills, the one which would cause the most trouble was the Fugitive Slave Act. The law allowed Southern slave owners to use the Federal Courts and U.S. marshals to seize runaway slaves and return them to captivity. Both in the Senate and then as Secretary of State, Daniel Webster, leader of the Whig party in Massachusetts, championed the Compromise as a way of preserving the Union. Over time, Webster's support for this solution would destroy his reputation and the Whig party itself.

Boston was as divided as the rest of the nation over the issue of slavery. Along with other reform movements, the anti-slavery movement began to gain ground in the city during the 1830s. Many of the city's elite saw this a part of a larger issue of moral reform and eagerly joined societies, committee and other groups to fight for emancipation. By 1850, two of the nation's leading abolitionist newspapers, *The Liberator* and the *Emancipator and Republican*, were published in Boston. Being an elite movement, while its influence and power were great, its numbers were relatively small. They were opposed by two large and vocal groups. The first were the so-called "Cotton Whigs" who saw the prosperity brought to New England by the cotton transported from the South to the developing textile mills. While many of them opposed slavery, they sought a gradual elimination rather than an immediate end.

The other large group in Boston opposed to the anti-slavery movement were the Irish. Boston always had an Irish population, most of which was on the lower end of the economic scale, but the Potato Famine of the late 1840s increased that number significantly. The Irish opposed the anti-slavery movement for a number of reasons. Because many of the Irish were unskilled workers, they competed on a daily basis with Boston's black population for economic survival, which inevitably led to racism. Also, many of the same people who were prominent in the abolition movement were fervently anti–Catholic and shortly would develop the "Know-Nothing" movement which was against both the Catholics and the Irish. In 1850, Boston, like the rest of the nation, was rent with divided loyalties.

The Fugitive Slave Act was passed by Congress on September 18 and little more than a week later a man was arrested in New York under the law. On September 30, a meeting of fugitive slaves in Boston was held to develop measures for their protection and a general meeting of anti-slavery supporters was held in Faneuil Hall on October 14 where a Committee of Vigilance was appointed to protect fugitives. The first warrants in Boston were issued on October 25 for the arrest of William and Ellen Crafts. They had come to Boston in 1848 after escaping from Macon, Georgia. Crafts was a cabinet maker and worked in a shop on Cambridge Street. When the warrants were issued, Ellen Crafts left the city but her husband William was reported to be waiting to see what happened. A conversation was reported between William Crafts and Frederick Douglass in which Crafts said, "I will never leave the state. Our people have been pursued long enough. For my part, if I can't live here and be free, I will die."

United States Marshal Devens was in an unpopular and difficult spot. The warrants for the arrest of William Crafts and his wife Ellen were issued to him. He knew that to serve them would cost him both professionally and personally. The *Emancipator and Republican* had already named him the "Slave catcher general of Massachusetts.." He was at first reluctant to get involved in the situation despite facing a $1,000 fine for not serving the warrants. Devens applied for help to Tukey and the Boston police but was flatly turned down. He thought of hiring his own men to grab Crafts from his house but a judge told him, as this was a civil proceeding, that he could not break open the door. As long as Crafts was in his house, he could not be touched. Rumors were abundant that Devens would resign, that he telegraphed Washington that a riot was about to occur and that he needed federal troops to aid in serving the warrants. For the time being, he did nothing.

The warrants charged the couple with larceny for having stolen their "body and clothes" in their escape. The man who sought the warrants was Willis S. Hughes, said to be a jailer from Macon, Georgia. He was seeking the reward from the owner for the return of the slaves. With him was John Knight, who was to identify the couple. He had worked in the same shop that William Crafts did before his escape. Knight reportedly made two friendly visits to William Crafts, supposedly delivering messages from Crafts' friends in Macon. He solicited a return letter from Crafts for his friends, saying he would stop by and pick it up. Instead, he sent a messenger saying he was busy and asking Crafts to bring the letter to his hotel. It is assumed that this was a ruse to get Crafts where they could seize him. On the same day that the warrants were issued for Crafts and his wife, posters were put up in various parts of the city, warning about "slave-catchers" in Boston and urging action be taken. Several newspapers hinted that tar and feathers might be involved.[33]

No violence occurred but both of the slave-catchers were sued by John C. Park on behalf of William Crafts for slander in saying he was guilty of larceny. Deputy Sheriff Rugg, assisted by several members of the Vigilance Committee, arrested Knight at his hotel. Hughes, while apprehended and taken to the Sheriff's office, was not arrested because he had checked into the hotel under an assumed name. Knight was charged with slander and was required to post a $10,000 bond for his bail. While in custody, Hughes was reported to have said "that he had come for Crafts and his wife, and added 'damn 'em, I'll have *them* if I stay here all eternity.'" He then said it was not about them, using a derogatory term, *but it's the principle of the thing!'* There was a large crowd outside the Court House but the men left by a back door.

The abolitionists' legal strategy was to make it impossible for the slave-catchers to stay in Boston. On October 28, two days after the first arrest, Hughes and Knight were arrested by Deputy Sheriff Coburn and members of the Vigilance Committee on a charge of conspiring to kidnap William Crafts. They were again taken to the Court House and each was required to give a bond of $10,000 for bail. That same evening they were again arrested, this time on a charge of conspiring to kidnap Ellen Crafts. This time, their bail was set at $20,000 each. At the same time, an unnamed but "noted Abolitionist" visited the hotel where the men were staying and tried to have the owner throw them out. The pressure must have been getting to the men from Georgia as both denied any intention of violence toward the couple. They both disavowed the statements attributed to them and Hughes stated "his intention to employ nothing but means strictly legal and peaceable in his undertaking." No one was fooled by these statements and the agitation against them continued. On October 30, Hughes and Knight took an express train to New York without having their warrants served on William Crafts. However, William Crafts and his wife no longer felt safe in Boston. In early November, they boarded a steamer for Halifax and eventually made their way to England.[34]

Shortly after the couple left Boston, another incident related to the Fugitive Slave Act rocked Boston. On November 12, an African American named Washington Ingraham was walking through the West End neighborhood then known as the Hill, an area where free blacks and fugitive slaves made their homes. He was recognized and a shout went up, "There's one of our betrayers, one of the spies!" He was accused of being a spy for slave catchers. Ingraham was suspected of having given information that led to the arrest, in August 1850, of William L. Chaplin while helping two slaves escape from the District of Columbia. A telegram from a friend of a fugitive slave had already warned the residents that he was coming. A mob developed, estimated at 500 people, and followed him, pelting him with rocks and other debris. Ingraham sought refuge in Plummer's grocery store on the corner of Garden Street. Marshal Tukey, alerted to a possible riot, arrived in company with the mayor and six to eight policemen. The marshal went in to the grocery, talked to Ingraham and escorted him out. Ingraham was taken to Tukey's own house until he could be safely transported out of Boston.[35]

In the midst of, and because of, all the excitement over the Fugitive Slave Act, George Thompson, member of the British Parliament, arrived in Boston on October 30. Thompson was a noted orator, abolitionist and reformer. His last visit to New England, in 1835, had caused widespread disturbances and he was forced to sneak away to avoid being mobbed. On this trip, he stayed at the home of William Lloyd Garrison. editor of the anti-slavery newspaper *The Liberator.* On November 7, Thompson in company with Garrison attended a large, Free-Soil meeting at Faneuil Hall. He did not speak and the meeting went off without any disruption.[36]

The anti-slavery forces planned a meeting at Faneuil Hall on November 15 to welcome Thompson and to allow him to address the issue of slavery in the United States. All the major Abolitionists were scheduled to attend and speak at this meeting. The announcement of the meeting alerted all in Boston to a coming storm. As early as November 7, the *Boston Herald* published a warning, saying, "We trust that no serious demonstration will be made against Mr. George Thompson, when he attempts to speak at Faneuil Hall." The editor was reading the mood of Boston when he said Thompson would "attempt" to speak. In his last tour of New England, Thompson had spoken out against the Constitution and various American institutions. He was accused of "making harangues against our government and institutions, and attempted to excite prejudice in the minds of our people against their own country."

Like Garrison, George Thompson saw the Constitution as an immoral document because of its recognition of slavery and favored a secession of the free Northern states from those of the South. In an era when most Americans were inordinately proud of their country and its institutions, a message like Thompson's was in for a rough reception. In the days prior to the meeting, a number of Boston newspapers published editorials denouncing Thompson and what they saw as his interference in American politics. One editor stated, "All true Americans, whatever may be their feelings and opinions in regard to the law will repel such impudent and sinister intrusion into their domestic concerns as the pretended apostleship of this foreigner."[37]

On the night of November 15, a large crowd assembled at Faneuil Hall, with men filling the floor and women in the galleries above. The crowd was a mixture of both blacks and whites and was estimated to number about 3,000. At 7 p.m. the meeting was called to order and Edmund Quincy, brother of the former mayor of Boston and a noted abolitionist, was appointed president. He introduced William Lloyd Garrison who gave a history of George Thompson's life and activism. The crowd was relatively quiet during Garrison's speech but when Wendell Phillips rose to speak there was a growing noise in the hall. He commented that the "scene was disgraceful to Boston." With this, the crowd broke into cheers for Boston, the Union and Daniel Webster. Phillips attempted to keep speaking but was drowned out by further cheers for Millard Fillmore and again for Daniel Webster.

Edmund Quincy got up and tried to get the crowd to listen to Phillips. At one point, he threatened to have the police on them, saying "the city marshal is present with a strong force of police.... This is our house for the night ... if you do not like our entertainment, there is the door." The crowd thereupon began to cheer for Marshal Tukey. Quincy then introduced George Thompson and there were alternate cheers and hisses for him. He stood at the podium with his arms crossed for ten minutes (it was said) waiting for the crowd to settle. He began speaking and the hall was filled with cheers for Webster and for the country. Eventually, he left the stage.

The organizers then introduced William H. Channing, another abolitionist, reformer and women's rights advocate. When he attempted to speak, the crowd gave three cheers for Jenny Lind. As he persisted, they again cheered for Lind as well as Webster, Bunker Hill and the ladies in the gallery. A number of people in the crowd began whistling *Yankee Doodle* and several other melodies. The crowd formed several rings on the floor and dancing was begun. The organizers declared the meeting closed and left the podium. When the organizers left, Police Captain Sam Adams mounted the platform and the crowd immediately quieted. He announced that the city marshal had asked him to announce that the meeting was adjourned. The hall lights were dimmed and eventually the crowd left. Throughout the entire event, the mayor, several aldermen, Marshal Tukey and a force of police were on the floor observing the crowd.[38]

The abolitionists were outraged that their meeting was sabotaged and that the city authorities did nothing to stop the crowd. At the next meeting of the mayor and aldermen, Edmund Quincy and other organizers of the meeting showed up to file a complaint against Marshal Tukey for "notorious neglect of duty." The mayor informed them that the proper way to lodge such a complaint was in writing and that a committee would be appointed to hear the charge. They presented their memorial at the next meeting on November 26. In it, they charged that Tukey was present with a large force of police but did nothing to quell the crowd even when asked by the president of the meeting. A hearing date was set a week later but the meeting was then postponed until December 9.[39]

After the mayor read the complaint aloud at the hearing,

Edmund Quincy began to present his case. He started by quoting a law, passed by the legislature just the year before, that made it illegal to disrupt a lawful meeting. He contended that there were only about 300 people making a demonstration and that the police could have removed them. He said that he sent Theodore Parker to the marshal to ask him to do so. Parker then said that he went to Tukey to relay the request from the president of the meeting (Quincy) and Tukey was said to reply, "I care nothing about your President." Wendell Phillips then got up to make remarks about the disturbance when he was disturbed by friends of the mayor who burst in to announce his re-election. After things settled down, the mayor told Phillips, "You perceive, sir, that other meetings besides your own are sometimes disturbed." Phillips replied, "I do, your Honor, and I also think I understand the difference between the disturbance of *friends* and that of *foes*." This "caused a great deal of laughter in the chamber, including the Mayor."

Several times Phillips and the mayor engaged in a back-and-forth over various points. When Phillips stated that no one in authority made any plea to the crowd, the mayor stated that he had given orders that if violence had been threatened to any officers or speakers at the meeting, then a response would have been made. He then said, "Do you wish to interfere when the audience express their feelings?" Phillips said he conceded the right of the audience to express its feelings but stated that the disrupters were not expressing a feeling but were trying to stop the meeting. Alderman Rogers asked if there was any violence and was anyone knocked down. Phillips replied that he knew of none but that was not the point. He claimed that the police entered the hall with their badges on but later took them off. Then, Phillips related that he had talked to the mayor before the meeting and that the mayor told him, referring to the abolition meetings the previous year, that it cost the City $80 to protect them and would they pay for it this year. Phillips used the argument that they were taxpayers and entitled to protection. However, he finally agreed that if it were a condition of using Faneuil Hall, they would pay for extra police. The mayor then asked if he had paid one cent and they fell to wrangling about whether they should have paid.

Alderman Grant then asked Tukey what his instructions were that evening. Tukey asked that he be allowed to answer in his own way. At this point an interesting exchange took place between the mayor and the marshal. As Tukey made ready to speak, the mayor expressed the opinion that he, "had better defer his defense to some other and more private occasion." However, Tukey stepped to the center of the floor and took out a number of written pages. The mayor called Alderman Rogers to take over the meeting and made to leave the room, saying he was not feeling well. Tukey then gathered his papers and declared that he would not proceed unless the mayor remained. Mayor Bigelow reluctantly conceded and sat down again.

Tukey began surprisingly by admitting to all the things charged in the petition except that he claimed the number of rioters was about 1500, which would have been half the crowd. He then went on to review what had happened in Boston since the passage of the Fugitive Slave Act. The peace of Boston was disturbed, he said, by the very men submitting the petition. They had vehemently urged citizens. both black and white, to arm themselves and take to the streets in resistance. Tukey brought up the mobbings of the slave catchers and of Washington Ingram. He stated that within the last five weeks there had been five mobs in the city, all incited by the petitioners, and that the crowd's reaction in Faneuil Hall was their "just deserts." Quincy objected and Alderman Rogers called Tukey to order. The mayor thought Tukey's remarks were in order but it was inexpedient for him to go on at length. The marshal was exceedingly upset and in an amazing leap of logic, stated that the city's population was 138,000 and only 1,500 of the petitioners supporters were dissatisfied with his conduct, therefore, 136,500 were satisfied with his performance.

Alderman Grant asked the marshal to calm down and stick to the complaint. In answer to a question from the Alderman, Tukey stated that Mayor Bigelow ordered him *"not to interfere, unless some actual attack was made on some speaker or officer of the meeting."* (italics in the original). He reminded Alderman Grant that this was the same order that had been given for the temperance meeting in 1847 where Grant had been forced off the platform. The police had swept in and quelled the rioters. In an aside to Quincy, Tukey commented that this was before the statute of 1849.

Quincy then asked him if he obeyed the mayor and aldermen in all things and he replied, "Yes, I obey them in preference to you or anybody else." Quincy, sensing an opening asked if Tukey obeyed them in preference to the Legislature and the law. He replied, "Yes, I would do anything they told me." Tukey said he recognized some of the rioters but did not know them personally. He admitted that the disturbance was as bad as it had been portrayed and that it was a disgrace to Boston. He said that if he had not been under orders, he would have tried to quell the rioters but did not think he would have succeeded. In answer to the allegation that the police had removed their badges and joined the disturbance, the marshal stated he did not see this and would discharge anyone who did so. His orders were to act only if the speakers were threatened; he had no right to interfere with any man for cheering or hissing. If the speakers had been threatened, he and his men were ready to defend them to the last. He concluded by stating that if he had violated any law, he was ready to resign from his office.

Much to the disaffection of the petitioners, the mayor brought the meeting to an end and announced that the aldermen would make a decision in the coming week. The Board of Alderman met on the night of December 16 and concluded, "it is the opinion of this Board that the Marshal acted under explicit instructions, and is therefore not liable for any disturbances which took place on the occasion referred to."

Despite the controversy over the Faneuil Hall meeting, Tukey and the police did protect George Thompson at another meeting shortly thereafter. On November 18, three days after the Faneuil Hall meeting, Thompson was invited to a reception at the First African Baptist Church on Belknap Street, known today as the African Meeting House, a National Historic Landmark. In preparation for the meeting, the police had strung a chain across the entrance to the court leading to the building. A force of police was stationed to maintain order and a member of the congregation was with the police to screen people going into the reception. Thompson talked for about an hour and there was no disturbance.[40]

As the year drew to a close, the tensions brought on by the Fugitive Slave Act were roiling the political waters. In the statewide election for governor in November, the Democrats adopted an anti-slavery platform and allied themselves to the Free Soil Party. Together, they defeated the Whig incumbent, George N. Briggs, who had held the office for seven years. In the Boston mayoral election, held on December 9, Mayor Bigelow was victorious, as noted. However, he was opposed by another Whig candidate as well as Democratic, Free Soil and temperance candidates. The vote was much larger than in the previous years but Bigelow's percentage was much smaller. In 1849, he garnered 80 percent of the total vote, while he received only 63 percent in 1850. When the election results were announced, a crowd of over 500 gathered around City Hall cheering for the mayor and interrupting the meeting about the disturbance at Faneuil Hall. The mayor went out on the balcony and spent 20 minutes addressing the crowd. Despite Bigelow and his Whig supporters retaining the office of mayor, major changes were in store for Boston and for the police in the next year.[41]

7

"Some men think ... that when a man becomes unfit for anything else, he is just fitted for a Policeman"

As the year 1851 began, the major problem for the police was that Boston Neck, the part of the peninsula which joined Boston to Roxbury, was again being used for sleigh races. This largely uninhabited area boasted a long, straight road with was perfect for fast sleighing. Unfortunately this was also the main land access to Boston. Sleighing was a Boston tradition, boasted of in many newspapers, and racing horses against each other was often part of the tradition. This New Year, a hard frost had turned the snow to ice and the sleighing was better than anyone remembered. Such speed, however, often led to accidents and the Board of Aldermen wanted it restrained. On December 31, Tukey and 15 of his men went to the neck to enforce a speed limit of seven miles an hour on the sleighs. The area was described by a contemporary: "The Neck, extending toward Roxbury, is a regular race course. Daily and constantly the fastest horses are tried over this road, and private passing is rendered nearly impossible." If the presence of the police should not be enough to slow things down, Marshal Tukey, using his favorite method for crowd control, was threatening to stretch a chain across the road.[1]

Mayor Bigelow, after the hotly contested election, organized the city government on January 7, swearing in the new aldermen and members of the Common Council. It might seem that he would mention the disturbances lately upsetting the city, or the aspersions cast against him, the aldermen, and the police. Instead, he painted a quite rosy picture, saying he was grateful for the confidence the people had placed in him. He said the city had experienced good health and "had been exempt from any serious calamities." As he had done in previous years, he praised the public education system but complained of cost. Mayor Bigelow again betrayed his narrow vision of Boston when he commented on the instruction in the public school, "A less number of studies, carefully reserving those having the most important practical bearing upon mental improvement, would secure the great ends of popular education better than ambitious endeavors to teach almost every thing." Most of the rest of the speech detailed various financial transactions and covering the city's debt.

When Mayor Bigelow briefly spoke of the police and night watch, he stated that they had actively and faithfully discharged their duties throughout the year, "as much as could be reasonably expected, from its paucity of numbers, and defective system of organization." He again stated that it would be too expensive to augment the numbers and renewed his call for the merging of the two forces under one department. In support he cited the report submitted to the City Council on December 19. The main complaint the report made against the watch is that they were at best part-time workers. Each had a job or profession he pursued during the day and then went on duty at night. They recommended that they be replaced by professional policemen. Undoubtedly, Tukey supported this development and contributed to the report.[2]

In January 1851, Marshal Tukey published the first annual report on the Boston Police Department, detailing its organization and describing its duties. This presents a unique chance to see how the police force was organized under Francis Tukey. This was the department he created and molded over the preceding three years. It was, in many ways, both the first of its kind in the country and a model for all later developments. Tukey used this report not only to describe what existed but to argue for changes that he thought were important to improve the department. One thing which stands out in the report is that Mayor Bigelow's repeated emphasis on cost cutting and reducing the city's debt was having an effect on the Police Department.[3]

The report begins by detailing the organization of the department. Interestingly, while he describes all of the other members of the police force, he says nothing of the position of city marshal.

Below the marshal is one deputy marshal, whose duty was to fill in for him when he was not on duty. He also had charge of the Health Department and oversaw the granting of licenses, collecting of fess and other activities. There were six officers of the day police who had specialized duties, including a clerk of the police, and superintendents of carriages, trucks, schools, secondhand and junk dealers, and employment offices. Their responsibilities include seeing that records are kept of all complaints at the office, that the city ordinances regarding vehicles are observed, and to check truancy, to look for and identify stolen property and keep citizens from being cheated.

A specialized portion of the day police was the detective force. It consisted of four men who were stationed at the Police Office. They kept records of all crimes reported, of men committed or released from prison, of boys sent to reform school, and of the comings and goings of known thieves and suspicious persons. Tukey reported that they kept a confidential record of crimes and methods which were only revealed by the "imperative requirements of justice." Specific duties included being present at all "unusual collections of people" in the streets to look for pickpockets and other thieves as well as gathering information on suspicious persons. If those persons were demonstrated to be criminals, they were to be taken to the Police Office to be " 'shown-up' at the roll-call, and thus made known to the whole of the Police." As discussed previously, in an era where there were no photographs and a person's identity was based primarily on what he said about himself, this was one deterrent to career criminals.

The rest of the day police, consisting of 28 men, were a generalized force assigned to walk specific beats within the city. They were the eyes and ears of the department. In their rounds, they watched for crimes being committed, violations of the city ordinances, and any situations that might develop into a riot. They generally worked a 12 hour shift beginning at 8 a.m. and ending, depending on the time of the year, at either 7 or 8 p.m. They were to report for roll call at the Police Office at the beginning of their shift and at 2 p.m. where they received "all necessary instructions." For this service, they received a salary of $2 per day. Tukey emphasized that, unlike the watch, when the police were required to testify in Court, the witness fees that they were paid were later deducted from their salary. This was so, in Tukey's own italicized words, *"no officer can derive any pecuniary benefit from complaints made by himself or other for violation of the laws."*

In his description of the night police, Tukey cleverly quotes the recent report submitted to the Common Council on the Watch and Police. The night force consisted of a captain and two sub-officers, along with 22 men. Their area of patrol was in the Commercial sections of Boston and they were specifically tasked with stopping burglars and preventing break-ins. Their shift began, depending on the time of the year, between 6 and 8 p.m. and was over at 7 a.m. and they patrolled between 12 to 13 hours each night for which they received $1.37½ per night. The 22 men were arranged in three watches of seven men each, with one extra to fill in. Two of the watches were on patrol each night while seven of the men were kept at the police office to respond to fires and answer calls from the public. To stop any hint of scandal, no policeman was on the same beat two nights in a row.

Tukey then went on to praise the night police, saying that they were generally "under 28 years of age, married, citizens, tax-payers," and, in his opinion, "a more useful body of men never were in the employ of the City." The marshal then went on to report that in the last quarter of 1848, according to court records, the night force, small as it was, caught more robbers than the entire watch, which consisted of 200 men. He commented that he was at one fire where 10 of the night police saved $7000 in goods from a burning building. The reason he went into so much detail on the night police was because "the City Government ... suffered this important branch of the.... Police to die out," reducing their numbers significantly. As proof of the effect of this neglect, he stated that in the last quarter of 1850 there were 168 robberies, burglaries and larcenies in Boston and 115 of these were at night. He also reported that the night police were used to test men and, if they seemed capable, they often advanced to the day police.

At the time of the Tukey's report, the night police consisted of one captain, one sub-captain and seven men, a two-thirds reduction in its manpower. Of the seven men, Tukey stated that three of them were now doing duties that should be done by the day police. Of the other four, "three of them, in my opinion, are not fit for Policemen." He argued that the appropriation for the Police Department was intended to and would cover a full complement of men and that deficiencies should be made up as soon as possible.

The next section of the report details the crime statistics for the year 1850 and shows that more than $30,000 of property was reported stolen and $22,000 recovered. There were 3,382 complaints and arrests for a wide variety of crimes. These are not much different than those previously discussed in type or percentage. Tukey stated that in 1850, though fines, forfeitures, witness fees and other sources, the efforts of the police yielded to the treasury a sum almost equal to the appropriation of the department.

Tukey then went on to describe things he thought should be changed or improved. First of these was the granting of police warrants to people who were not members of the department. These included employees of railroad companies and other special warrants. He stated that their interests were not those of the city but those of their employers. That they often caused complaints against the police, even though the department was not involved. Tukey recommended the revocation of all police warrants except for those people who worked in the department and the passing of an ordinance that made it illegal to wear a police badge unless one actually worked for the city.

A second item of concern to the Marshal was the amount of time, effort and money his Department expended in helping other jurisdictions, for which it received no compensation. He recounts several recent examples where his officers were required to help other jurisdictions in recovering several thousands of dollars in stolen property. During these efforts they incurred several hundred dollars in expenses, all of which came out of his budget. He stated that this did not include his own time or services. Further he pointed to the recent Parkman murder case where he claimed the Boston Police accrued over $2,000 in expenses which were in no way reimbursed. He asked the mayor and Board of Aldermen for guidance in how much to continue this process if no recompense was offered.

The marshal quoted from a recent grand jury report which spoke of the number of assaults on officers, "the jury feel it to be their duty earnestly to recommend more severe enactments for the punishment of persons assaulting them while discharging their duties." Surprisingly, Tukey suggested that there were too many complaints about assaults on officers and that they should be restricted to aggravated assaults. He reported that in the period from 1848 through 1850, there were fewer than 30 such complaints made, in part because he reviewed each one and dismissed those he thought frivolous. However, he went on to say that some were quite serious but the punishment was minor. He reported two cases where the injuries were severe but the culprit was only sentenced to a $5 fine. Tukey felt that if the complaint was serious, the punishment should be as well, stating, "Either the Courts must impose sentences sufficiently severe to protect the officers in the performance of their duties, or you must allow them to protect themselves."

In the same regard, Tukey also advocated for greater fines and punishments for those who ran venues dealing with vice. Quoting again from the report of the Grand Jury, Tukey cited the most notorious district in Boston: "In some parts of the City, particularly in Ann Street, there exists an amount of iniquity so great that the jury feel bound to call the attention of the court and community to it." They went on to report that on this street alone there were 72 dance cellars and brothels as well as innumerable liquor shops. Further, they deplored the number of assaults and robberies that take place there. Tukey then quoted from two affidavits that had been taken on January 5, 1851, describing the sordid and squalid conditions in one of these places. He went on to list all of the criminal complaints derived from this street in the past year. Tukey stated that the one officer, whose beat encompassed this street had, in 1850, "made 123 arrests for larcenies, robberies and burglaries, 55 for assault and battery, 10 for receiving stolen goods and 211 as drunkards." The reason why such crime flourished on this street, and others in the city, according to the marshal, was that it was still profitable. Those who ran such dens of iniquity could pay all the fines imposed by the courts and still make a profit. No significant reduction in such places would occur until the courts made it unprofitable to keep them open.

A subject close to Tukey's heart and for which he had been advocating for several years was to get destitute children off the streets. The end of the report contains a large exposition on the problem of young criminals. He began by saying, "Allow me to renew my appeal to you, in regard to the young in this City, and of the large and increasing number of poor and destitute children of both sexes who are growing up in vice and crime." He went on to cite a number of crime statistics showing the number and types of crimes juveniles were charged with over the years. Both the grand jury report and a petition from a number of prominent citizens pleaded that juvenile criminals not be put in with adults because it would only make them harder criminals. Young boys, below the age of 7, were being used by older boys to commit crimes because the courts had decided they were too young to actually be a criminal. The older boys would wait for them and then take most of the loot without any risk of being caught.

Tukey recounted several life stories of both boys and girls to show how they progressed into a life of crime. He then suggested that some people think an increase in the number of police would take care of this problem but he flatly denied this. The only solution, in his mind, was for the city to take control. If the police found a child in the streets who appeared to be up to no good, they should be allowed to bring him before a tribunal and, if the parents could not show cause, the child should be bound out as an apprentice. He cited the new jail being built in Boston and the expansion to the state prison and suggested that if nothing was done on this issue, the capacity of both those institutions would, in ten years, need to be doubled.

The end of the report contained Tukey's recommendations for what should be the size and compensation of the Police Department. He stated that there were two ways of organizing a Police Force,

> *First.* To pay a fair compensation, get good men, have the work done properly, *and without expense to the citizens other than their taxes.*
> *Second.* To give a poor compensation, get unfit men, have the work half done, and allow them to *sponge* the citizens to make a living.

In his opinion, the Boston Police would compare favorably with any other city in the country. The main difficulty, he said, was to get good men. He commented that some people believed that "when a man becomes unfit for anything else, he is just fitted for a Policeman." This opinion was, to Tukey, a great detriment to any department. He had in his office 125 applications for the position of policeman but would not recommend more than ten of them. His recommendation was that the day force be increased to 38, the night force be restored to 25 and that a special group of 10 "Water and Wharf" police be appointed.

The newspapers were complimentary about the report and the marshal himself. One commented that it was gratifying to see that while Tukey was exposed to the worst of humanity, he had not lost his philanthropy. The emphasis he put on the plight of destitute children was widely praised and supported. Another said that the report contained excellent recommendations, "which are characterized by the usual intelligence, wisdom, and practability of the Marshal. Mr. Tukey has individually trod the very ground on which he treats with so much force and ability in his Report." They agreed with Tukey that the police force needed to be "filled by the most vigorous and efficient men that can be found in the community, and that such should be amply paid for their services."[4]

Tukey's report seemed to suggest that Mayor Bigelow and the Board of Aldermen decided to save money by reducing the number of men on the police force. One way to do that would be by not replacing men who left and not hiring any new ones. This would not be an official policy and is very difficult to assess at this point. In the years 1849 and 1850 only two men are actually reported in the newspapers to be appointed as police officers. Another way to look at this is how many applied for a position on the police, even though most were not accepted. In 1849, there were at least 36 reported applications to be police officers while in 1850, this number fell to only 11. Did the city government put out the word that they were not interested in new hires?

Whatever the case, Marshal Tukey's report, describing manpower shortages and recommending what needed to be done in the city, led the Board of Aldermen to make major changes. One of the first of these changes was to hire a lot of new officers. On February 10, 1851, Marshal Tukey nominated, and the board confirmed, 11 men to join the night police. It is interesting to note that this group of men are the first to be specifically nominated by Tukey. It is possible that his new understanding with the Board of Aldermen was that he would select the men to be appointed.[5]

Among the men confirmed by the board was Edward H. Savage, who would have a long and successful career in the Boston Police Department. When he joined the police in 1851, he was already 39 years old and identified himself in the 1850 census of Ward 1 as a grocer. Ward 1 was in the North End and the term *grocer* was often a euphemism for a liquor dealer. One source referred to him as a "hand-cart jobber." It was reported that he wanted to join the police so that he could pay his debts. Tukey may have seen himself in Savage's history. Within three years, Savage was promoted to captain and in 1870 was appointed police chief. He held that office for eight years. In 1873. he wrote a remarkable history of the Boston Police Department detailing its development from the Colonial period and offering his observations as a patrolman.[6]

Although Savage's book is mostly anecdotal in nature, he is the only officer who served under City Marshal Tukey and left us his impressions of the man and his methods. According to him, Tukey was "truly one of the smartest executive officers I ever knew." A characteristic of Tukey's administration was his secrecy. Savage described him as "shrewd and sly in his nature, his plans were deep laid and secret." He seemed delighted at being able to pull off a surprise. In Savage's opinion, "his tact in planning, and not less to the secrecy with which he managed his plans, may be attributed most of his success." Tukey's orders were "short, tart and to the point" and he expected them to be obeyed without question. If an officer obeyed orders, the marshal would "back him up to his utmost." Savage and all the patrolmen attended roll call at 8 a.m. and 2 p.m. where they received orders for the day from the police clerk. Marshal Tukey was in an adjoining office and they did not see him unless he had a special order to give. In that case,

> When he had something to say to us, you could see his office door open slowly just before [the Clerk] had finished the call, and then that peculiar Roman nose and keen black eye of the Marshal's would make its appearance. Then came the order, short and quick, and he was gone,—*and so were we too, very shortly.*[7]

Savage did not have to wait long to be involved in one of Tukey's "deep laid and secret" plans. The Board of Aldermen took to heart the recommendations made in the police report. On February 6, it passed a number of orders. First, there was to be no police service out of the city unless authorized by the mayor. This was one of the questions Tukey had posed to the Board. Secondly, all "special police" were to be placed under the control of the Police Department. This meant that no police warrants were given to outsiders, as the marshal had recommended. Then the Board went on to deal with the horrible situation on Ann Street which Tukey so graphically described in the report. The city marshal was ordered to survey the cellars on the street and report those that were damp or underwater. The mayor was requested to see what could be done to light the street with gas so there were no deep, dark places. Finally, the city marshal was authorized to make complaints against all "vagabonds, rogues, common pipers and peddlers, and lewd, wanton, and lascivious, persons found in Ann Street."[8]

Tukey may have begun his survey and was planning what to do about Ann Street but matters soon swamped Boston in another controversy related to the Fugitive Slave Act. On February 14, George T. Curtis, Commissioner of the United States Circuit Court for Massachusetts, issued a warrant for the arrest of a man identified by the name "Shadrach," who had escaped from Norfolk, Virginia, in May 1850 and was now living in Boston. The warrant was given to Charles Sawin, one of the United States deputy marshals for execution. The man identified as Shadrach in the warrant was known in Boston as Frederick Wilkins or Mimkins and he worked as a waiter at Taft's Cornhill Coffee House. Unlike the previous fugitive slave case in Boston, preparations were made secretly, well in advance, and came as a surprise to many. At the time, United States Marshal Charles Devens was away in Washington answering for his actions in the previous fugitive slave case. In his stead, he had left Deputy Marshal Patrick Riley in charge of the office.

Riley was informed of the potential arrest before 8 a.m. the next day, Saturday, and this was the first notice given to the Marshal's Office despite the issuance of the warrant to Sawin the night before. Another deputy had come to ask Riley where they should hold the prisoner, once he was arrested. The federal government had no prison facilities of their own in Massachusetts and had been forbidden to use Massachusetts facilities for holding fugitive slaves by an act of the legislature in 1843. Riley told him that the man should be held in the United States Courtroom in the City Courthouse. This was a space rented by the government for the holding of federal cases in the state.[9]

Riley arrived at the office and discovered that things were in disarray. No one knew what the fugitive looked like and the man who was to act as informer had not showed up as agreed. Finally things were arranged to happen at 11 o'clock at the coffee house. Riley and nine other officers went to the scene but the informant had still not shown up. To allay suspicions, he and another officer went into the dining room and ordered coffee. They were served by a black waiter and sat waiting for the arrival of the informant. After a time, they paid the waiter and proceeded to leave. As they passed through the barroom, Sawin showed up and arrested the man who had waited on them as the fugitive. He was escorted out of the building and across the square to the courthouse.

Riley then crossed the street to City Hall where he found City Marshal Tukey in his office. He informed Tukey of the arrest and told him that he expected trouble. He suggested that the police might be needed to keep order and protect the city's courthouse. According to Riley, Tukey stated that "it should be attended to." Riley next went upstairs to the mayor's office where he repeated his request for assistance. The mayor responded, "Mr. Riley, I am sorry for it." Riley was correct in assuming that there would be trouble. Despite the surprise of the arrest, crowds were already gathering around the courthouse and the Boston Vigilance Committee had already gathered a team of lawyers to defend Wilkins.

While the deputy marshals held the doors to the courtroom, they allowed a large crowd to gather and hear the proceedings. Riley sent one of his men to the Navy Yard in Charlestown to ask if the prisoner could be held there, in case of a delay. The commissioner, Curtis, had various depositions from the slave owner read and asked the defendant's counsel if they were ready to proceed. They claimed, rightly, they had no time to prepare and asked for a delay. Curtis granted their request and set a hearing for the next Tuesday. The lawyers who volunteered to defend Wilkins asked if they could remain and consult with their client. This request was granted and the room was cleared except for the prisoner, his lawyers, a few reporters and a number of men under the command of the deputy marshal. Riley then heard that his request to house the prisoner in the Navy Yard was refused. He then sent several of his officers out to try to find additional help, leaving nine men in the court room. Meanwhile a crowd still surged around the courthouse and in the corridor leading to the U.S. court room. About 1 o'clock, Riley sent the court messenger to Marshal Tukey saying he needed all the men he could spare.

The city marshal replied that he "had no men in, but would send them over as they came in."

At 2 o'clock, Elizur Wright, editor of the *Commonwealth* newspaper and a rabid abolitionist, and the last of Wilkins's lawyers, Charles G. Davis made to leave. The door, which swung outward, was opened for them to leave. The crowd of blacks in the corridor grabbed the edge of the door, yanked it open and flooded the courtroom. They quickly overpowered the officers and surrounded the prisoner. One of Riley's men immediately went to the City Marshal's Office but did not find him. He then went to the Mayor's Office and was told that the mayor was at dinner. Returning to the City Marshal's Office, he found Tukey in his private office and told him of the pending trouble at the courthouse. He asked that Tukey send any men he had and offered to help gather such men. Tukey told him that his assistance was not needed.

Meanwhile, back in the courtroom, the crowd grabbed Wilkins and hustled him down the stairs and out a side door. They proceeded to the neighborhood known as "The Hill," where most of the black population lived and Wilkins was hidden away. Although Riley sent officers in pursuit, they were not able to find where Wilkins was stashed. Very soon after the rescue, Deputy Marshal Riley gave a deposition to the U.S. Circuit Court regarding these events and was very critical of the mayor and the city marshal:

> ...in my opinion, it was the pre-determined purpose of both not to do their duty in keeping the peace in and about their Court House; for the City Marshal, when requested by Henry S. Hallett, Esq., to disperse a similar mob, which had collected about the office of his father, a United States Commissioner, during the excitement in the "Crafts" case, said that he had orders not to meddle in the matter, as I am informed by the said Hallett,—and that the City Marshal gave a similar answer to Watson Freeman, Esq., who asked him, at about the same time, why he did not disperse the mob....

During the "excitement" over the first fugitive slave case, the police were strangely absent and it appears that was the strategy of the city authorities. During the present case, they seemed to have maintained that same position. They were in a very difficult position being criticized by both sides. They did not break up the mobs favorable to the abolitionists but they also did not stop the disruption of the abolitionists' Faneuil Hall meeting. Tukey, ever ready for action, was restrained by the orders of the mayor, who wanted nothing to do with the troubles caused by these actions.

However, Francis Tukey was not one to take criticism lightly. On the same day that the deposition from Riley was published, the newspapers also published a letter from the city marshal to the mayor. In it, Tukey recounted that the deputy marshal came to his office at 11:30 that Saturday and told him of the arrest, saying, "I merely notify you, so that if they make trouble, you may be about." Obviously, Riley was not expecting much from the police. Tukey then consulted with the mayor, who told him to prevent any breach of the peace outside the courthouse. In consequence, he sent men out to monitor the crowd. When the court messenger arrived at 1 o'clock, asking for all the spare men he had, Tukey told him he had none. Most of his men were on patrol and would not return to the police office until roll call at 2 o'clock. The men who were not on patrol, were already out in the crowd. He stated that about 10 minutes of 2 o'clock, he did send a man to the court room but he was denied admission. Tukey stated, "I learn, and believe it to be true, that Mr. Riley said he did not want any others than those he had employed, to remain in the court room, and added that 'we can take care of the man.'" Tukey claimed that when the last messenger came, around 2 o'clock, he immediately began to go to the courthouse but before he left City Hall, Wilkins was already spirited away.[10]

As he did in his recent report, Tukey challenged the mayor and Board of Aldermen to make a decision about how to handle this issue. He stated that he found no mention in the ordinance establishing the office of the city marshal that he was to do the work of the United States marshal. If they wanted him to do it, all they had to do was pass an ordinance stating so and he would "arrest the Fugitives, and keep them, or I will resign." The tone of his letter is very frustrated and he was seeking advice on whether to take action or not.

Tukey was not the only one frustrated by this conflict. The fragile nature of the national Compromise of 1850 led to agitation on both sides. In the Senate, Henry Clay, one of the architects of the Compromise, presented a petition asking the president for information regarding the freeing of the fugitive and inquiring whether further legislation was required to enforce the Fugitive Slave Act more vigorously. President Millard Fillmore issued a proclamation on

February 18 deploring the violation of the laws of the United States and calling on all leaders, civil and military, to aid in the capture of the fugitive and in preventing future breaches of the law. He further ordered that all persons involved in the rescue should be prosecuted in the Federal Court. Numerous rumors about a federal response were reported. It was stated that the president was going to call out the state militia or that a company of U.S. Marines would be stationed at the Charlestown Navy Yard to hold fugitive slaves during their trial.[11]

The mayor and aldermen of Boston reacted to the pressure from Washington and the challenge of the city marshal by passing a new ordinance on the afternoon of February 18. The new law began by regretting that the "integrity of the laws and the dignity of the Commonwealth and city, had been damaged by the violent removal of a Federal prisoner from custody." It ordered the city marshal to assist any public officer, when properly informed of a threat to the obstruction of justice by a mob. When so informed, he was to immediately go to that place, with all of his police force, and "use the same in the most energetic manner possible, in support of the laws, and the maintenance of the public peace." This ordinance by the Board of Aldermen was transmitted to the president in Washington by Mayor Bigelow. Tukey now had his orders should a new threat arise over the Fugitive Slave Act.[12]

Perhaps because of the frustration he felt in being inactive during the rescue of Wilkins, Tukey decided to take decisive steps in combating other problems in the city. Making one of his "deep laid and secret" plans, the Marshal himself went round to suspected locations of gambling dens in the city, carefully noting the doors and secret stairways. On the night of March 8, Tukey gathered 60 of his men at the Police Office, without telling them why they were assembled. He divided them into 11 divisions, each under an experienced officer, to raid known gambling dens throughout Boston. The squads were sent to their destinations to be in place by 10 o'clock and the raids were made simultaneously at the sound of a signal bell. This was so that no warning could be given to others. This was the first of Tukey's famous "descents" where he would gather a large force and send them to make mass arrests. Tukey himself led the raid on 29 Sudbury Street, the largest of the gambling dens. In all, 86 persons were arrested,

40 at the location Tukey raided.[13]

At each location, the building was surrounded and the head of the detachment led the rest of his men into the establishment to inform the gamblers why they were there, "assuring the astonished gentlemen of the impossibility of escape, requested all present, principals and accessories, to surrender, which most did without further ado." A few tried escaping out windows but were soon captured by the men outside. Tukey, knowing that there would be many prisoners to be transported to the jail, had prepared chains with handcuffs welded to them, spaced three feet apart. The men were handcuffed in pairs with eight couples per chain. Once secured, they were marched off to the Lever-

CAUTION!!

COLORED PEOPLE

OF BOSTON, ONE & ALL,

You are hereby respectfully CAUTIONED and advised, to avoid conversing with the

Watchmen and Police Officers of Boston,

For since the recent ORDER OF THE MAYOR & ALDERMEN, they are empowered to act as

KIDNAPPERS

AND

Slave Catchers,

And they have already been actually employed in KIDNAPPING, CATCHING, AND KEEPING SLAVES. Therefore, if you value your LIBERTY, and the *Welfare of the Fugitives* among you, *Shun* them in every possible manner, as so many *HOUNDS* on the track of the most unfortunate of your race.

Keep a Sharp Look Out for KIDNAPPERS, and have TOP EYE open.

APRIL 24, 1851.

Poster printed by the Vigilance Committee during the Fugitive Slave crisis in Boston. Tukey had his force ignore Federal requests for assistance in two of the cases. In the third one, the Boston Board of Aldermen passed a specific ordinance requiring Tukey and the Police to assist the Federal officers. Because of this, the poster warns against talking to the watchmen and the Police (Library of Congress).

ett Street Jail where they stayed until their appearance Monday before the Police Court. The gamblers took the arrest in stride and were said to be joking and laughing as they marched to jail. One is reported to have said, "Here goes a train of brothers bound in the chains of a universal brotherhood." The number of men brought to jail strained the limits and there were as many as 20 men in a cell.

While arrests were not made at each of the locations—in several there was no gambling observed at the time of the raid—any

gambling equipment was seized. The raids are said to have net-
ted $2,000 to $3,000 in equipment. A detailed list was published
of what had been taken. It ranged from dice and packs of playing
cards to a roulette wheel. Items associated with the game of faro
were very common as were those used in a game called props. This
was a unique Boston game, perhaps imported from whalers who had
picked up a similar game from the native peoples of California. It
involved the modification of cowrie shells by filing one side and filling it with red wax. Then the shells were tossed and people bet on
how many red sides would appear. Bostonians were fascinated by the
paraphernalia of the gamblers and Tukey exhibited the material to
the public in the Police Office. As many as 20,000 people stopped by
to see this exhibit. After the trials, all the material was destroyed.

On Monday morning, the prisoners were transported to the
court in police vans and a large crowd was there to see them. Both
the gamblers and the crowd were in a good mood and exchanged
jibes. The procession into the courtroom was led by Marshal Tukey
and the first persons brought forward were those arrested by him.
Most all pleaded guilty and were fined $4 plus costs. As the prison-
ers were led to the judges' chamber to pay their fines, Tukey, and his
men, looked at each in a mini "show-up."

The descent on the gamblers had the effect that Tukey desired.
He was praised by all the Boston newspapers for his direct action
and energetic enforcement of the laws. Some made a comparison
between the city police and the U.S. marshals, saying that the police
were "competent to enforce and execute the laws of the land. Instead
of twaddling and dawdling about, until imprisoned behind a green
baize door, our efficient City Marshal laid careful plans—had a competent force, well organized, and carried his plans into effect." The
reference to the "green baize door" was to U.S. Deputy Marshal Riley,
who deposed that when the crowd rushed into the courtroom, he
got trapped behind the door. Other notices praised Tukey in particular: "…our City Marshal conceived and carried out the plan in a
manner that reflects great credit upon him, as a shrewd and efficient
officer." The amount of publicity generated by these actions, both in
Boston and across the country, made one New York newspaper complain, "The papers are full of the exploits of Marshal Tukey of Boston. There seems to be no end to them." In Tukey's mind, this sort of

public notice was needed to counter charges leveled against him in the Shadrach case.[14]

He continued his brand of personal police action by visiting one of the raided establishments where no arrests were made. By himself, he boldly entered the room where as many as 15 men were gambling. Afraid that this was another raid, they made a rush for the door but Tukey blocked it. He told them that there was no way to escape but the window, which was an 18 foot drop. He then seized the gambling equipment and "two drab overcoats" which were left in the room. One editor stated. "The Marshal displayed his usual chivalry and manly bearing.... A brave man can do almost anything— when on the side of law and right." The futility of these raids must have been obvious to Tukey when he, later that week, led another group of police to the house at 29 Sudbury Street. They observed that the gamblers had now placed a guard at the door who kept a key to let in patrons. Tukey had the man quietly removed, took the key and entered the building. They found 27 men playing props. The props table they had seized in the earlier raid had been replaced within the week. The players were brought to Police Court the next morning and it was reported that nine of the men had been arrested in the original raid. The judge doubled the fine for all the men. All but two pleaded guilty and paid their fines. The other two were held over for trial in the Municipal Court.[15]

While Tukey's publicity campaign to show the efficiency of his department was in full swing, he also took steps to strengthen his control over the force. In his report, he had commented not only on the lack of men hired but also on how hard it was to get rid of men who were unsuitable. On March 25, he again nominated six men to be police officers and the Board of Aldermen agreed. More importantly, he recommended the dismissal of 12 men from the police and again the Board agreed without argument. Unofficially, at least, Tukey had made it a precedent that he would control the make-up of the Boston Police.[16]

While Tukey may have restored the reputation of his department, continuing furor over the Fugitive Slave Act would once again engulf him and his men. On the afternoon of April 3, U.S. Commissioner George T. Curtis issued a warrant to Deputy Marshal Frederic D. Byrnes for the arrest of Thomas Simms, allegedly a fugitive from slavery in Georgia. Knowing that the arrest was likely to cause trouble and aware of the recent ordinance by the Board of Aldermen, Byrnes applied to City Marshal Tukey for help. In response, Tukey sent two officers, Asa O. Butman and Alfred Sleeper, to go along with Byrnes and several other deputies to capture Simms. Tukey's orders to the men were to keep the peace and prevent bloodshed while the U.S. marshals made the arrest.

Byrnes knew, from an informant, the neighborhood where Simms often loitered at night so they waited to the evening to seek him. The search party seems to have gotten separated and Butman and Sleeper were alone when they encountered Simms and several companions. In order to get Simms away from the others, Butman decided to arrest him on a ruse of being "drunk and noisy." Simms resisted this and stabbed Butman in the leg with a knife. The officers subdued Simms and he was handed over to Byrnes, who put him in a carriage to take him to the courthouse. While he was being taken out of the carriage, he realized what was happening and began to shout that he was being kidnapped.[17]

The actions of Butman seemed to put the Boston police squarely in the middle of the controversy, not only supporting but actively arresting and detaining fugitive slaves. Marshal Tukey would later testify before a Massachusetts State Senate Committee that this was not his choice. He reported that he sent his officers to prevent "riot and bloodshed" and that Butman thought the arrest was the way to do that. Showing the loyalty that Edward Savage claimed he had for his men, he took responsibility for Butman's actions. However, he stated quite clearly that his department did not have "anything to do with arresting a fugitive slave. Have no orders to make such arrests. I would not arrest a fugitive slave, and I would not ask others to do what I would not do myself." Later in his testimony, Tukey claimed that had the U.S. deputy marshals made the arrest there would have been a riot and added, "Still I should not have ordered the arrest; but the arrest having been made by officers.... I uphold them for what they have done." The city marshal might have regretted the arrest being made by his officers but was not going to question their judgment.[18]

Whatever his personal feeling on the matter, recent events indicated that there could well be a major riot at the courthouse. Acting on orders from the mayor, Tukey took immediate steps to prevent a recurrence of what happened the last time the U.S. marshals were holding an alleged fugitive slave. By 3:30 in the morning, the day after the arrest was made, the police surrounded the courthouse with chains to prevent intrusions and the entire force was on duty to maintain order in Courthouse Square. Over the past few years, Tukey had repeatedly made use of chains for crowd control. This time, however, they took on a more sinister meaning. When the judges arrived in the morning, they faced a decision about getting into the courthouse. Chief Justice Lemuel Shaw and Judge George T. Bigelow, both of the Supreme Court of Massachusetts, ducked under the chains to gain admittance. The symbolism of these judges passing under chains to a building where a fugitive slave was being held did not pass unnoticed by the abolitionists or the newspapers. Daniel Wells, chief justice of the Court of Common Pleas, refused to bow under the barrier. As a result, an opening was made at the south door of the courthouse which allowed visitors to enter without going under the chains. Every visitor was questioned by the police. If they could show they had business in the building, they were admitted. This did not apply to "idlers and spectators" and they were turned away. The marshal reported that he had 60 men on duty during the day in and about the courthouse and 25 men there at night.[19]

The crowds around the courthouse were large but not unruly. There was no organized attempt to rush the building. The rhetoric however was still quite violent. During a meeting of the abolitionists on the Boston Common the next day, Wendell Phillips addressed the crowd, advising his listeners to "fill their pockets with pistols ... to crowd the streets and surround the Court-House, so that if the fugitive should be taken away, it must be over their dead bodies." He exhorted the people of the country around Boston to flood the streets and aid in the rescue. The city authorities took these threats seriously and Tukey and his men went into the crowds, searching for weapons. He reported that two or three pistols were found. These actions brought him trouble however. A black man, John Randolph, was reported to have been carrying a weapon in the Square. He was searched by Tukey and no firearm was found. Randolph objected to this treatment and sued Tukey for $1,000 in damages. Deputy Sheriff Coburn arrested Tukey on April 7 for trespass on Randolph. The

Early photograph of the Courthouse where fugitive slaves were kept. The U.S. Court Room, from which Shadrach was freed, was on the second floor. It was from here that Tukey escorted Thomas Simms to the boat which took him back to slavery (Library of Congress).

city marshal was required to post a bail of $5000. Remarkably, on the same day that he was stopped by Tukey, John Randolph attempted to assault the slave owner's representative with a club as he was entering his hotel.[20]

While the legal wrangling went on inside the courthouse, outside both the abolitionists and the police were preparing for the worst. The Boston Vigilance Committee held a meeting on April 8, where Thomas Wentworth Higginson argued strongly for a rescue of Simms but the other members refused to endorse this course of action. Higginson, along with Leonard Grimes and Lewis Hayden, the two black men who arranged the Shadrach rescue, agreed on a plan to get Simms out of custody. They would not be able to storm the courthouse, as in the last rescue, so Simms had to get out of the building. They arranged to have several mattresses stored nearby and Simms agreed to jump out the third floor window at the appointed time. Once out of the building, he would then be whisked away in a carriage. Unfortunately, on the appointed day, Higginson went to set things up and saw that workers were installing iron bars on the window. Tukey, having sworn to hold onto the prisoner or resign, began his own preparations to thwart a rescue. The police spent time training to make a hollow square, maneuvering, and in the use of a mariner's cutlass. The weapons were supplied by U.S. Marshal Devens from the Navy Yard and, when not in use, were kept in Tukey's office at City Hall. On the waterfront, it was noted that the brig *Acorn*, which would take Simms back, was building a deck cabin for passengers.[21]

On Friday, April 11, 1851, U.S. Commissioner Curtis rendered his opinion on the case and granted a certificate for the return of Simms to slavery in Georgia. Preparations were made for him to leave Boston the next day on the *Acorn*. A large force of police and watchmen were marched to the courthouse at 3:30 a.m. In front of the east door, the police, armed with their swords, formed a hollow square, while the watchmen, two deep, formed a ring around them. At 4 o'clock, Tukey came out of the courthouse followed by Marshal Devens and other officers, who escorted Thomas Simms to the center of the square. The group them marched down State Street to Long Wharf, where Simms and those who were to accompany him to Georgia boarded the *Acorn*. The brig was immediately towed out of the harbor. A crowd of about 100 was said to follow the procession but no resistance was offered. After the ship pulled away, Edward Savage, reflecting the feeling of the entire department, offered a final thought on the affair: "The Police, like true citizen-soldiers, surrendered up the sword—for the *rattan*, and quietly returned to duty on their beats, wondering, in the innocence of their hearts, *how one man could own another.*"[22]

Other than his own admission that he would never arrest a fugitive slave, Tukey never talked about his feeling in this matter. However, other people, generally hostile to Tukey, did report things he said about it. Dr. William F. Channing, who was intimately tied to the abolitionists though his cousin Thomas Wentworth Higginson, testified before the same Senate Committee that Bigelow and Tukey had. In that testimony, he recounted a conversation he had with the city marshal. Tukey told him that the police would be engaged in taking Simms to the ship. Channing told Tukey he was breaking state law, referring to the 1843 personal liberty law. According to Channing, Tukey replied, "I know no orders but those of the Mayor and Aldermen. If his orders had been the other way, he said he should act the other way. He said it was a painful duty; nevertheless he should perform it." Channing concluded that Tukey was sincere and acted according to the orders he was given.[23]

While the Fugitive Slave controversy occupied much of Tukey's time, preparations were still underway for another of his "deep laid plans." After the mayor and Board of Alderman authorized him to survey the notorious dance cellars of Ann Street on February 11, Tukey assigned two officers, Ham and Taylor, to walk the street with "neither badge or baton" and observe and report on illegal activities. One, perhaps romanticized account, referred to them as "continually passing up and down the sidewalks in Ann Street, peering into dance-halls and cellars, and carefully taking notes of the various passing transaction." Those notes were secretly presented to the Grand Jury which found indictments against a number of owners and operators. On the night of April 23, a combined force of 100 men from both the police and the watch, made the famous "Descent on Ann Street."[24]

Edward H, Savage joined the Boston Police, under Tukey, in 1851. He later left an interesting retrospective of Tukey's methods of dealing with his men. Savage eventually served as chief of police from 1871 to 1873.

The men assigned to make the raid were told to proceed to Ann Street from different directions and not to congregate too closely to their intended targets. At 9:45, a signal bell was rung and all the targets were raided at the same time. As with the raid on the gamblers, all exits were guarded so there was no route of escape. That night, the police arrested 153 people on

various charges. Of these, 61 were men and 92 were females. Most of
the females were charged with being a "lewd, wanton and lascivious
person." City Marshal Tukey addressed the court and detailed the
nature of the arrests and reported that they were made at the direction of the grand jury. As they were paraded in front of Judge Cushing of the Police Court, he noted whether they had been before him
on the same charge previously. If they had, he sentenced them to pay
a fine of $3 and two months in the House of Correction unless they
removed from Boston within 24 hours. Those who were new to the
Court, he fined $3 and released them. Tukey commented that their
fine was a dollar less than had been given to the gamblers he brought
to court. Judge Cushing reportedly acknowledged this, adding "$3 is
probably more for these women than the $4 to the gamblers."

The next day, 15 pipers and fiddlers were brought before the
Police Court and each fined $3. The charge of being a "common piper
or fiddler" was one that dated back to Colonial days and indicated
one who plays for rogues and dissolute persons to dance. Most of
the men captured in the raid were arrested on warrants related to
the grand jury investigation and were taken directly to the Municipal Court. They were charged with operating brothels or disorderly
houses or violating the license law. Each of these men or women were
required to post a bond of $200 against their future appearance at
trial.[25]

The "Celebrated Descent on Ann Street" was successful in dis-
rupting the criminal activities for a time. Tukey was widely praised
again for his active policing. However, he had already warned the
city fathers that unless they made it unprofitable to run such places,
they would be back in business in a short time. Ann Street continued to be the main red-light district in Boston for decades to come.
Edward Savage claimed that those women who could not pay their
$3 fine were saved from going to jail by being placed in homes to
work as domestics. As a result of this unsuccessful experiment, he
claimed, home robberies and burglaries went up for a time. While
the police continued to watch Ann Street, gradually things returned
to normal.[26]

Tukey was up for reappointment in June and, as they did the previous year, the mayor and aldermen nominated and reappointed him
to the position of city marshal without dissent or comment. What

little notice there was in the newspapers was favorable, one editor saying, "His services during the six years past have been signally beneficial to the city." The hiring of additional police, an emphasis on enforcing city ordinances and the campaign against vice in Boston led to much more active policing and this was reflected in the crime statistics presented by the city marshal for the quarter ending July 1, 1851. During the previous three months, the police made 1711 arrests, an average of 570 per month. This was considerably more than previous crime reports where the average per month was only about 200. Some of this increase could be directly attributed to the "descents" made on the gamblers and dance cellars. However if those arrests, totaling 239, were subtracted from the total, the average number of arrests per month would still be 490. Another significant increase in the reported crimes was in the category of violating the city ordinances. In the second quarter of 1851, there was an average of 90 such violations a month. Previously this accounted for an average of 20 violations a month. Similar statistics could be reported for those who broke the liquor license law. It appears that Tukey was encouraging his men to be more vigilant, perhaps in response to the recent criticisms.[27]

Another test of his police force came in September of this year. The city planned a three-day celebration called the "Railroad Jubilee" to commemorate the final connection between Boston and Montreal, as well as the beginning of steamship service between Boston and Liverpool. Both Mayor Bigelow and his predecessor, Josiah Quincy, Jr., had boosted the railroads connecting Boston to the West and this was a major accomplishment. Committees from the city called on President Fillmore and on the Governor-General of Canada to extend invitations, both of whom accepted. The celebration was to consist of three days, the first day for the reception of visitors and tours of public institutions, the second taken up with excursions around the harbor and the final day featured a massive procession through the city ending with a dinner under a pavilion on the Common and fireworks. This would prove to be an even larger crowd than for the introduction of Cochituate Water in 1848.

While the organizing committee made their arrangements, City Marshal Tukey took steps to maintain order during the celebration. The mayor and aldermen were particularly concerned that no violence occur during this event as President Millard Fillmore, whom they had invited, had recently been very critical of the city over the escape of the fugitive slaves. Tukey was authorized to raise a force of "special police" numbering 500 men to watch the depots, the docks and the hotels for pickpockets, thieves and other con men, as well as keep the peace. In his usual manner, Tukey organized this as a military campaign, dividing this force into groups of ten, each led by one of his regular officers. Most of the men hired were described as "mechanics and artisans" and had little experience with the professional criminals that were expected to prey on the crowds.

To familiarize these men with Boston's seamier side, Tukey arranged for a "grand show up" of known rogues in the City. This was held on the Common a few days before the big event. The police rounded up 76 men and women, known to be criminals, and paraded them before the whole force. As each was brought forward, Tukey recounted their criminal pasts to the assembled men and the gathered public. While this tactic was effective in letting the regular police know who to look for, this large a gathering was unusual and raised some concerns. The editor of the *Commonwealth* commented, "An entirely new legal institution seems to have grown up under the efficient marshalship of Mr. Tukey, which is very embarrassing to rogues, and still more puzzling to legal theorists. We may say it appears to be equally arbitrary, illegal, necessary and useful." He goes on to point out that these people were collected without warrant, they were insulted by being called rogues and having their history exposed, then let go without any charges against them. Nevertheless, the "specials" were now aware of who these people were and how they operated.[28]

The celebration went off without any serious trouble. On the third day, as the procession was readied, 12 policemen formed a line in the street and led off the parade. They were followed by Marshal Tukey, on horseback, accompanied by two aides. The procession, as it wended its way through the streets was said to take two and half hours to pass one point. It was reported to be the largest and most magnificent ever seen in Boston. For this occasion, Tukey had borrowed a superb horse known as "May Fly" which was said to be worth $2,000. There was universal praise for the police and how they kept things under control during the celebration. The official Canadian visitors were said to be amazed how the police could handle a crowd of 200,000 to 300,000 without any serious disturbance and they called Tukey, "the Napoleon of City Marshals." An even more amazing description of Tukey was provided by the Vermont editor of the *Burlington Free Press*:

> Prominent in all the glorious displays of the occasion, was a slightly-built, neatly dressed, gentlemanly man, about five-feet-six, with the darkest hair, and the mildest black eyes in the world, kind and courteous in his demeanor, though quick, determined and resolute in his movements, and about the last man in the world who would have been selected, by the casual observer, as the monarch of the Boston police. This man was Marshal Tukey—the ever-present, ever-vigilant, ever-efficient, ... Marshal Tukey is the best police chief in the world....[29]

Despite all the praise and success, political forces in Boston were about to impact the police department and lead to Tukey's downfall. In part, this can be traced to the previous year's election when the power of the Whig Party in Boston and Massachusetts had broken over the issue of slavery. A large number of voters had rejected Daniel Webster and the Compromise of 1850, electing a Democrat as governor and giving the Democrats control of both houses of the legislature. The remaining Whigs were reeling from this defeat and began to seek an alliance with the one block of voters who might be sympathetic to them—the Irish. The conservative Whigs and the naturally conservative Irish sought to counter the progressive movements which were characterized as elite and Protestant. As was common in 19th-century politics, if a party wished to court a group of voters, they favored them with patronage jobs. The mayor and aldermen decided it was time to open the public jobs to Irish-Americans who were naturalized, including the police department. Consequently, on September 29, Mayor Bigelow nominated a Bernard McGinniskin, known mostly as "Barney," to be a police officer. The board unanimously agreed to this appointment.[30]

This appointment was made quietly and without fanfare. It was one line in the report of the activities of the Board of Aldermen. However, it quickly became notorious. In an article entitled "Foreigners on the Police," the *Boston Evening Transcript* reported this unusual event and suggested that it was due to the coming election. Rumors abounded that the man appointed had just recently arrived in the country, that he was not a citizen, that he was a drunk, and that his appointment had been "smuggled" through the Board. In the next meeting of the Board, on October 6, Alderman Abel B. Monroe asked for a reconsideration of the appointment, saying that in the last meeting, "his attention was withdrawn from the proceeding, and he wished the privilege of voting on the question." In many recently-published, popular histories, Monroe is reported to have said, "Irishmen commit most of the city's crime and would receive special consideration from one of their own wearing the blue." This quote is unattributed and clearly anachronistic as the police at this time wore a badge but not a uniform.[31]

Monroe's reaction to an Irish American being appointed to the police elicited a passionate response from Mayor Bigelow. He began by addressing the rumors about McGinniskin, denying them all. The mayor indicated that the nomination process had been the same as it always was. A petition was presented to him by a number of well-known and prominent businessmen who strongly supported McGinniskin's appointment. The mayor then asked Marshal Tukey to investigate the candidate. Tukey, in a report to the mayor dated June 9, stated "he found that the man was 42 years old, and had been 22 years in this country, and had the reputation of being a 'temperate and quiet man.'" Bigelow then went on to praise various Irish-born men who served Boston in the other government positions and in the community in general. He described McGinniskin's coming to America, his becoming a citizen and his peaceful living in the city for many years. The mayor asked what kept McGinniskin from being treated like other respectable applicants? His answer was "You were, without your own consent, born on the wrong side of the ocean. It is true you came away as soon as you could, and all your adult life has passed in the nest of the Eagle; but we cannot forget that you were cradled in the bower of the Shamrock. You cannot be trusted." After the mayor's speech, the Board voted again with Monroe being the only vote against.[32]

Whether the mayor edited Tukey's comments or the marshal had second thoughts, he met with the majority of the Board of Aldermen on October 8 and expressed his opposition to McGinniskin's becoming a policeman. Apparently the city marshal refused to employ him. Matters were at an impasse until November 3, when

McGinniskin showed up at the police office with a letter from Mayor Bigelow ordering Tukey to put the Irishman to work. To fulfill this order, Tukey took another officer, J.C. Oliver, off his beat in the South End and put McGinniskin in his place. Within days, a petition was begun to have Oliver returned to his beat. It was presented to the Board of Aldermen on November 11, having been signed by 300 residents of the area.

At the same meeting of the Board of Aldermen, Tukey presented a letter, outlining his objections to McGinniskin. He reminded the Board that earlier in the year they had decided no one would be appointed as a policeman without Tukey's own recommendation. However, McGinniskin had shown up at his door on November 3 with the letter from the mayor ordering him to be put to work. The marshal claimed that he had never met McGinniskin nor had he recommended him. He vehemently believed that he was not fit to be a policeman and "respectfully protested" against his being in the department. Tukey gave three reasons why McGinniskin was not fit. The first was that he was reported to be a "noisy, quarrelsome, meddlesome Ann street cabman." Secondly, when he showed up for work on the first day, he introduced himself to the other police as "Barney McGinnisken, fresh from the bogs of Ireland" which Tukey claimed was said in an "impudent, insulting manner." Finally, Tukey reported that in 1842, McGinniskin had been convicted for being "engaged in a riot on the Lord's day in church."[33]

Naturally, McGinniskin replied to these statements, defending his appointment. He answered the marshal's contention that they had never met by stating that he had gone to Tukey's office on June 2, after his petition was first presented, met him, and shook his hand. After a few brief questions by the marshal, McGinniskin left with the feeling that Tukey was pleased. As to not being recommended, he cited Tukey's own report to the mayor which termed him a "temperate and quiet man." McGinniskin then went on to address the three reasons for Tukey's opposition. He wondered why, if Tukey had diligently made the inquiries into his background in June finding him quiet, how he could now call him a troublemaker? McGinniskin admitted to owning and driving a cab for 11 months in the past. His being on the notorious Ann Street was due to his being assigned a station there by the superintendent of carriages, who worked for

Tukey. As to his greeting his fellow officers, he claimed that it was intended as a joke and that they received it as such.

Finally, he dealt with his conviction for rioting in a church. This incident occurred in St. Mary's Catholic Church on Endicott Street in the North End. At the time, there were two priests serving the parish and each had his own group of followers. The dispute arose from differences about how the church should deal with the issue of temperance. One side believed that it should be actively preached from the pulpit. The other side, while supporting the need for temperance, did not feel that it belonged in the church service. As tensions grew, the bishop removed one of the priests to another parish. His supporters objected and 400 signed a petition to the bishop. When it seemed like he would not relent, they disturbed Sunday Mass and refused to let the other priest speak. The dispute went on for 15 minutes until the city marshal was called and dispersed the crowd. Ten men were convicted of rioting and were given fines ranging from $10 to $20. McGinniskin was assessed the lower fine. In his defense, he stated that he was a pew holder in the church and was resisting those who sought to disturb the service and that it did not imply he was "riotous or quarrelsome." He pointed to his continued employment at some of Boston's largest merchant houses and presented recommendations from their owners. All of this information was presented in a sworn statement made before a justice of the peace in Boston.[34]

All Tukey could say was that he had never recommended McGinniskin and never would. He claimed that the report he gave in June was not a recommendation. Further, he stated that three hours before McGinniskin was nominated by the mayor, he, Tukey, positively refused to recommend him. Despite the marshal's objections, McGinniskin remained on the job. It is clear that politics was a major factor in this episode. The mayor and most of the aldermen wanted to attract Irish voters and political patronage was an accepted way of doing this. Tukey may have objected so strenuously because the Board made the appointment without his recommendation, a procedure which he had fought hard to have them affirm. In discussing this case, Lane, in his history of the Boston police, persuasively argues that under Tukey, the police force thought of themselves as a unit rather than individuals. They were developing a sense of professionalism. The blatant introduction of politics into the appointment process, offended not only Tukey, but the men's sense of themselves.[35]

The confrontation with the mayor was only one of the problems facing Tukey in the fall of 1851. Once again, he had over extended himself and on October 20, he filed for insolvency for the third time. Two creditors came forward to seize his estate. The first was the Boston Gas Light Company, to whom he owed $107.75. Their detailed list of charges showed that in April 1851, Tukey was having gaslighting installed in his house at 48 Russell Street. There were 13 gaslight fixtures as well as iron and copper pipes to bring in the gas. The second creditor was a firm identified as Black & Company, and he owed them $3,118.46. This firm was a lumber company, located on Francis Wharf, with strong connections to Maine lumber interests. This debt may represent Tukey's shipment of supplies to California on speculation.

Another factor was that he had begun speculating in property. In 1849, he bought a house on West Centre Street for $2,000. In 1851, he bought a brick house on London Street for $3,000 and two brick houses on May Street for $7,000. Over those three years, Tukey purchased $12,000 in property while his salary remained at $1800 per year. The house on West Centre Street was not a problem as he sold it in 1850 for $2,025, probably using the money to finance the purchase of the other houses. As he purchased the three brick houses, he mortgaged them to his close friend and subordinate, Asa O. Butman, for a total of $7,500. When his finances began to look shaky, Tukey signed a quit claim deed to Butman for the two houses on May Street. This was just two weeks before he declared insolvency.

However, the main reason Tukey had to declare his insolvency was his association with Josiah Quincy, Jr., in stock of the Vermont Central Railroad. Quincy was a major booster of railroads, serving on the boards of several different lines. The completion of the Vermont Central line was the reason for the recent Railroad Jubilee in Boston. It was the railroad that completed the connection between Boston and Montreal. To finance the line, Quincy took no salary but bought huge amounts of stock on margin with the idea that when the line was completed, its value would go up and he would profit. It is likely that he persuaded Tukey to invest on the same basis. However, in 1851, the money market was very tight and the company had trouble raising cash. With Quincy's mixed support, the board of directors began issuing stock and bonds at discounted rates. This led to a precipitous drop in the value of the stock and bonds already issued. Both Quincy and Tukey were forced to pay up the rest of what they owed on stock that was worth much less than they paid for it.

The insolvency went through the usual process, first being advertised in two of the Boston newspapers. It must have been embarrassing to see his name again in the news for debt. The first meeting of his creditors was held on November 11, the day after his conflict with the mayor and aldermen. Thomas B. Hall, a lawyer involved in many insolvencies, was appointed assignee of the creditors and took possession of all Tukey's estate. By the time of the third meeting, in May 1852, it was determined that there remained no assets in Tukey's estate and he was discharged. The significance of this insolvency for Tukey can be seen in the fact that when his daughter Adelaide died in 1910, her obituary still mentioned her father's losing all his money even though it was almost 60 years earlier.[36]

November 11 was a busy day for Tukey. Not only did he have the first meeting of his insolvency hearing, but in the afternoon, he married Carsilla Haycock. They were married by Joseph Banvard, pastor of the Harvard Street Baptist Church, in the South End. She had been a member of that church since 1849. In many ways, Carsilla was just what Tukey needed. She was about his age, she was born in Maine, and she was a very wealthy widow. No specific information exists on when or how they met each other but several things may have aided their romance. Tukey seemed well connected to the community of Maine merchants that had been established in Boston. His organization of these men to provide a charitable ball for the California Packet Company, a venture originating in Maine, was one sign of this. Perhaps he met Carsilla at the ball. Besides both of them being from Maine, she and Tukey shared an interest in the California excitement. Before he died, Jesse Haycock, the husband of Carsilla, became the image in Boston for the Gold Fever.

Jesse Haycock, also a Maine native, had been a lumber dealer in Boston with an office at 29 Long Wharf. He specialized in importing timber from Maine for Boston's developing expansion. Haycock was often in financial trouble and in one case, testimony revealed that he substituted inferior lumber for what had been agreed upon and increased the price for goods beyond what had been negotiated. In March 1849, Haycock sailed on the *Harriet Neal* as a member of the Massasoit Mining and Trading Company, a band of 24 Boston men headed for the gold fields. It was said that he was in great debt when he left. His reputation did not improve on the voyage when he charged another member of the group $70 for the use of $100. By September, he was in the gold fields and making money. Haycock returned to Boston in May 1850 and was showing off his "gold lumps." He took out advertisements in the newspapers stating that he was ready to pay off all his debts. After paying his debts, it was reported that he still had over $100,000 in gold dust and no desire to return to California. His was the dream of thousands of Americans, to make it rich in California. Despite his remark, Jesse Haycock returned to California where he bought a large property in Sacramento and began building a house for his family. However, he died of cholera, in 1850, before he could complete it.

A little over a year later, his widow married Francis Tukey. They left for a honeymoon in Baltimore the day after the wedding. It was from there that Tukey wrote his response to McGinniskin's defense. Returning to Boston, they set up a household with six children, Tukey's four and her two teenage sons. Despite Carsilla's wealth, the insolvency process continued into the next year.[37]

On his return from Baltimore, Tukey found himself involved in perhaps the most contested mayoral election in Boston's history. Not only had the shift in politics forced the Whigs to seek Irish votes but the mayor and aldermen had a serious controversy with the Fire Department, reorganizing it and firing many members. For various reasons, the Whigs knew they were in trouble. On November 11, Mayor Bigelow announced to his party that he would not seek reelection and he was joined by five of the eight current aldermen. The Whig convention eventually nominated John H. Wilkins, a Boston paper merchant, as their candidate for mayor.

In response to the growing influence of the Irish, a new party, known as the Native Americans, was formed. In a letter to the editor of the *Boston Herald*, a writer who termed himself "22 Years in Boston" expressed the sentiments of many who favored the new party. He called the controversy between Tukey and the Board of Aldermen over McGinniskin ridiculous and, somewhat loosely, said "If Marshal

Tukey had raised the same objections against the appointment of an American citizen to the police ... who believes that he would be appointed?" Of course, McGinniskin was a citizen, although a naturalized one. The writer attributed the controversy to an attempt to stay in power by "means of the foreign vote" and exhorted all the "American citizens" of Boston to elect men who would resist this influence.

The Native American party held their meeting on November 22. One of the first speakers to address the convention set the tone for what followed. Mr. C.W. Dennison reviewed the controversy over the Irish policeman and decried the great influx of "ignorant and priest ridden foreigners." The committee in charge of nominations proposed three names for the office of mayor: Dr. J.V.C. Smith, Edward Brooks and Francis Tukey. When the vote was held, Smith won the nomination with 19 out of 37 votes. However, Tukey had a strong showing, receiving 16 votes. There is no indication that Tukey was at this meeting or was even aware that he had been nominated. When his name was again proposed for mayor in December, Tukey took out ads in a number of newspapers clearly stating his refusal to offer himself for election, saying "I have positively refused to allow my name to be used as a candidate for that office."[38]

The election was held on December 8 and no one secured a majority of the votes. Wilkins, the Whig candidate, received 4,425 votes, more than 400 votes short of a majority. Smith came in a distant second with 2,661 votes. By tradition, Wilkins withdrew from the race and the Whigs then nominated Benjamin Seaver, former president of the Common Council, to run for mayor. The second election was held on December 17 and the results were again undecided. Seaver received fewer votes than Wilkins and failed to secure a majority. A third election was scheduled for December 24 and Seaver was again at the head of the Whig ticket. Two things changed between this election and the previous one. On December 22, there was a meeting of the "adopted citizens" of Boston at St. Joseph's Church on Moon Street in the North End, and they voted to support Seaver for mayor. Secondly, Tukey influenced the police to also vote for the Whigs. The men of the night police took this seriously and marched to the polls as a body to vote for Seaver.

When the results were tabulated, Seaver squeaked by with a very small majority and was elected. The vote totals reported by various newspapers were different with Seaver's majority ranging from 33 votes to a single vote. In any case, the support of the "adopted citizens" and the police made a difference. When Edward Savage later recalled this election, he said that the police were "in very good spirits at the close of the year, in anticipation of a longer job."[39]

8

"After you left the City Hall, others came, with whom I had but little sympathy"

The mayoral election of 1851 marked a watershed for Francis Tukey. It was the first time, as city marshal, that he became involved in politics. Prior to becoming marshal, Tukey's sentiments had been with the Democratic Party and he was mentioned several times as a ward organizer. When Whig Mayor Josiah Quincy, Jr., appointed him city marshal, all of that stopped. For almost five years, respecting his office, Tukey remained apolitical. This began to change with the appointment of an Irish policeman for political purposes. He saw this as a personal rejection of his leadership and was vehement in his opposition. Mayor Bigelow and Tukey, despite a rocky start, had come to respect and trust each other. When Bigelow decided not to run again, it was a betrayal to Tukey.

It is easy to see Tukey's opposition to McGinniskin as a sign of his Nativism, and certainly when he moved to California, he would join the Native American Party. However, up to this point, Tukey had never shown any particular bias to the Irish or any other "adopted citizens" living in Boston. The police force under him was well known for delivering food and fuel to Irish families who were having difficulties. One of the first things Tukey did after becoming city marshal was to take into his own home two Irish children until their father, whom he had arrested, could arrange for them to be taken care of by relatives.[1]

However, Tukey's opposition to McGinniskin made him a hero to the newly formed Native American Party in Boston. In a vote for

170

whom members of the party wanted to be their candidate for mayor, Tukey's name received only three votes less than the man they eventually nominated. Still, Tukey took to the newspapers and let it be known that he had no desire for his name to be used in such a way. Ultimately, Tukey's views were expressed by the way he organized the police to vote in the last election. They voted not for the Native American candidate but for the regular Whig nominee.[2]

Having supported the winning candidate in the mayoral election, Tukey may have thought he was secure in his position. However, his support had been only for the top of the ticket and it was reported that he worked against several of the aldermen and Common Council members. In addition, everyone, including Tukey, knew that it was a shift in the Irish voting that allowed Seaver to be elected by his small majority. The controversy over the hiring of McGinniskin still rankled the city marshal and he was vocal in his opposition. These factors combined to create a hostile relationship with the new city government. In his recollections of this time, Edward Savage commented that while they helped get the mayor elected, "no sooner had we got our man *in*, than he began to get us *out*."[3]

Tukey, who usually had good instincts about which battles to fight and which to let go, made a serious mistake in regard to the new mayor. The day before the new government was to be installed, Tukey dismissed McGinniskin from the police force without giving a reason. He had no authority to do so as policemen were appointed or dismissed by the mayor and this Board of Aldermen. Virtually every newspaper in the city, no matter their feelings about the Irish policeman, decried Tukey's usurpation of the mayor's power. He must have known that Mayor Seaver would bring McGinniskin back, given his need for the Irish vote. Whatever his motives, Tukey had created a bad feeling with the mayor even before he was sworn into office. His opposition to McGinniskin continued unabated despite the mayor's rebuke. On January 9, a notice was published in several papers stating that "Policeman McGinniskin" was seeking the owner of a bag containing money found in Washington Street the previous morning. It was reported that City Marshal Tukey refused to take charge of it. The editor of the *Boston Evening Transcript* expressed what many Bostonians were feeling, "the Marshal has taken a position he cannot sustain, and which the highest interests of the public require he should be made to retract at once, or else vacate his office." McGinniskin, despite Tukey's hostility, remain an active policeman through the rest of Tukey's tenure and beyond.[4]

Mayor Seaver organized the government of the city on January 6, 1852, swearing in all of the aldermen and Common Council members. Like all mayors, Benjamin Seaver addressed the City Council, and the citizens of Boston, when he was sworn in. This was traditionally where the mayor would provide his vision of how the city should be governed and where he would make specific proposals for the Aldermen to consider. In his extremely short address, Mayor Seaver did very little of what was expected. The six previous inaugural addresses, from Quincy and Bigelow, averaged about three columns of newsprint. Seaver's address barely filled one quarter of one column. The only significant insight into how Seaver viewed his office was when he compared the City Government to running a corporation. He stated that he viewed the office of mayor as a business office. As to the scope of his office, "Whatever the city charter, general laws or the city ordinances authorize me to do, shall be done; and nothing more *must*." Perhaps in a refer-

Benjamin Seaver

ence to Tukey, he said that he would hold those under him to the same. As for the lack of any details in his address, Seaver pleaded that he had not had time to understand the "great interests and expenditures of the city."[5]

As was required, Tukey presented his annual report on the Police Department to the new mayor and aldermen on January 19. This report is very similar to that presented the previous year, using much of the same language. It does reveal the state of the department and discusses several significant points for the

Benjamin Seaver, mayor of Boston 1852–1854. Elected by the liquor interests of Boston, he worked to smear Tukey and remove him from office.

coming year. As far as manpower, the Police Department was now fully staffed. There were two more day police than in 1851 but more importantly the night police were fully restored. In 1851, the night police had been reduced to one officer and seven men. Now they had a full complement of three officers and 22 men. As mentioned in the previous chapter, this revitalized force was more vigilant and active. Arrests had risen from 3282 in 1850 to 5449 in 1851. This was a 37 percent increase in one year. Tukey was aware of the increasing amount of crime and, once again, attributed it to the leniency of judges and juries in Boston. He gave examples of the low fines given to offenders, commenting that they made much more money per week than any fine imposed on them. He compared the fines to a license system whereby the offenders were allowed to continue their business.[6]

A major issue continued to be the regulation of the sale of spirituous liquor. In June 1851, Maine took the lead in the fight for temperance when they passed what became known as the "Maine Liquor Law." This was the first law to completely ban the manufacture and sale of spirituous liquors and was widely hailed as a major advance. Previously, Mayor Bigelow and the Board of Aldermen, which included a majority of temperance supporters, responded to this by authorizing the city marshal, himself a temperance advocate, to conduct a census of the sale and use of alcoholic beverages in Boston. With his usual efficiency, Tukey completed and presented his report on November 10 and now included it in his annual report. The police counted 1500 places that sold alcohol and not surprisingly, these were concentrated in Wards 1 (North End), Ward 4 (Waterfront) and Ward 7 (Fort Hill). All of these areas were close to the shipping and crammed with Irish immigrants. The Board asked that the ethnicity of the sellers be determined and 60 percent of the total were Irish. The final question that the Board asked Tukey was what he could recommend to check the progress of intemperance. His answer was simple and direct, "Execute the law."

There was already talk about Massachusetts passing a law similar to that of Maine. These statistics were praised as a way of pushing that initiative. Unfortunately for Tukey, the new mayor and Board of Aldermen were not temperance advocates. The city marshal's answer to the final question was seen as his intention and that did not sit well with those now in power. Nor did his being initiated into the Honor Lodge of the Order of the Sons of Temperance in early February.[7]

While his relations with the mayor and aldermen may have been shaky, Tukey's men appreciated his leadership. In February, they organized a subscription to have a silver tea service made for him. The policemen, and their wives, attended a "soiree" hosted by "Mr. & Mrs. Tukey" at their home on March 4. The presentation of the tea service with a silver salver was made by Deputy City Marshal Hezekiah Earle, a long time associate of Tukey's. The silver bore the engraved message, "Presented to Francis Tukey, Esq., City Marshal, as a Token of Respect, by the Boston Police Department. March 1852." On the other side it read, "Honor, the Reward of Fidelity." They also gave Tukey a gold watch. It would be interesting to know if Officer McGinniskin was invited or attended the soiree. However, one newspaper, the same week, reported that he remained sick at home.[8]

Within a month, however, Tukey was the one to get sick. It was reported in mid–April that he had rheumatic fever, an inflammatory disease resulting from an untreated strep throat. There are a whole host of nasty symptoms associated with the disease but generally it is very debilitating. Both Tukey and his deputy, Hezekiah Earle, were out with this sickness and had been ill for several weeks. Almost two months later, in early May, Tukey was recovered enough to go out in public and finally return to work. When he did, he was facing a major crisis.[9]

While Tukey was sick, events were moving that would force major changes in his life. Since the previous year, temperance advocates in Massachusetts were pushing for a law similar to that of Maine. By May of 1852, it was obvious that such a law would soon be enacted. On April 26, the new mayor and aldermen, who counted on support from the liquor interests, revived the old license system for selling spirituous liquors. Within a few weeks, they had granted several hundred licenses. Previous administrations, not wanting to appear in favor of drinking, avoided the issue by not issuing licenses. Mayor Seaver and his Board of Aldermen believed that if they issued licenses prior to the adoption of the new liquor law, they would remain valid for a year despite the new strictures. However, they also knew that City Marshal Tukey would have a contrary vision of their actions and decided it was time for him to go.[10]

The first step in this process was a decision to eliminate the night police. Tukey had developed this branch of the police department and he used it not only for patrolling the business district at night but they had become his tool for the famous descents he had made the previous year. When Boston let the night police wither away in 1850, Tukey fought to have the entire complement restored to duty. It was reported that they had marched to the polls as a body to vote in the mayoral election of 1851. Such loyalty and concerted political activity were seen as dangerous. On May 17, the members of the night police were abruptly informed that they would no longer have a job the following week. Of the three officers and 22 men, only four were kept. At the same time, the Board of Aldermen reduced the number of watchmen by 30 and were ready to reduce the day police as well. All of this was put forth as a cost-saving measure.

While it had been recently stated that this reduction was not "seriously protested in the press," there was, in fact, considerable opposition in Boston's newspapers. The *Boston Herald*, long a critic of Tukey and the police, stated, "We have known no action of the City Government for several years past which has caused so great and general dissatisfaction, as the discharge of the subordinate officers of this city, known as the 'Night Police.'" The editor of the *Boston Daily Times* went further in condemning the move: "Seriously, there never was a more flagrant or egregious blunder than that which the city government has committed in this instance." A petition in favor of the night police, signed by a large number of merchants, was presented to the Board of Aldermen but was dismissed.[11]

At the same time, Tukey became aware that two members of the Common Council, Harvey Jewell and Daniel Haskins, were taking depositions about his activities and his running of the department. They were talking to men who had been discharged from the department by Tukey as not suitable to be police officers. Not one to sit by idly while his enemies were getting ready, Tukey wrote, on May 24, directly to Mayor Seaver and the Board of Aldermen stating that he had heard the rumors that charges were to be made about his conduct. He asked, if such charges were submitted to them, that he have a public hearing before the Board to answer them. He received no reply to this letter. It was reported that these depositions were an effort to get Tukey to resign.[12]

The Massachusetts legislature, on May 22, passed the strict liquor law that many feared. While this was a state law, the enforcement of it fell on the individual cities and towns. The law specifically mentioned that city marshals were responsible for seizing and destroying liquor. As early as February, the city of Roxbury sought to get around this issue by proposing to eliminate the office of city marshal. Boston considered this same tactic in June. The rationale was that if the city marshal were to seize liquor and destroy it, the city would be liable for damages if the law were later deemed unconstitutional.

The mayor and the Board of Aldermen held a special, secret meeting on the morning of June 24 to work out the new police ordinance. The solution was to replace the city marshal with a chief of police, and thereby avoid the letter of the law. In the afternoon, in a public session, they approved the ordinance. That evening, the ordinance was passed to the Common Council for its approval. As the vote was about to be held, James B. Allen, from Ward 2, asked the committee that presented the ordinance: what was the reason for the new ordinance? He was given no answer and the Council then moved to vote. Allen spoke up again, saying that the city government "had adopted as their motto 'Rum and Economy'" and he further mentioned that this was passed "in order to carry out the feelings of some individuals by the overthrow of others." In this he was referring to the campaign against Tukey. Led by Harvey Jewell, the Council passed the ordinance 27 to 11.[13]

Under the new police ordinance, the office of city marshal expired at midnight on June 30. The mayor and Board of Aldermen held a secret meeting that afternoon to appoint the chief of police. They had achieved their goal, as Tukey let it be known that he would not be willing to accept the position if it were offered to him. Remarkably, the Board adjourned the meeting without appointing anyone to the office. Either it could not agree on a candidate or could not find anyone to take the job. As the next scheduled meeting was not until July 6, more than a week away, there would be no head of the police department during that time. One editor was very critical of this lack of action, stating, "We cannot at this moment foretell the evils to result from the indecision, not to say unpardonable delinquency of the Mayor and Board of Aldermen in this instance."

Tukey, who agreed to continue to supervise the department until an appointment was made, became, by default, the first "Chief of Police" for the city of Boston.[14]

The mayor finally got around to nominating someone to be chief of police on July 14. At a meeting of the Board of Aldermen, Gilbert Nourse was first appointed as a policeman and several minutes later nominated by Mayor Seaver to be chief of police. He was unanimously confirmed by the board. Nourse was a local merchant and politician whose most recent job was as deputy clerk of the Faneuil Hall Market. He had no experience in either the law or law enforcement. In commenting on Tukey's replacement, one editor gave him faint praise saying, "But we have no reason for doubting that Mr. Nourse will do his duty, if not as well, at least to the best of his ability." This was a minor remark compared to what the editor of the *Boston Journal* had to say:

> So far as we have heard, there is but one feeling in regard to this appointment, and that is disaffection and regret. It is looked upon as throwing away the services of the most capable, faithful and efficient City Marshal which the City of Boston ever had, for those of a person totally inexperienced in the duties of the responsible office to which he has been elected, and who, so far as is known, has no peculiar qualifications to fit him for the station.[15]

Now ex–Chief of Police Tukey was also at the Board meeting. After the vote to confirm Nourse, Tukey asked Mayor Seaver if he could ask a single question of the Board and the mayor granted this. He asked, "If any act of his, or any neglect, either of omission or commission, had influenced the action of the Board?" There was no immediate reply but eventually Alderman Cary replied that there was not as far as he was concerned. Tukey then put the question directly to Mayor Seaver, who replied that he was not ready to give an answer. Still resentful of the underhanded attempt to smear his name, Tukey, the next day, addressed individual letters to the mayor and each board member, again asking the same question. Two of the aldermen, Benjamin James and Benjamin L. Allen, replied that they had no problem with his performance of his duties and, had he been nominated by the mayor, they would have voted for him. Tukey claimed that three other Aldermen gave him verbal reassurances. There was no answer from the mayor.

Tukey's last official act was on July 17 when, at 8 a.m. he turned over the city property he held to Gilbert Nourse. Tukey then made "a few appropriate remarks" to the assembled force which were answered by the new chief of police. After this, Tukey individually introduced each of the policemen to their new chief.[16]

The shockwaves from Tukey's removal continued to move the community. In the Common Council meeting on the afternoon of July 15, Samuel R. Spinney proposed a resolution that Francis Tukey was a valuable city officer and that reasons should be given for his removal. He stated that there was a feeling in the community "that an outrage had been committed" and that the public was amazed. There was "considerable animated discussion" led by members Jewell and Haskell, the men who collected the depositions against Tukey, and the matter was tabled. On that same night, Tukey attended the Suffolk County Temperance Convention and was selected as a vice-president of the meeting. The Rev. Rufus W. Clark addressed the meeting concerning the enforcement of the new liquor law. He stated, "to loud and repeated cheers" that if the city government did not need Tukey, the people will take him. It was reported in one newspaper that posters were already put up around town seeking the nomination of Francis Tukey for mayor.[17]

For his part, Tukey moved on from his official duties and went back into practice as a lawyer. He rented an office at 30 School Street and began advertising in the newspapers on July 15. The office on School Street was very different from his previous one on Court Square. While still in the center of town, it was opposite City Hall and a block removed from most other lawyers' offices. Perhaps it was all that was available or the rent was much cheaper. His ad stated that he gave particular attention to the settlement of estates and the care of real estate. This same ad would run uninterrupted until March 30 of the next year. There is little information mentioned as to what Tukey did as a lawyer, most of his work being private. He was counsel for two separate divorce cases before the Massachusetts Supreme Court in October. Both of the men he represented were granted divorces.[18]

While he pursued his legal career, Tukey was still involved in politics. In October, he addressed a Webster Club meeting in Ward 6, his home territory. Webster Clubs were formed to support Daniel

Webster in his effort to become U.S. president. Although the Whig Convention, held in Baltimore in June, had nominated Winfield Scott, New England Whigs and Southern Whigs continued to push for Webster's inclusion on the ballot. None of that came to fruition as Webster died on October 24.

The Union Whigs did not entirely give up their struggle, however. While their ticket had no candidate for president, they did support Charles J. Jenkins of Georgia for vice president. He was a Whig and gained national attention as the author of the Georgia Platform, which endorsed the Compromise of 1850 but warned that no further intrusion on states rights would be allowed. This was credited with keeping the South in the Union for another decade. As they organized for the election, the Union Whigs of Ward 6 chose Tukey as one of vote distributors for the ward.[19]

Tukey supported the Webster Whigs in the national election but in the municipal election that year, the Webster Whigs, while putting forth their own ticket for Board of Aldermen, supported Benjamin Seaver for mayor. The ex–city marshal, both because of his temperance beliefs and his personal dislike, could not support this ticket. Instead, he threw his support to a new party called the Citizen's Union Party. This party was supposedly "independent of all party and political considerations" and was made up of disgruntled voters from many different parties.

What attracted Tukey most was their staunch support of the new liquor law. On December 3, the convention nominated Dr. J.V.C. Smith as their candidate for mayor. Tukey became an active campaigner for Smith and against Seaver. The *Boston Daily Atlas*, a prime supporter of Mayor Seaver, complained about the ex-officials who were rallying against their candidate, most notably the ex–city marshal, commenting they "doubtless feel that the City requires their services, as they do the city's pay." The mayoral election of 1852 was not as contested as the previous one but did generate more votes than any previous election. All together, 11,973 votes were cast and Seaver won with 6018 votes for a 31 vote majority. The total vote was 20 percent greater than in the first election of 1851 and 33 percent greater than the third election which gave Seaver his first term.[20]

The large number of votes could have been as a result of the controversy over the liquor law. However, some viewed the total with suspicion. The day after the election, a petition was filed with the mayor and Board of Aldermen which alleged voting fraud. It was signed by five men, including Francis Tukey, all supporters of Dr. Smith. They stated that an examination of the voter lists made at the polling places, compared to the aggregate totals, showed that there were 232 votes more than there should have been. Since Mayor Seaver's victory had been by only 31 votes, this discrepancy could have cast doubt on the results. The mayor gave the petition to a committee of three aldermen for investigation; the election of all three of these aldermen would have been overturned by this petition. Not surprisingly, the report they produced, after an "uncalled for stab at the protestants," concluded that the results showed no evidence of fraud. The city solicitor was called upon and opined that the mayor and aldermen could not go behind the returns that had been certified by the Ward officers. The only remedy, he said, was by a civil suit. Mayor Seaver, again by the slimmest of margins, was elected for a second term.[21]

Tukey's continued opposition to and campaign against Seaver and certain other politicians did not go unnoticed. They decided now to use the information they collected in May when they feared they would have to force him out of office. In a relatively new newspaper, the *Boston Chronicle*, an editorial was published which was critical of Tukey's time as city marshal. It apparently included derogatory remarks attributed to Mayor Seaver. One newspaper stated that the editor of the *Boston Chronicle* was "shooting his wild shots at Tukey." On the same day it was published, December 8, Tukey fired off an indignant letter to the mayor asking if the statements were "MADE BY YOUR ATHOURITY, OR IF YOU ENDORSE THEM?" The capital letters are from the original. Not receiving an answer, Tukey took out an ad in the *Boston Herald* on both December 13 and 14 which reprinted the letter.[22]

Even more serious was a report prepared by the Committee on Ordinances describing its hearings about uniting the police and watch departments. Although attributed to the committee as a whole, the report was authored by Harvey Jewell and Daniel N. Haskell, the members of the Common Council who had been taking depositions about Tukey's time as city marshal. It was rumored that the report would be highly critical of Tukey but in the end, the criticism was mild. It commented on the use of the night police to work against candidates of the Common Council (i.e., Jewell and Haskell) and that "highly profane and abusive language" was used in the Police Office.

While they could not put their real charges in the report, Jewell and Haskell used the debate about the report to bring out serious charges against Tukey, which were reported in the newspapers. The main charges were that unclaimed items in the Police Office were often sold in private auctions to members of the force for much less than their worth, that the gambling equipment so prominently displayed by the city marshal had been sold back to the gamblers and that the house Tukey lived in was owned by one of the gamblers. The editor refused to take responsibility for reporting these charges, saying, "We merely report the facts as detailed by members of the City Council, speaking in their places in the Council Chamber, in defense of an official report." Conveniently, neither the City Councilors nor the editor could be sued for slander yet the charges were out there.[23]

Tukey did not take this slander on his reputation lightly and the day after the debate occurred, it was reported that he was "going to fire into certain 'reports' and sayings lately indulged. ... Feathers may be expected to fly." He attended a meeting of the mayor and aldermen on December 27 and presented them with a memorial asking that charges against him be investigated. In his memorial, he recounted the many times he asked the mayor and Board of Aldermen if there were any objections to his time in office and the deafening silence from any of them. In discussing the debate that took place in the Common Council, Tukey related the charges made against him and that Jewell and Haskell said they had evidence to sustain these charges.

He wanted the Board to do one of three specific things. First, that a joint special committee be appointed to investigate and that he be allowed to confront his accusers. Or, secondly, that the Board instruct the City Solicitor to present the evidence gathered by Jewell and Haskins to the grand jury and, if it was sufficient, he be prosecuted. Or finally, he asked the Board to request that Jewell and Haskins make the charges "in such a manner that they can never pretend that they are protected from actions of slander, by their official capacity as members of the Common Council." Tukey was ready to defend himself in any way the Board desired. For its part, the Board was not going to do anything and, citing "discourteous terms" used against city officials, it tabled the petition. Clearly, the members of the Board did not want an investigation but were happy enough that the slander succeeded.[24]

Not having been given a chance to answer the innuendos against him, Tukey would later address them in a public meeting. As to the auction of abandoned items in the Police Office, he commented that there was a written record of all such items and how much was realized from them. He had been authorized by various mayors to sell these items and the money was given to the poor. Mayor Seaver himself authorized such a sale in 1852. The results of the sales were open to all members of the government who might want to look at them. He reported that the gambling equipment was currently in the City Stables in Harrison Avenue for anyone to see, and that the pigeons roosted on them every night. Finally, as for living in a house owned by a gambler, he stated that he lost that house in his insolvency but has since paid rent on it and had the receipts. While he burned with indignation, there was not much he could do.[25]

The report on the watch and police departments is instructive because it presents the City Council's view on what the role of the police should be and how that differs from the police under City Marshal Tukey. It argued for a much more passive approach to policing. The report emphasized that the main purpose of the Police Department was in enforcing the ordinances of the city. Its view was that the police should be unseen and unheard but quietly do their duty. At one point it argued that all the publicity about rogues and crimes was both morally degrading and bad for the city's reputation. Over the past year, it claimed, the mayor had begun these changes and "although there may be less *eclat* in the results, the public good has been more faithfully cared for." As to combining the watch and police departments, which was why the committee was formed, it, like others before, said that the issue should be taken up by the next City Council.[26]

An unexpected chance for Tukey to continue the fight arose when Alderman Lyman Perry died suddenly on January 5. Perry had been one of the men elected along with Mayor Seaver in 1851 and was reelected to the Board in 1852. The Citizen's Union Party chose

Tukey as their candidate to fill this vacancy. The Whigs chose Samp-son Reed as their candidate. Reed had run in the election of 1852 and received enough votes to be elected but there were eight others ahead of him so he lost out.

While the nomination of Reed for alderman raised no concern in the newspapers, some editors were outraged that Tukey should run. They compared Reed, an esteemed and respected gentleman, to Tukey, who, they said, was running in a spirit of vengeance. In an allusion to Tukey's checkered past, they stated that several years ago, no one would have thought him qualified to run for such an hon-ored post. As to his supporters, they described him as "the head of an army of radicals and malcontents, who have more desire to pull down than to build up." Another editor was as direct: "Found faith-less in one responsible post, we are forsooth asked to promote him to yet another more important." Tukey was fighting not only the hum-bleness of his past but the smears that had been put forth about his time as city marshal.[27]

It was in this campaign for Alderman that Tukey had the chance to address a large crowd of both supporters and detractors. He sub-mitted a petition, with 115 signatures, to the mayor and Board of Aldermen on January 27 for the use of Faneuil Hall for a political meeting on the 29th. The next day he advertised in several news-papers announcing the meeting. His ad reported that he had been nominated for office by the Citizens' Union Party and "having been charged by members of the City Government, with committing crimes, ... and they having refused to give me a hearing thereon," he promised to speak on City Affairs and reply to the charges. The ad ended by saying, "Hear both sides, then judge."[28]

Meetings at Faneuil Hall were often raucous and Tukey was very familiar with them, having policed a number of such meetings. If this was the only way he could publicly answer the charges against him, he would rise to the occasion. Faneuil Hall was filled to capac-ity, both on the floor and in the galleries, before the meeting began. It was reported that numerous people were turned away because the hall was full. The meeting was called to order at 8 p.m. when Tukey and those supporting him entered the hall to loud and sustained applause and cheering. In addition to Tukey, there were 17 men on the platform. Some such as Benjamin F. Cook, Jr., were personal friends of Tukey. Two of the members had run for alderman in the last election on the Citizens ticket. They selected George Odiorne, a prominent iron manufacturer and real estate developer, as president of the meeting.

Just before 8 o'clock, Odiorne rose and addressed the assembled crowd. He stated the object of the meeting, reported that it had been called at the request of members of the Citizens' Union. They wanted to offer Tukey the opportunity "to speak on subjects personal to himself and interesting to the citizens generally." Odiorne went on to say that "Tukey had been dealt with ungenerously, not to say meanly, by the late city government." With that he introduced Tukey to what was called "a perfect storm of applause" mixed with cat-calls, hisses, and "sounds infernal." One report described Tukey as standing there among the tumult with "sublime nonchalance."[29]

Tukey was not a shy orator. He reportedly had 76 pages of notes and spoke for three hours and twenty minutes. In general, it was said, "he contrived, during this extended period, to command attention." He began by telling his listeners that, for the first time in his life, he found himself talking to a crowd on his own behalf. This was the only course left to him as he had been denied a hearing by the city government. The first topic was the recent reports on the watch and the police, and the annual report made by the chief of police, both of which he used to comment on the level of crime in Boston. He stated that, by their own numbers, the number of burglaries had increased by 50 percent over the past year. During his time as city marshal, he said, the highest total of stolen property in a single year had been $45,000 while this year it was approaching $140,000. Because of the increase in crime, he reported that one firm in the city had sold over 300 revolvers this year.

As he moved on to other topics, there was a lively exchange with one of the audience members over recovered stolen property. Tukey was saying that "Under my administration, when I received a dollar—" and he was interrupted by a "Man in the Gallery. You put it in your pocket." Not missing a beat, Tukey replied, "That's what they say at City Hall. But for every dollar collected by me, there is a receipt in black and white." This was received with a round of cheers. Shortly after this, the hall was disturbed by the cry of "Pickpockets" and the crowd erupted in general panic. During this disturbance, Tukey "rested himself with one leg over the table, ... with the coolest phiz in the world."

Eventually, Tukey addressed the innuendos reported about his actions, as has already been discussed. He reported that his sale of property was well documented, the proceeds were given to the poor and his actions were authorized by the mayors, including Mayor Seaver. The gambling equipment he was supposed to have sold back to the gamblers was in a city stable gathering dust and other things. Then he turned to the thing which most rankled him.

> Two cowardly assassins have made foul and malicious libels against me. I asked to be heard in my own defense, and petitioned respectfully, or if that was denied me, I asked the libellers to stand out from their official protection, and stand with their charges where I could reach them with law. This too was denied. They were determined to crush me if they could.

He then spent a long time questioning the motives and the morals of the two men who accused him, much to the delight of the audience. His main point was that the charges against him were politically motivated and false. They stemmed from the fact that he had opposed several candidates for the Common Council, including Jewell and Haskell. He challenged them to say that the charges were political and "he would say Amen." He concluded the speech by telling the voters to vote for whomever they wanted and thanked the audience for their patience and attention. As he left the platform at 11:15, the crowd gave him three cheers.

Responses to the speech were predictable. Both the *Boston Herald* and the *Boston Daily Bee*, newspapers that supported the Citizens' Union and temperance, were complimentary of both Tukey and the crowd. On the other side, the *Boston Courier* called the speech "low, vulgar and abusive" and described the crowd as "disorderly beyond description." The *Boston Daily Atlas*, the main supporter of Jewell and Haskell, said, "The speech, if such a tissue of personal slang can be thus denominated, will serve to render even more manifest the total unfitness of Mr. Tukey." Still, Tukey had his public defense.[30]

The special election for Alderman was held on January 31 and a total of 7845 votes were cast. This was significantly less than in the general election. Sampson Reed, the Whig candidate, won easily with 4,935 votes, or 62 percent of the total. Tukey came in a distant second with 2,350 votes. With his reputation still tarnished and his nascent political career over, Tukey turned his eyes elsewhere.[31]

He began to take a more serious interest in California. Many men had recently made a new start in the new state. Also, a major part of his wife's fortune was tied up in land near Sacramento. With a new administration coming into power in Washington, he renewed his quest for a federal position. In 1850, it was rumored that he was seeking an appointment as the U.S. marshal for California. Then he made a trip to Washington to lobby the Fillmore administration for the post but was unsuccessful. With no prospects in Boston, he made another trip, trying to interest the new Pierce administration in his law enforcement experience. On February 24, he checked into Willard's Hotel, his place of choice when he was in the city. While he was in Washington, he applied for and was admitted to practice law before the United States Supreme Court.

He and Carsilla made a second trip to Washington in March, again checking into Willard's on the 15th. While in D.C. this time, he is reported to have attended the auction of Daniel Webster's personal effects, buying some tea cups and saucers. His quest for a federal position in California was unsuccessful. In fact, those already in the state were growing increasingly resistant to the government appointing Easterners to jobs they thought could be filled by Californians.[32]

Having determined to go to California, Tukey had three ways to choose. He could go overland but that would take a long time and was very dangerous. He could take a ship around Cape Horn but it was again a very long voyage and full of different dangers. The most popular route since the beginning of the California Gold Rush was to take a ship to Panama, cross the isthmus and then take another ship to San Francisco. Over the past few years, this route had been considerably improved. It was now possible to buy a through ticket which included steamships on both the Atlantic and Pacific runs. The frequency of ship departures had increased from once a month to weekly. The most difficult part of this passage was through the jungles of Panama. Entrepreneurs were currently building the Panama Railway, which after 1855 would whisk passengers from one side to the other. However, at the time Tukey was planning his trip, the railroad only extended halfway from the Atlantic into the interior. The rest of the trip, about 23 miles, had to be made by donkey or on foot. While this route was shorter, there was still the serious threat of violence and disease.[33]

The combined Tukey and Haycock family had to make some tough decisions. A trip to California was a major life changer and many who went to California never returned. The combined family had six children, ranging in age from 9 to 17. Traveling with such a large party would not only be expensive but would increase the dangers. But who would go and who would stay and what would happen to those left behind? Carsilla's two boys, 17 and 14 years old, were both in school and would finish their education. Tukey's two older girls, 17 and 16 years old, went to live in Weymouth with relatives of Tukey's first wife, Mary Gay. Tukey's youngest boy, Greenleaf Storey, 9 years old, went to live in Salem with Elizabeth Butman, sister of Tukey's close friend and associate Asa O. Butman. The only child the couple took with them to California was Francis Tukey, Jr., who was 13 at the time. At the time of departure, the newspapers reported that Tukey left with his wife and one son.[34]

The Tukeys made their way to New York where they boarded the SS *Georgia* operated by the United States Mail Steamship Company. The ship was a typical wooden, side-wheeled steamer which had been making the journey from New York to Panama since 1850. They sailed on April 5 and the trip to Panama generally took seven days. One of the passengers on the *Georgia* wrote a letter to the *Buffalo Republic* which took notice of Tukey, saying, "His failing to obtain from President Pierce the appointment of Marshal of California did not deter him from migrating thither. He is a fine looking fellow of about forty, and has an eye as keen as a hawk." Their through tickets called for them to board the SS *Tennessee*, after crossing the isthmus, for the trip to San Francisco. They did not make that ship but took a slightly later ship, the SS *Panama*. The trip from Panama to San Francisco generally took 12 days and they reportedly arrived in the harbor on May 6, 1853, to start their California life.[35]

9

"Emigrants from Every State in the Union, and all the Nations and tribes of the Earth"

Soon after his arrival in San Francisco, Tukey wrote a letter to a friend in Boston which was reported in the *Boston Daily Bee*. It was stated that Tukey "is in full feather, and is astonishing the 'natives.' It is rumored that he is already talked of for the City Marshalship of that city." Where that rumor stated is unknown but Tukey always intended to head straight to Sacramento. That plan was delayed by four weeks while Carsilla recovered from an illness she suffered on the trip. However, by the time the letter reached Boston, the Tukeys were in Sacramento. This was to be their home from now on. Carsilla's deceased husband, Jesse Haycock, had a significant amount of land in downtown Sacramento as well as a large ranch nearby in Sutter Township.[1]

Before his death in 1850, Jesse Haycock was said to be building a large house for his family. This was probably located at the corner of C and 13th streets and was described as consisting of "Parlor, Sitting Room, Dining Room and Kitchen, also four large Bed Rooms, with Out Houses, and 100 feet of land." This is where the Tukeys set up their home. Some other buildings built by Haycock were located at the corner of 5th and J streets; these were one-story wooden structures. Tukey used one of these for his new law office. As he had in Boston, he again advertised that he gave "particular attention" to the buying and selling of real estate, the searching of titles and negotiating loans.[2]

As he had in the past, Tukey got involved in the community and its activities. He may have begun teaching Sunday School at the 6th

Street Congregational Church. As the Fourth of July approached, Sacramento began to think about how to celebrate the National Anniversary. The main activity planned for that day was a procession of the town's Sunday School children. Tukey was appointed chief marshal for the event and headed the committee that made the arrangements. This was much more than a parade of children through the streets but involved ceremonies in town, a steamship excursion and a day of activities in a rural location. The children, their teachers and their parents assembled at their respective churches early in the morning. From there, they marched to the Congregational Church. When they assembled, there were 400 to 500 children and many more adults. Chief Marshal Tukey called the assembly to order; prayers and addresses were made to the crowd. The procession was formed, led by the Sons of Temperance and accompanied by a fire company brass band. The children were lined up, by school, and proceeded two by two to the levee along the Sacramento River. There they boarded a pair of river steamers which took them up river to Wilson's Grove, described as "one of nature's cool, shady retreats," about a mile and a half above Sacramento. The children played games, the adults were entertained by vocal music and they all ate a large meal. After more speeches and prayers, the steamers returned to Sacramento at 5 p.m.[3]

Just about a year after arriving in Sacramento, Tukey wrote a letter to his friend and former boss, Josiah Quincy, Jr., back in Boston. It is known that they exchanged letters for a number of years but this is the only one to be preserved. The letter is five pages long and filled with chatty gossip, facts about California, Tukey's impression of a number of groups and a description of his first year in Sacramento. In his discussion of his residence in California, Tukey boasted of three "public matters" to which he turned his attention.

The first of these was his involvement with a volunteer fire company. Without an organized, professional fire department, Sacramento relied, as did many cities, on voluntary associations of its citizens to combat the ever-present danger of fire. The Eureka Engine Company No. 4 was founded in August 1853 and its organizational meeting was held at the "office of Marshal Tukey, Fifth Street, near J." At this meeting, W. Henry Jones was elected the first foreman but by September, advertisements listed Tukey as the foreman and the company continued to meet at his office. Tukey organized a subscription campaign for the new company and raised $1000. This money was used to build a brick station house and order a new fire engine. The company, while it waited for a new engine from the east, was given an old pumper that had been left exposed for a year. This was repaired as much as possible and the company acquitted itself well in trials against other companies held in mid–September. At the end of the month, Tukey, as foreman of the company, presented a silver trumpet to John H. Burgess, who was the assistant foreman but was moving back to the east coast. Tukey would go on to represent the company as a delegate to the Sacramento Board of the Fire Department when that was organized. His association with Eureka Engine Company No. 4 would continue until his resignation in 1864.[4]

The second "public matter" of which Tukey boasted to Quincy involved the opening of public schools in Sacramento. Tukey had always had an interest in education and he advocated for the beginning of public schools in California. In the letter, he reported that he "kept talking to the Governor … to the Mayor about schools" and that two were finally opened. There had been private schools in the city for some time but many could not afford the fees. It was estimated that there were 1,500 children in Sacramento but only 300 regularly went to school. The City had a Board of School Commissioners and they had advertised to open a school on August 1, 1853, soon after Tukey arrived, but it never materialized. It was not until February of 1854 that Sacramento opened its first public school, located on 5th and K streets, only a block from Tukey's office. In 1855, Tukey would be appointed School Superintendent for the city.[5]

The final item of which Tukey boasted was his involvement with the plan for a new county jail. Tukey stated that he "gave a young Carpenter an idea of the Boston Jail, and he got the *premium for his plan*." The "young carpenter" that Tukey spoke to was Seth Babson who would become one of the most famous architects in California in the 19th century. Tukey and Babson were natural allies. Both had been born in Maine and moved to Massachusetts before coming to California. Babson, like Tukey was intimately involved with the Sons of Temperance and the Sons of New England in Sacramento. Babson's office was on 5th Street between J and K and may have been in one of Tukey's buildings. When the county began soliciting proposals for a new jail, it was natural for Babson to seek out Tukey. The former Boston city marshal was very familiar with criminals and their incarceration. Moreover, Tukey held his office during the time that Suffolk County, Massachusetts, built a new, model jail known as the Charles Street Jail. The "Boston Jail" was based on ideas of reformation then current and classed under the term the "Auburn Plan." This involved putting prisoners into individual cells instead of congregate cells and separating the cells from all outside contact. In effect, the cells were a "building within a building."[6]

Babson's plan called for the construction of a three-story, brick building, 50 by 70 feet, described as "within which, and ten feet from the walls, another house is to be raised, containing three stories or tiers of cells, each surrounded by a gallery, which does not connect with the outside, or main walls." His estimate of the costs was $60,000. On May 25, 1854, the County Court decided that his plan was the best submitted. Almost immediately, objections were raised about the decision. It was thought to be too expensive, too elaborate and more than needed by the county. Further, it was said that a three-story building might be appropriate where land was scarce but in Sacramento, there was ample land to expand a one-story building. After all the criticism, the Court decided on another plan that was lower, cheaper and less elaborate.[7]

Any letter between the former city marshal and the former mayor of Boston was bound to have a discussion of politics, both in Boston and in California. Tukey received a letter from Quincy dated April 28, in which Quincy said that he had not heard a report from Tukey concerning his new life. Tukey responded that he had not "forgotten our long official connection." He used a quote from Edward Everett on the death of Daniel Webster, saying, "scenes to me our acquaintance, all clean, all bright, no dark clouds," and thanked Quincy for kind words said about him and reported to Tukey by others. Tukey boasted that he was happy with the 2400 votes he received in the election for alderman. He went on to recall his last year in Boston, saying,

> After you left City Hall, others came, with whom I had little sympathy, and having no one to "hold the reins" I acknowledge *to you*, I did occasionally make a mistake, but Sir, *I did not forget my promise.* I did nothing wrong or criminal, nothing which would bring reproach upon *you* or me, and since I

left, every one of those parties who quarreled with me, have *been laid upon the shelf*, by the people.

Turning to California, he reported that the state was torn by the same politics that would soon lead to the Civil War. In imitation of their origin, settlers from slave states dominated the southern part of the state while New Englanders were dominant in the northern area. Tukey commented that "The political interests of the State are *North* and *South*." He commented that the controversy surrounding David Broderick, leader of the anti-slavery Democrats, was because "Broderick is from the *North* and hence the opposition." Both because of the politics and because they were so far away from their homes, settlers tended to congregate with others from their own region. As early as 1850, New England Societies were organized in California with the purpose of fostering "good fellowship, they extend an helping hand to the distressed, and they bury the dead." One of the major events sponsored by the Society was the commemoration of the landing of the Pilgrims on December 22. Naturally, Tukey joined the Sacramento New England Society soon after he arrived in the City and, at an organizational meeting on December 13, he was appointed chief marshal of the upcoming Forefathers' Day Celebrations.[8]

The day was planned to begin at 1 p.m. with a procession originating at the Orleans Hotel, Sacramento's largest and most impressive hotel, on Second Street. There were 250 men in the procession with Tukey leading the way. At the head of the procession was a blue silk banner, trimmed in gold with gold lettering which read "Sons of New England." The marchers were divided into six divisions, each with its own banner, representing the six New England States. The parade proceeded to the Sacramento Theater on Third Street, where the program was presented to 700 gentlemen, on the floor, and 100 ladies in part of the balcony. The meeting began with prayers and then the Reverend Benton, of the Congregational Church, gave a speech detailing the development of the Protestant religion in England and the setting out of the Pilgrims for the New World. After the speech, the "New England Choir" sang "America" and Mr. J. Proctor, lead actor and proprietor of the theater, gave a reading of the Whittier poem "New England" to great applause. A brass band played "Hail Columbia" and the choir sang several other themes. When the program ended, the guests went back to the Orleans Hotel where, at 9:30, 150 were seated for a dinner which prominently featured turkey. After the dinner, there were a number of toasts made, including one for each New England state. Various guests responded to each toast and Tukey chose to respond to the Massachusetts toast. The gathering broke up at 1:30 a.m.[9]

After the political discussion, Tukey wrote a more personal report to Quincy which sheds valuable insights on his first year in California. He began by jokingly stating, "But I see the order from 'His Honor the Mayor' was a 'detailed report of your position and prospects.'" Tukey detailed his voyage and arrival in Sacramento. He reported that he found the family property badly managed and neglected. It yielded about $600 per month but he had reordered things, and it now rented for $1,000 to $1,200 per month. One of the problems Tukey faced was that squatters had taken over much of the land that Jesse Haycock had bought with his gold money. Land in Sacramento was very expensive and much of it was not developed. Squatters, who called themselves settlers, took over land that had no improvements on it, stating it was public land. They claimed that the old Mexican Land Grants, under which John Sutter had sold lots in the city, were invalid and undeveloped land was in the public domain. According to Tukey, the squatters, mostly Irish, held $8,000 to $10,000 worth of his property. He assured Quincy that "we expect to have our title settled in one or two months." This was very optimistic and, in fact, title to lots in Sacramento would remain uncertain until 1859, when the U.S. Supreme Court confirmed Sutter's original claim to the land.[10]

Despite certain problems, the move to California seems to have been very good for Tukey. In his last paragraph, he assured Quincy that he was doing well and concluded by writing, "allow me to add that we have enjoyed excellent health since our arrival at this place, and we feel that our present prospects were never better."

Just a month after Tukey wrote this upbeat ending to his letter, disaster struck Sacramento. A huge fire swept through downtown, burning 12 blocks to the ground. The fire reportedly began by someone overturning a spirit lamp in the block bounded by 3rd, 4th, J and K streets. However, it was reported that a man was seen trying to start a fire in the area after the initial fire was discovered but he was not apprehended. While two fire companies responded quickly, the fire still spread to the Sacramento Hotel on K street. There were four companies stationed on K street, including Eureka Engine No. 4, and they prevented the fire from moving in that direction. The temperature was reported to be a hundred degrees in the shade and the heat of the fire added to that greatly. Many firemen were overcome with heat exhaustion. The fire continued to spread and eventually crossed J street between 5th and 6th streets, burning all of Tukey's buildings, the Congregational Church he attended, and the brick engine house of Eureka Engine Company No. 4 that he helped build. His engine company fought hard to keep the fire from spreading further, losing much of their hose to the fire.[11]

The disaster was a wake-up call for Sacramento as it was the second devastating fire in the last two years. Several brick buildings with iron shutters had withstood the blaze. The newspapers recounted the story of Kreaner & Quivey, a general merchandise store on J street located in one of the fire-proof brick buildings. When they saw the fire approaching, the employees shut themselves up in the building, closing the doors and the shutters. While it was extremely hot in the building, they were able to survive with no injury. As people began to think about rebuilding, brick became the building material of choice. Multiple buildings in the burned area were replaced with brick structures. The Reverend Benton of the Congregational Church led the drive to build a new church in brick. The brick walls of the Eureka Engine Company, No. 4 were still standing and builders determined that they remained sound so the structure was soon rebuilt.[12]

It was reported that Tukey lost $2,000 due to the fire, a not inconsequential amount. Despite the enthusiasm for rebuilding in brick, Tukey chose to put up new wooden structures. Perhaps he could not afford to use brick or wanted to quickly get renters back to the properties. A later report described these buildings as "twelve feet high and wooden frames of the lightest material." In any case, the structures were being erected and rented by late July, barely two weeks after the fire.[13]

After his loss in the alderman election in Boston in 1853, Tukey had little to do with politics but his letter to Josiah Quincy, Jr., showed that he still burned with the ambition for political office. That desire and his unflinching advocacy of public education led to an opportunity in Sacramento. Early in 1855, the California State

Legislature passed amendments to the Sacramento City Charter, creating an elected school board consisting of a Superintendent and two School Commissioners. When the Sacramento County Democrats met in convention to nominate candidates for the upcoming election, Tukey was unanimously acclaimed for the office of superintendent of public schools. However, the Democratic nomination was not the only one that Tukey received; he was also nominated by the Know-Nothing party.[14]

The Know-Nothing party was a response to the rise of Irish and German Catholic immigration in the 1840s. At its core, it was nativist, anti–Catholic and anti-immigrant. In Boston, Tukey was involved with the beginning of the movement as part of the Citizen's Ticket. In 1854, after Tukey left Boston, this group became part of the Know-Nothing party, which swept the city election. In Sacramento, Tukey's association with the movement was useful. In 1855, Tukey was one of three candidates (out of 23) on both the Democratic and Know-Nothing tickets. When the election was held on April 2, the Know-Nothing candidates overwhelmingly won election. Tukey received 1,281 votes which represented 70 percent of the total and was elected to his first political office in California. Two weeks after his election, Tukey advertised that the school commissioners would meet at his office on 5th Street, on Tuesday evenings each week. By the end of the month, he was advertising an examination for prospective teachers. Tukey's circumstances changed by October when he advertised the house on C Street for rent and moved to his ranch outside the city. He resigned the superintendent's office in February 1856.[15]

Tukey's involvement with the Know-Nothing party did not end with his election as school superintendent. As the 1856 presidential election approached, the party nominated Millard Fillmore, former president, as its candidate. While Fillmore was a Whig and out of the country when the convention chose him, nevertheless he accepted and campaigned. Fillmore clubs were formed across the country, particularly in New England. Whether it was specifically to participate in this excitement or for personal reasons, Tukey made a trip back to Boston in June, arriving in New York on the 28th. On September 16, in Boston, the "Fillmore Convention" of Suffolk County was held with Benjamin F. Cook, Tukey's boarder from Harvard Law School days, elected president.

In an unofficial poll for the candidate for county sheriff, Tukey got the most votes but when a formal ballot was taken, he lost to the then chief of police. While the convention did not support him for sheriff, they recognized his organizational abilities and appointed him chief marshal of the large, torchlight parade they planned for October 15. The procession was in nine divisions consisting of Fillmore clubs from all over Massachusetts. The divisions assembled in various places, then proceeded to Washington Street, where they were organized in line. At the order from the chief marshal, the torches were lit and the parade began. The paper reported that torches were available for rent at $6 per hundred. Events were to begin at 7:30 p.m. and be over "in season" so that participants could take trains out of town by 11 p.m. Nevertheless, the festivities did not end until after midnight.[16]

When the Suffolk County Fillmore Convention reconvened on Saturday, a proposal was made that the party align itself with the Whigs in Boston for the election. At about 10 p.m., Tukey rose to address the convention. He stated that he was opposed to any compromise with the Whigs. Some have claimed this was because they were the ones who forced him from the position as city marshal. In any case, he claimed that he would talk until doomsday unless the convention agreed with him. In the end, he talked for almost two hours until he was forcibly required to take his seat. For a man who had made his residence and place of business in California, Tukey seemed very involved in Massachusetts politics. In his 1854 letter to Josiah Quincy, Jr., he wrote "Hardly a mail comes that I do not have letters to come home, *they say they want me*." This trip in 1856 was his attempt to satisfy that desire.[17]

What Tukey did in Boston from the election in November until April of the next year is unknown. He is mentioned as one of the mourners at the funeral of Hezekiah Earle, a friend and long-time member of the Police Department. Earle served as deputy marshal during the time that Tukey was city marshal and then continued as deputy chief of police until his death on March 30, 1857. The funeral included a large number of mourners, including former Mayor Josiah Quincy, Jr., the current mayor, and the current chief of police. The entire police force attended the funeral and then led the funeral cortege from Earle's house to the burial ground on the common. When they arrived at the burial ground, they split and formed lines on either side through which the hearse and mourners proceeded.[18]

While Tukey was in Boston, odd things were going on in Sacramento. Early in February 1857, someone cut through the clapboards in the rear of one of his buildings on 5th street where he was storing his furniture. It was not readily apparent it anything had been taken. The nature of the frame structures Tukey built is illustrated by this and subsequent events. The walls consisted of clapboarded studs without interior finish. To make it look better, cloth was attached to the studs on the inside. On the night of February 18, a fire was started in a building occupied by one of Tukey's tenants on 5th street between J and K streets. This was quickly extinguished. On the morning of February 20, another fire was started below a building occupied by a jeweler in the same block. This caught some of the cotton lining but it too was quickly extinguished by a force pump that Tukey kept in the yard. A burglary and two suspicious fires in the same neighborhood within the space of two weeks led one newspaper to suggest "some infamous scoundrel is determined to burn the block having some spite possibly towards the owner, Frank Tukey."

While it is possible this was directed specifically at Tukey, it is also possible that these frame buildings were easy targets for an arsonist. During the disastrous fire of 1854, a man was seen in the area trying to light a building on fire. Most of the structures destroyed in 1854 were replaced with brick buildings. Tukey's frame structures were an exception. Things went quiet for a few months but the arsonist was not finished. Early in the morning of July 19, a fire was started in a pile of rubbish at the corner of 2nd and O streets. Two of the city's fire companies responded to the blaze. While they were fighting that fire, another fire erupted in an empty store on J street near 5th street in what the newspaper called "a most combustible neighborhood." It was presumed that the first fire was started to attract the fire companies away from the area of the second fire. In all, ten of Tukey's frame structures were destroyed. It was estimated that the tenants lost over $7,000 in goods and that Tukey's loss for the burned buildings was $2,500.[19]

An indication of how fast communication was improving between California and the East Coast was how soon Tukey heard of the event. Less than a month after the fire, Tukey reportedly left

Boston "having received news of a loss by fire in Sacramento." Travelling to New York, Tukey booked passage on the U.S. Mail Steamer *Central America*, which left on August 20 and arrived in Panama by August 30. It was on the return trip to New York that the *Central America* sank on September 12, with the loss of 425 people and $550 million in California gold. At that time, Tukey was nearing San Francisco on the Pacific Mail Steamer *Golden Age*, which arrived in the Bay on September 14.[20]

Back in Sacramento, Tukey began to contemplate rebuilding but in brick this time. He voiced this thought as early as 1856, but the fire forced him to invest the money. On September 19, the newspapers reported his intention to build a large brick building and that he had men working on the property. They were clearing away the debris from the fire and were getting ready to tear down any wooden structures that survived. The new building would fill the entire lot at the corner, stretching 80 feet along J street and 150 feet along 5th street. The building was designed by Seth Babson, the "young carpenter" he talked to about the Boston Jail. Tukey began advertising for half a million fine quality bricks and had teams excavating the full basement. The structure contained four stores on the bottom floor and offices and meeting rooms on the second floor.[21]

The brick block was ready by December 1857 when businesses began advertising their presence in "Tukey's Brick Building." An employment office and a jewelry store occupied two of the ground floor stores. "Old Joe's Saloon" opened in the basement and advertised billiard tables, good liquors and a "substantial lunch." Such a large and elegant space was highly coveted and there were rumors that the County Courts and County Offices might lease the second floor. There was considerable opposition to this but when the grand jury complained about the room it was given in the old building, a new one was found on the second floor of Tukey's building. One of the long-term tenants on the second floor was the Sacramento Public Library, which moved to the building on February 8, 1858. Also the California State Agricultural Society met at Tukey's building. This structure would remain a landmark in Sacramento long after Tukey passed from the scene.[22]

With the coming of the Civil War, California, with its

population made up of adventurers from all the Eastern states, was deeply divided. Sacramento was heavily settled by Northerners and especially New Englanders. With the news of the bombardment and surrender of Fort Sumter, loyalists began looking for ways to support the Union and Union Clubs were formed across much a California. The purpose of these clubs was to eschew party politics and express loyalty to the Union. The Sacramento Union Club was formed by the end of April 1861 and Tukey was a member of its executive board. The rapid development of this movement can be seen in the fact that less than a month after being formed, the Sacramento Union Club had over 1,500 members and sponsored two military companies. Tukey was one of several speakers asked to address a mass meeting on May 30, which 2,000 people attended. In May, the Union Club had already begun making preparations for the celebration of the 4th of July in reverence to the formation of the Union. Probably because of his previous experience, Tukey was appointed chief marshal of the celebration.[23]

According to the program, the procession would begin at 10 a.m. and would be escorted by six military companies and the Sacramento Fire Department. They would be followed by four divisions made up of politicians, tradesmen, clergy, Union Clubs from other communities in Sacramento County and ordinary citizens. The procession would be followed by a program featuring a flag raising, singing of the "Star Spangled Banner" and a presentation of patriotic songs and poems. The military companies would fire a national salute and the bells of the city would be rung, for half an hour, at dawn, at noon, and at sunset. The day would end with fireworks and music at 9 o'clock. The night before the celebration, someone entered the building where the cannon that was to be used in the salute was stored, and spiked it with the end of a file. Fortunately it was discovered early enough that the damage was fixed. In the procession, instead of carrying a baton, as was usual, Tukey carried an American Flag made of silk.[24]

The tensions of the Civil War caused many Americans to question their political affiliation and Tukey was no different. A seemingly life-long Democrat, Tukey switched to the Republican Party in 1861, being listed as a candidate for their state convention. Two slates of candidates were put forward for selection to go to the

State Convention, known familiarly as the "Swell-heads" and the "Sore-heads." The Swell-heads, of whom Tukey was a member, were known as the Regular Republican ticket and supported Leland Stanford for governor. Their motto was "The Union must and shall be preserved." The "Sore-heads" were known as the Unpledged Union Administration ticket and vowed to support whichever candidate for Governor seemed the best man. The Swell-heads carried the day and Tukey was chosen as a delegate to the State Republican Convention.[25]

Before that event, Sacramento County held its own convention to nominate candidates for county offices and Tukey was chosen as the chairman of the meeting. In a speech to the delegates, he recalled how just a few years ago, the Republicans had very few members in California and how, when they tried to hold a meeting in Sacramento, they were mobbed. He went on to say that he had opposed "Every man, in every place, at all times and on all occasions who dared to utter a sentiment against this glorious Union." In speaking of the recent election, Tukey said, "I confess that I belong to the Swell-heads, but the swelling has gone down, and now, if I can do anything to take the soreness from any man's head, I shall be glad to do it." He said he had asked for names from all parties and would appoint them to committees in a "Spirit of Fairness." Tukey expressed his support for Stanford as governor but said that if the State Convention chose someone else, he would support him, for it was the success of the Republican party that was important in this election.

In July, the Sacramento Republicans met again and among the candidates chosen, Tukey was selected to run for police judge. When the election was held in September, Stanford, the Republican candidate, easily won the office of governor but the Union Democrats took the Sacramento City election. Tukey lost to T.W. Gilmer, the Union Democratic candidate, by 164 votes. While he lost the election, Tukey remained active in Republican politics in Sacramento. In 1862, he served on the levee board for the City to build and maintain levees along the American and Sacramento Rivers. He was also appointed Assistant U.S. Assessor for the city and county of Sacramento. He served as chairman of the "Union Administration County Central Committee, whose motto was 'Our Country First—Party Last.'"[26]

Most citizens of Sacramento were very loyal to the Union, but there were others with different views. On October 10, the U.S. Marshal arrested Major George P. Gillis for treasonable language against the Federal Government. Gillis was an outspoken supporter of the Confederacy, even before the War he had vilified Northerners and reportedly "no epithet was too vile." In Sacramento, on the previous July 4, Gillis was drunk and "flourished a secession flag..., dared anybody to take it from him and hurrahed for King Jeff." After his arrest, the Marshal sent him to the Provost Marshal in San Francisco, where rebel sympathizers were being confined on Alcatraz Island. Gillis was put on a steamer in the custody of "Deputy Marshal Tukey," who delivered him as instructed. It is unknown if Tukey's brief return to law enforcement was a one-time event or if he filled this position for some time.[27]

During the state Republican conventions of 1862 and 1863, Tukey served as a delegate from the First Ward of Sacramento. In June 1863, Tukey was chosen as a candidate for the office of Assemblyman from Sacramento. In the election held in September, Tukey won a seat in the California Assembly. This was his first and only election to a legislative body and he took an active part in the deliberations. He followed his strengths and was appointed to the Judiciary and Education committees. He also became chairman of the Committee on the State Prison. Tukey proposed a bill for the erection of a branch prison at Folsom on the American River, northeast of Sacramento. This was not enacted and it would be almost 20 years before the prison was built. As part of the education committee he made visits to the State Normal School and the reform school. He was part of a three-man committee to consider the use of lands offered by Congress for the founding of an Agricultural and Mechanical Arts College.[28]

Perhaps the most important and contentious issue Tukey took on as an Assemblyman was that of supporting a national currency made of paper and not backed by gold. When the Civil War began, the only money the Federal Government issued was in metal coins but private banks had issued paper banknotes, which were backed by their reserves of gold. Because of very high interest rates, the Lincoln administration found it hard to raise the money necessary to prosecute the war. In 1862, Congress passed the Legal Tender

Act, authorizing the printing of $150 million dollars in paper currency not backed by gold. These notes were printed on the back in green ink, becoming known as "greenbacks," and almost immediately began to lose value against gold. California, where gold was abundant, opposed this currency and passed the "Specific Contracts Law" in 1863, which stated that contracts had to be paid in the currency specified in the document. While this law did not ban the use of greenbacks to fulfill contracts, few contacts were written for the devalued currency. The passage of this law divided California between San Francisco banks and politicians who favored it and the interior of the state where the gold was produced. Those who produced the gold, particularly in the Sacramento area, felt they could get a better price for their gold if it were valued in greenbacks. Also, the notion of a national currency was seen as a test of loyalty in California during the Civil War.[29]

Both the idea of supporting the Union and his representation of a gold-producing area led Tukey to be a champion of national currency in the Assembly. In December, the State of California was having trouble finding coinage to pay the per diem of the legislators in the current session. Tukey first proposed a bill to allow those who so chose to accept greenbacks on par with gold for their per diem. Not surprisingly, the legislators turned this down. In January, he proposed seven bills which would have radically changed the way California did business. These included repeal of the Specific Contracts Law, a bill making it a misdemeanor for anyone to write a contract not in the National Currency and a bill making State and Local taxes, assessments and other obligations payable in greenbacks.[30]

While the Assembly considered these matters, a large meeting was held on February 4 in San Francisco in favor of hard currency. The attendees approved resolutions in favor of retaining the Specific Contracts Act, declaring their loyalty to the Federal Government and decrying any attempts to question their loyalty. After the resolutions were approved, D.W. Cheesman, sub-treasurer of the United States Mint at San Francisco, tried to address the crowd. Since he was a well-known advocate of the new currency, the crowd would have none of it and he was shouted down. After the meeting, Cheesman was assailed by members of the meeting and forced to flee. In the California Assembly, a resolution was proposed to allow Cheesman to use the Assembly Hall to address the question of a national currency. Naturally, this began a vigorous discussion.

Tukey rose to speak in favor of inviting Cheesman, saying, "the idea that there were no talkers in the Assembly was being refuted; they were all talkers. The question was, should Cheesman be allowed to make a few feeble remarks in that hall on the currency question. He (Tukey) would make a few feeble remarks in the affirmative of that proposition." He went on to comment on the violence offered Cheesman in San Francisco, stating that he would surround "Cheesman with knives and pistols so he shall be heard." If, after the speech, the other side wanted to use the hall to present their views, Tukey said "let them have it." One of the opponents of legal tender rose and offered a resolution naming Tukey "Generalissimo of a knife and pistol brigade" to widespread laughter but was ruled out of order. The Assembly voted to invite Cheesman to speak, which he did on February 8. Despite a telegram from Treasury Secretary Chase saying that California's gold standard was against national policy, the California Senate rejected the repeal of the Specific Contracts Act on March 2 and greenbacks continued to devalue.[31]

Despite his strong support of a National Currency, on one issue, Tukey let that principle go. In April, the Assembly began to debate a bill for issuing bonds to aid the construction of the Central Pacific Railroad. This was an issue of vital, national importance and was supported by the Federal Government and Abraham Lincoln personally. A number of Southern-leaning Democrats proposed amendments that were designed to doom the bill, including requiring the bonds to be redeemed in greenbacks. Tukey voted against the amendments and supporting the use of gold for the redemption of bonds. Naturally, he was severely criticized for his change in attitude. Tukey rose to address the Assembly about the bill and began by recounting his experiences—both good and bad—with the building of railroads. He stated that in New England they appreciated and honored railroads. He quoted a letter from his friend, Josiah Quincy, Jr., that said the East was depending on California to finish the road. To great laughter, he said, "Abraham Lincoln had also proved himself the friend of the Pacific Railroad; he had moved mountains in its behalf with his strong, awkward right arm; he had shoved the Sierra thirty miles nearer to Sacramento." The bill was written for the use of gold, the legislature had defeated repeal of the Specific Contracts Act and, having talked with railroad men, he concluded that "the necessities of the case demanded that greenbacks should be waived for the present, in order to push the road along. ... He believed it was right and patriotic to waive the currency question for the time being." The amendments were voted on and defeated and the main bill was then approved by the Assembly.[32]

For a period after the Assembly ended, Tukey remained active in politics. In November 1864, he was one of the speakers at a Union meeting in Sacramento. It was announced in May 1865 that he would once again be a candidate for Assemblyman in the upcoming September election. However, when the election was held on September 6, he was not on the ballot. It seems likely he was too ill to continue. It was reported that he had a long-standing illness and that he had retired to his ranch. On November 19, the *Sacramento* Bee stated that he was lying at the point of death. He died on his ranch on November 23, 1867, at the age of 52 years.[33]

Sometimes the best understanding of what a person accomplished in life is what was recorded by contemporaries in the obituary. Francis Tukey had played a part on the national stage during his life and obituaries were printed for him all over the country, not just in Sacramento or Boston. Those that mentioned any detail stated that he began with nothing but educated himself in the law. They talked about his successful practice and his appointment as City Marshal of Boston. While most were complimentary, a few mentioned that he dabbled too much in politics and was let go. His time in California was mentioned, plus the fact that he served in the Assembly. Tukey's legacy remains his organization of the Boston Police Department as one of the first active police forces in the country.

Chapter Notes

Chapter 1

1. A good discussion of the "magnetic attraction" of Boston to the New England area can be found in Knights, "Yankee Destinies," 1991, p. 15–23.

2. Location and type of business of Tukey's father is from advertisements in the *Portland Gazette*, June 17, 1823, June 25, 1824; Anonymous, "Narrative of life and adventures of Francis Tukey," 1848:3–5

3. His name appears in the list of letters left in the Post Office in July 1833, *Boston Morning Post*, July 1, 1833, p. 4.

4. Tukey's ad in the *Salem* Gazette ran from October 23 to December 2, 1834. Samuel Berry's prominent role in the Methodist Church of Salem is found in Almy, "Methodism in Salem," 1887:277.

5. The editor's comments on Tukey's cake appeared in the *Salem Gazette*, November 11, 1834, p. 2.

6. An early recipe for Dyspepsia bread, which included "one gill" of molasses was in Child, *The American Frugal Housewife...*, 1835:78. A discussion of dyspepsia, and its bread can be found in Civitello, *Baking Powder Wars*, 2017:13–14.

7. For Sylvester Graham and the effects of diet on cholera, see Iacobbo and Iacobbo, *Vegetarian America*, 2004:19–24.

8. Sylvester Graham lectured in Boston in October, *Boston Recorder*, October 16, 1835, issue 42, p. 167. In October, the Salem Lyceum advertised a lecture by Graham as part of their upcoming lecture series, *Salem Gazette*, October 20, 1835, p. 3.

9. *Salem Register*, June 25, 1846, p. 2.

10. Tukey's marriage record is available on the Ancestry.com website in the Massachusetts Town and Vital Records, 1620–1988. Charles Gay was a partner in the firm Howard & Gay which advertised that pilots for Boston Harbor could be contacted at Howard & Gay's store, *Boston Patriot & Daily Chronicle*, May 13, 1830, p. 1. Blagden's obituary lists him as pastor from 1830–1836, Yale University, *Obituary Record*, 1880:226. For Adelaide Tukey's birth see her obituary, *New York Tribune*, February 7, 1910, p. 7. When Sarah Elizabeth Tukey was married in 1869, she listed her birthplace as Chelsea. For his loss of the Chelsea bakery, Anonymous, "Narrative of life and adventures of Francis Tukey," 1848:7.

11. Charles E. Gay's career as a grocer is evidenced by newspaper advertisements in *Boston Patriot & Daily Chronicle*, May 13, 1830, December 28, 1830. He is listed as a grocer in the 1831 and 1839 Boston City Directories with an address at 237 Ann St. The exception allowing grocers to sell spirituous liquors is discussed in Lane, *Policing the City*, 1967:41–42. Reference to the Black Sea was from *Bacon's Dictionary of Boston*, 1886:45. A good description of the Black Sea can be found in Wilhelm, *Wicked Victorian Boston*, 2017:20–26.

12. Lane, *Policing the City*, 1967:40–41. Krout, *The Origins of Prohibition*, 1925:108–109 reports that "Others got around the regulations by taking out grocery licenses and then converting their

establishments into grog-shops of a low order."

13. Krout, *The Origins of Prohibition*, 1925:263.

14. The original "striped pig" was reported in the *Columbian Centinel* (Boston, MA), September 12, 1838, p. 2. This evasion of the law was looked on as an example of Yankee shrewdness and was widely reported across the country. The play was put on, about a week later, at the National Theater in Boston and was advertised in the *Columbian Centinel* (Boston, MA), September 22, 1838, p. 3. The controversy was of nationwide interest and the *Philadelphia Inquirer* of September 22, 1838, p. 2 reported that in New York, upscale hotels like the Astor were now offering a new beverage called the "striped pig." A report of the "striped pig party," a derogatory name for those opposed to the 15 gallon law, was published in the *Norfolk Advertiser* (Dedham, MA), October 6, 1838, p. 2.

15. On the undemocratic and elitist nature of the 15 gallon law see Lane, *Policing the City*, 1967:43 and Krout, *The Origins of Prohibition*, 1925:265. For Boston's sentiment against the use of spies to enforce the law see *Boston Courier*, June 20, 1839, p. 2.

16. The testimony at the initial hearing for Cummings before the Police Court was reported in the *Columbian Centinel* (Boston, MA), April 17, 1839, p. 2. In this hearing Cummings was found guilty by the judge and fined $20. The appeal of this case went to the Municipal Court, where the jury produced its verdict, *Boston Traveler*, May 31, 1839, p. 2. For the June disturbance see *Boston Courier*, June 13, 1839, p. 2. The handbill trying to cause a disturbance was reported in the *Gloucester Telegraph*, November 23, 1839, p. 2.

17. The first indictments that Savels and Coleman were mentioned in was reported in the *Columbian Centinel* (Boston, MA), October 10, 1839, p. 4. The incident in Chelsea occurred less than a week later. The extended testimony about the incident is best reported in *The Expostulator* (Boston, MA), October 24, 1839, p. 2.

18. Robert Rantoul, Jr., is eulogized in a biography published in 1854, two years after his death. It outlines his life, offers excerpts from his many writings and discusses his views on many of the issues of the day. Edited by Luther Hamilton, *Memoirs, Speeches and Writings of Robert Rantoul, Jr* is a basic reference for his life. On Rantoul's 1839 temperance speaking tour see Krout, *The Origins of Prohibition*, 1925:270.

19. Unlike his opponent, John C. Park got no laudatory biography when he died. Details of his life have been pieced together from various newspaper accounts. His name appears frequently in the Boston papers as a defense lawyer. His obituary, printed in the *Boston Journal*, April 22, 1889, p. 1, refers to him as an ardent Whig and stated that early on he joined the Republican Party. The *Boston Herald*, April 22, 1889, p. 1 also published a long and informative obituary for John C. Park.

20. The comment of "strange swearing" was published in the *National Aegis* (Worcester, MA), October 23, 1839, p. 3.

21. For a thorough discussion of contemporary bankruptcy and insolvency laws see Cutler, *The Insolvent Laws of Massachusetts, with Notes of Decisions*, 1853.

22. Tukey's insolvency case in 1840 is listed as Case #2218 and the records are held in the Archives of the Massachusetts Supreme Judicial Court in Boston. The following discussion is based on those records.

23. The new business arrangements were reported in the 1840 Boston Business Directory. Tukey's home address was still at the rear of 107 Hanover St.

24. On the repeal of the 15 gallon law and the subsequent confusion over licensing, see Lane, *Policing the City*, 1967:43–45.

25. *Columbian Centinel* (Boston, MA), April 8, 1840, p. 3. The applicants were divided into three groups: retailers, innholders and victuallers. Of the 152 applicants, the majority (106) were listed as victuallers with innholders representing 32 and retailers with 14. In the end, the Mayor and Alderman granted at most 60 licenses for selling liquor, *Bay Sate Democrat* (Boston, MA), April 14, 1840, p. 2.

26. Both the Aldermen's resolution

and the editor's complaint were published in the *Bay State Democrat* (Boston, MA), June 25, 1841, p. 2.

27. The original editorial was in the *Hartford Weekly Review.* It was reprinted in the *Bay State Democrat* (Boston, MA), July 31, 1841, p. 2. It mentions as many as thirty people a day presented for the crime of illegal liquor sales in Boston.

28. The *Boston Post*, July 9, 1841, p. 2 listed all those accused of selling liquor without a license along with the location of their establishment. Tukey's place was on Ann St. while Gay's was on Commercial St. A large number of those indicted on July 8 were also listed as applying for licenses in the *Columbian Centinel* (Boston, MA), April 8, 1840, p. 3. Obviously, they did not get a license.

29. The trial was covered by a number of newspapers with varying degrees of detail. The most complete was that of the *Weekly Messenger* (Boston, MA), August 25, 1841, p. 2. However, both the *Boston Daily Atlas*, August 23, 1841, p. 2 and the *Boston Post*, August 23, 1841, p. 2 added important details.

30. Pfaff's trial was reported in the *Boston Daily Atlas*, September 22, 1841, p. 2.

31. *Ibid.*, November 16, 1841, p. 2. *Boston Post*, November 16, 1841, p. 2.

32. The original letter was published in the *New Hampshire Patriot* (Concord, NH) and was reprinted in the *Boston Post*, November 18, 1841, p. 2.

33. The attack on Gould's house was reported in the *Boston Post*, November 19, 1841, p. 2. The attack on Loring's house and the supposition that Ira Gibbs was the intended target was published in *The Liberator* (Boston, MA), December 17, 1841, p. 2. Gibbs had testified at the trial. The reward was advertised in the *Boston Post*, December 13, 1841, p. 1.

34. The best description of the assault, including the quote about Lewis's eye was in *ibid.*, August 3, 1841, p. 2. For a discussion of the development and historical use of the slungshot see Escobar, *Saps, Blackjacks and Slungshots*, 2018. The resolution of the case was reported in the *Boston Daily Atlas*, August 12, 1841, p. 2.

35. Parker expressed his regret at having to prosecute during the trial of Jeremiah Brown, *Boston Post*, November 16, 1841, p. 2. The cases were postponed in December, *ibid.*, December 28, 1841, p. 2. Again in January, *ibid.*, January 17, 1842, p. 2. Postponed again in April, *ibid.*, April 27, 1842, p. 2. The compromise was reported in *ibid.*, May 11, 1842, p. 2.

Chapter 2

1. Tukey's presence at the school in 1842 is in Harvard Law School, *A Catalogue of Students of Law...,*" 1842. This book also give general information on the course of study, the requirements and describes the instruction. Tukey entered the Law School in 1841 as reported in 1851 in *Gleason's Pictorial*:1(2):25 and in the *Boston Journal*, December 16, 1867, p. 2. He is listed as a student in the August term of 1841, Greenleaf Papers, Harvard Law School, Academic Miscellani, Box 23, Folder 17. A good history of the early years of the law school is Harvard Law School, *Centennial History, 1817–1917*, 1918. On p. 138, the percentage of entering students who were college graduates during the time 1830–1850 period is mentioned. The *Salem Register*, June 6, 1846, p. 2 recalled Tukey's time in Salem and commented on his becoming a lawyer. The fee structure is reported in Coquillette and Kimball, *On the Battlefield of Merit*, 2015:161

2. The description of the usual law education under a preceptor and the quotes from Sumner and Greenleaf are from Harvard Law School, *Centennial History, 1817–1917*, 1918:1–3, 14–15. The attitude of Harvard undergraduates in the 1830s is reported in Coquillette and Kimball, *On the Battlefield of Merit*, 2015:176–177.

3. Information on the structure of the course and its requirements are from Harvard Law School, *A Catalogue of Students of Law...,*" 1842. The quote on the "peculiar jurisprudence" of states in on p. 5. A modern perspective on the teaching of law at this time is found in Coquillette and Kimball, *On the Battlefield of Merit*, 2015:166–173.

4. The listing of residences is in Harvard University, *A Catalogue of the*

Officers and Students...," 1842. Benjamin F. Cook became a lawyer and was associated with Tukey in a petition against voter fraud in 1852. Sedgwick L. Plummer did get a law degree from Harvard. His obituary, *St. Paul Globe,* December 28, 1884, p. 5, states that he died in an almshouse in Gardiner, ME. His father had left him $50,000 and he squandered it in "riotous living."

5. The listing of students is in the Greenleaf Papers, Harvard Law School, Academic Miscellani, Box 23, Folder 17. The Moot Court Case was preserved in Greenleaf Papers, Harvard Law School, Moot Court Cases, 1841–1842, Box 20, Folder 2. The catalogue stated that the course was arranged to be completed in two years, Harvard Law School, *A Catalogue of Students of Law...,"* 1842:6. The notice of Tukey's passing the bar was published in *Boston Evening Transcript,* March 8, 1844, p. 2.

6. Wilmot was listed in the catalogue of all students in 1842, Harvard University, *A Catalogue of the Officers and Students...,"* 1842:8. He is listed under the Senior Class and is described as from Lenox, MA. He was staying at "Mr. Griffing's." In the 1845 Law School catalogue, Wilmot is listed as leaving the school in 1843, the same year as Tukey, but was not granted a Bachelor of Law degree, Harvard Law School, *A Catalogue of Students of Law...,"* 1845:45, 61. In the Greenleaf Papers is a letter of recommendation, dated August 29, 1842, for George D. Wilmot from a lawyer in Lenox named H. W. Bishop. It revealed that Wilmot had studied law in his office and had already passed the bar, Greenleaf Papers, Harvard Law School, Recommendation Letters for Admission, 1842–1843, Academic Miscellani, Box 22, Folder 5. The ads in the *Trumpet and Universalist Magazine* (Boston, MA) for Tukey & Wilmot appeared every week from September till the end of January 1845.

7. For a biography of Frederic Tudor see Carl Seaburg, *The Ice King: Frederic Tudor and his Circle,* 2003, H. W. Bishop's connection to George D. Wilmot is in the letter of recommendation in Greenleaf Papers, Harvard Law School, Recommendation Letters for Admission, 1842–1843, Academic Miscellani, Box

22, Folder 5. Biographies of George N. Briggs and Julius Rockwell can be found in Davis, *History of the Judiciary in Massachusetts,* 1900:250, 256. A short biography of Charles A. Dewey is in Clark, *Antiquities, Historicals and Graduates,* 1882:294.

8. The report of the original case is published in *Salem Register,* February 17, 1845, p. 3. The law regarding pilotage fees is set out in Metcalf, *General Laws of Massachusetts,* 1822:529–531. The detailed Supreme Court decision is reported in Metcalf, *Reports of Cases,* 1847:371–380.

9. The case in the U.S. District Court was titled "Wachs vs. the ship *Sophia Walker"* and was reported in the *Boston Daily Atlas,* November 10, 1845, p. 1. The divorce case was reported in the *Boston Daily Atlas,* November 12, 1845, p. 2.

10. Wilmot is mentioned in the Boston newspapers as late as October 10, 1845. He is not listed in the Boston City Directory for 1846. The next reference to him in Boston occurs in the *Weekly Messenger* (Boston, MA) of September 27, 1848, p. 3, when he is again practicing law in Boston. Tukey's advertisements in the *Boston Daily Atlas* ran weekly from March 25 till June 17, 1846. They are in the *Boston Daily Bee* daily from March 25 till June 19, 1846. Finally, the advertisement in in the *Boston Semi-weekly Atlas* ran weekly from March 25 through June 17, 1846. He also ran the advertisement in the *Boston Post* in 1846 until June 29, 1846, a week after his appointment as Marshal.

11. *Boston Post,* June 23, 1846, p. 2. The information from the *Boston Mail* and the *Boston Eagle* are quoted in the *Boston Daily Bee,* June 26, 1846, p. 2. The last quote is from the *ibid.,* June 27, 1846, p. 2.

12. List of Boston tax payers who pay tax on more than $100,000 in property was published in the *Newburyport Herald,* May 20, 1845, p. 2. Biography of Josiah Quincy, Jr., in Boston, City Record, *Boston's 45 Mayors,* 1975:10. The relationship between Quincy and Tukey is based on an article in *Gleason's Pictorial Drawing Room Companion,* May 10, 1851, p. 25, which stated, "Mr. Tukey was appointed city marshal under Josiah

Quincy, Jr., as mayor in 1846 (who by-the-by, is a firm and consistent friend of the marshal)."

13. A discussion of the men who held the office of City Marshal before Tukey is in Lane, *Policing the City*, 1967:46.

14. Quincy's Inaugural Address was printed in Boston City Register, *The Inaugural Addresses of the Mayors of Boston...*, 1894, p. 323–332. The quote in on p. 325.

15. The discussion of what type of man the City Marshall should be was in the Inaugural Address that Josiah Quincy, Jr., delivered on January 4, 1847 as published in *ibid.*, 1894, p. 342.

16. *Ibid.*, 1894, p. 325. The restrictions on the constables and watch were discussed in Lane, *Policing the City*, 1967:36. This source is the best history of the development of the police in Boston. The requirements for the marshal were described on p. 16.

17. A general account of the riot can be found in Stevens, *Hidden History of the Boston Irish*, 2008:46–50. Also see Elliot, "Being Mayor ... a Hundred Years Ago," 1936: 154–173. *Columbian Centinel* (Boston, MA), June 14, 1837, p. 4.

18. Elliot's proposal of a "new police" and the aldermen's enthusiastic response to it is in Lane, *Policing the City*, 1967:34. Their purpose and responsibilities are detailed on p. 36- 38. The statute authorizing the new police was passed on April 17, 1838 and is in Massachusetts General Court, *Private and Special Statutes...*, 1848:52.

19. Tukey's swearing in was reported in the *Boston Pilot*, July 4, 1846, p. 6. The addition of new men at this time is described in Lane, *Policing the City*, 1967:60.

20. The indictment of newsboys for being a nuisance was reported in *Boston Traveler*, February 17, 1843, p. 2. The epic battle between a group of newsboys and the "Irish apple girls" was described in the *Boston Daily Bee*, June 23, 1846, p. 2. The order of the Common Council to the mayor was in *Boston Evening Transcript*, June 26, 1846, p. 2 and the Aldermen's regulations regarding newsboys was in same paper, on page 2 on June 30, 1846. The use of a badge is reported in the *Brooklyn Eagle*, July 13, 1846, p. 2.

21. The licensing of newsboys was reported in *Boston Evening Transcript*, July 7, 1846, p. 2. Information on the badge and the restriction on crying their papers was in the *Boston Daily Bee*, July 11, 1846, p. 2. The economics of selling newspapers was described in the *Emancipator and Republican* (Boston, MA), April 24, 1844, p. 200.

22. For the opposition of those without licenses and their violent response, see *Boston Daily Bee*, July 18, 1846, p. 2. The *Brooklyn Daily Eagle*, July 13, 1846, p. 2 commented on the issue of licensing. The four boys who lost their licenses were in the *Boston Daily Bee*, July 28, 1846, p. 2.

23. The right to regulate traffic in Boston, granted in 1809, was discussed in the *Boston Intelligencer*, July 19, 1828, p. 2. The placement of notices in standing carriages was reported in *Boston Evening Transcript*, July 8, 1846, p. 2. Tukey's letter to the mayor and aldermen was printed in the *Boston Evening Transcript*, July 14, 1846, p. 2.

24. A biography of William Pope is available in Pope, *History of the ... Pope Family*, 1888:200–206.

25. The badges were reported in the *Boston Daily Bee*, July 8, 1846, p. 2. The letter from "A Bostonian" was published in the *Boston Daily Atlas*, June 16, 1846, p. 2.

26. A sensationalized and undocumented look at Boston's early detectives was published in *Boston Globe Magazine*, April 28, 2016, "The Incredible Untold Story of America's First Police Detectives," https://www.bostonglobe.com/magazine/ 2016/04/28/the-incredible-untold-story-america- first-police-detectives/jewdTrdVzkQZJuVZEEc9TJ/story.html. See also Lane, *Policing the City*, 1967, p. 60–61, 68–69.

27. The Hamilton St. riot was widely reported in the Boston newspapers. The best coverage was in *Boston Post*, July 21, 1846, p. 2 and the *Boston Semi-weekly Atlas*, July 22, 1846, p. 4. The marshal's exhortation to "Die first" rather than letting Sweeney go was published in the *Boston Daily Bee*, July 21, 1846, p. 2. It also reported the crowd urging them to kill the city marshal.

28. Tukey's offer to care for Sweeney's

children was published in both the *Boston Post*, July 21, 1846, p. 2 and the *Boston Semi-weekly Atlas*, July 22, 1846, p. 4. The sentencing of the rioters was in the *Boston Daily Bee*, August 16, 1846, p. 2.

29. The comment about enforcing the non-smoking ordinance was in *Massachusetts Ploughman and New England Journal of Agriculture* (Boston, MA), March 1, 1845, p. 4. The report on John Diamond's brutish behavior was published in *Emancipator and Republican* (Boston, MA), July 29, 1846, p. 56. Officer Ripley's violation was covered in the *Boston Evening Transcript*, September 30, 1846, p. 2. The report about this being the first such citation of a city officer was in *Boston Daily Bee*, September 30, 1846, p. 2.

30. Regulation of cabs and omnibuses was published in *Boston Evening Transcript*, October 27, 1846, p. 4. The use of non-slippery hole covers was reported in *Boston Daily Bee*, October 6, 1846, p. 2. The order for clearing obstructions from the streets was in *Boston Evening Transcript*, November 3, 1846, p. 1.

31. The text of the ordinance was reported in *Boston Daily Bee*, September 15, 1846, p. 2. An interesting description of the "third tier" and other aspects of Boston theaters was printed in the *Liberator* (Boston, MA), September 18, 1846, p. 152.

32. The arrest of the pickpocket was in the *Boston Evening Transcript*, November 9, 1846, p. 2. A somewhat fuller account is in the *Christian Reflector* (Boston, MA), November 12, 1846, p. 3.

33. Tukey's enforcement of the Sunday law is reported in *Boston Daily Atlas*, October 20, 1846, p. 2.

34. The fullest description of the snow campaign was originally in the *Boston Evening Herald* and reprinted in the *Fall River Monitor*, December 5, 1846, p. 2.

Chapter 3

1. Quincy's nomination was reported in the *Boston Evening Transcript*, November 18, 1846, p. 2. His opponents and the results of the election were published in *Boston Semi-weekly Atlas*, December 16, 1846, p. 4. The New Year's Day editorial

was reported in the *Boston Daily Bee*, January 1, 1847, p. 2. The latter editorial, entitled "Mr. Quincy's Address" was in *ibid.*, January 9, 1847, p. 2.

2. The meeting was published in the *Boston Evening Transcript*, January 4, 1847, p. 2. The full text of the mayor's address is in Boston City Register, *The Inaugural Addresses of the Mayors of Boston...*, 1894, pp. 335–349.

3. The fullest report on the elopement/abduction was in the *Weekly Messenger* (Boston, MA), February 3, 1847, p. 4, as reprinted from the *Boston Journal* on January 29. Woodman's interaction with the law was reported in the *Boston Evening Transcript*, January 29, 1847, p. 2. The description of the building at 22 Oneida St. is from an advertisement for the sale of the building which reported that it was a four-story, brick building with 16 rooms, *Boston Herald*, September 13, 1864, p. 1.

4. There was considerable confusion, early on about how the robbers gained access to the stores. One idea was from a storeroom above while another suggested they had a set of keys. Most reports settled on the cellar window without giving a reason. Early reports of the robbery were published in the *Boston Daily Bee*, February 1, 1847, p. 4 and the *Boston Evening Transcript*, February 1, 1847, p. 2.

5. The description of the safe having three doors was in the *Boston Evening Transcript*, February 1, 1847, p. 2. The work done on the safe by the robbers was reported in the *Springfield Republican*, February 2, 1847, p. 2 which reprinted it from the *Boston Traveler*. Further description of the safe was in the *Alexandria Gazette*, February 5, 1847, p. 2, again reprinted from the *Boston Traveler*.

6. The most complete account of the stolen goods that I found was in the *Salem Register*, February 4, 1847, p. 2, reprinted from the *Boston Traveler*. The original value for the reward of $500 was cited in the *National Police Gazette* (New York, NY), February 6, 1847, p. 6. The increase to $1000 was reported in the *Boston Evening Transcript*, February 3, 1847, p. 2.

7. The initial report of the arrest was in the *Boston Daily Bee*, February 8, 1847,

p. 4. Their first appearance in the Police Court was reported in *ibid.*, February 8, 1847, p. 2. The description of Tukey recognizing the accomplice of Hall and finding the men at Suffolk House was in the *Worcester Palladium*, February 10, 1847, p. 3.

8. The articles in the *National Police Gazette* (New York, NY) were published on February 13, 1847, p. 4 and February 20, 1847, p. 4.

9. The description of the examination in the Police Court was taken from several accounts published in the *Boston Evening Transcript*, February 10, p. 2, February 11, p. 2 and February 12, 1847, p. 2; *Boston Daily Bee*, February 11, 1847, p. 2.

10. Information on Marks and Gore appeared in the *Boston Evening Transcript*, February 20, p. 2 and February 25, 1847, p. 2. The information on George Bell was published in the *National Police Gazette* (New York, NY), February 27, 1847, p. 4.

11. The indictments were reported in the *Boston Daily Bee*, March 6, 1847, p. 2. The postponement was in the *Boston Semi-weekly Atlas*, March 17, 1847, p. 2. The second postponement was in *ibid.*, March 31, 1847, p. 2.

12. The *Boston Daily Bee*, April 20, 1847, p. 2 stated that they had published the testimony from the Police Court and would not repeat it, but would be "publishing whatever new testimony may be elicited." The description of the trial was taken primarily from *ibid.*, April 21, 1847, p. 2 and the *National Police Gazette* (New York, NY), May 1, 1847, p. 6.

13. The reward advertisement was published in the *Boston Daily Bee* between April 26 to May 12, 1847. The mistaken arrest of Joseph Brown was first reported in the *Boston Evening Transcript*, May 1, 1847, p. 2. His eventual release was in the *Boston Daily Bee*, May 3, 1847, p. 2. For the story of the watches found in the canal see the *Hingham Patriot*, July 16, 1847, p. 2. The capture of Morton in Lawrence was reported in the *Boston Evening Transcript*, December 9, 1847, p. 2. Morton's sentence was reported in the *National Police Gazette* (New York, NY), April 29, 1848, p. 2.

14. The recovery of $300 worth of goods was reported in the *New York Evening Post*, February 24, 1848, p. 1 as reprinted from the *Boston Traveler*. The arrest of "Black Bill" was reported in the *New York Herald*, February 22, 1848, p. 5. His being discharged was printed in the *Commercial Advertiser* (New York, NY), March 25, 1848, p. 2 and the *National Police Gazette* (New York, NY), April 1, 1848, p. 3.

15. The notice for licensing of dogs was printed in the *Boston Evening Transcript*, March 8, 1847, p. 3. The extensive coverage of the trespass case was published in the *Weekly Messenger* (Boston, MA), March 10, 1847, p. 4.

16. The appeal for the Home for the Destitute was published in the *Christian Register* (Boston, MA), March 13, 1847, p. 3. One source for the story of the USS *Jamestown* is in Laxton, *The Famine Ships*, 1996, p. 49–52. A large meeting was held at Faneuil Hall to organize a committee to raise money and the Mayor, Josiah Quincy, Jr., was named its head, *New Bedford Mercury*, February 26, 1847, p. 4. The Day Police contribution and Tukey's involvement was in the *Boston Semi-weekly Atlas*, February 27, 1847, p. 4.

17. The Tukey insolvency case in 1847 is listed as Case #2268 and the records are held in the Archives of the Massachusetts Supreme Judicial Court in Boston. The following discussion is based on those records.

18. The insolvency notice was published in the *Boston Post*, March 5, 1847, p. 4. The report of the raise in salary was in the *Boston Daily Bee*, March 29, 1847, p. 2.

19. The raid on the gamblers was well covered by the Boston newspapers. The description printed here is based primarily on the *Boston Daily Bee*, March 22, 1847, p. 2; the *Boston Evening Transcript*, March 22, 1847, p. 2; *Weekly Messenger* (Boston, MA), March 24, 1847, p. 3. The game of props was popular in Boston in the 19th century and was believed to be based on a game played by California Indians and transmitted by the Massachusetts whaling fleet, Stearns, "On the Nishinam game of 'Ha' and the Boston game of 'Props' " *American Anthropologist*, 1890, 3:353–358.

20. *Boston Evening Transcript,* March 23, 1847, p. 2; *Boston Daily Bee,* March 24, 1847, p. 2.

21. The story of the handcuffs and the note accompanying them was published in the *Boston Evening Transcript,* March 26, 1847, p. 2. The lad who returned them was reported in the *Trumpet and Universalist Magazine* (Boston, MA), April, 24, 1847, p. 3.

22. The arrest of Michael Tubbs was reported in the *Boston Daily Bee,* October 27, 1846, p. 2. His acquittal was in the *Boston Daily Atlas,* October 30, 1846, p. 2. The case against Tukey is in the *Boston Daily Bee,* May 8, 1847, p. 2. This case eventually went to the Massachusetts Supreme Court and was reported in Cushing, ed., *Reports of Cases ... Supreme Judicial Court of the Commonwealth of Massachusetts,* 1865, p. 438–442.

23. The content of the articles in the *Chronotype* were reported in the *Boston Semi-weekly Atlas,* May 12, 1847, p. 2. The libel case was published in *ibid.,* May 22, 1847, p. 2. This case also went to the Massachusetts Supreme Court where Wright was acquitted, not because the statement was not libelous but because the indictment did not contain the actual words of the libel, *ibid.,* March 25, 1848, p. 4.

24. Tukey's request for the city to cover his expenses and its agreement was in the *Boston Daily Atlas,* October 2, 1849, p. 2.

25. The "Special Police Notice" first appeared in the *Boston Daily Bee,* May 26, 1847, p. 3. It ran until September 4th. The notice also appeared in the *Boston Evening Transcript* and the *Boston Daily Atlas.*

26. Tukey addressing his officers was reported in the *Boston Evening Transcript,* July 13, 1847, p. 2. The information about Tukey's report to the city was published in the *Boston Daily Bee,* October 5, 1847, p. 1.

27. The report of the arrest of Silsby was in the *Boston Daily Bee,* October 10, 1847, p. 1. A detailed description of the counterfeit bills was published in the *Weekly Messenger* (Boston, MA), October 20, 1847, p. 2. The disposition of this case does not seem to have been reported.

28. The arrest of Herbert was so swift

that the first report of the robbery was when he was brought before the Police Court on November 2, 1847, *Boston Daily Bee,* November 2, 1847, p. 1; *Boston Evening Transcript,* November 3, 1847, p. 2. The recovery of the money was widely covered in the Boston papers, *Boston Daily Atlas,* November 15, 1847, p. 2; *Boston Evening Transcript,* November 15, 1847, p. 2. The story was published in the *Boston Daily Bee,* November 17, 1847, p. 2. Herbert's discharge was reported in *ibid.,* November 20, 1847, p. 2.

29. The story of the Temperance meeting was reported in the *Boston Evening Transcript,* October 22, 1847, p. 2.

30. The arrest of Burns was reported in the *Salem Observer,* November 27, 1847, p. 3 as well as the *Boston Evening Transcript,* November 22, 1847, p. 2.

31. The article in the *Boston Post* was published on December 14, 1847, p. 2. The editorial was published in the *Boston Daily Bee,* November 27, 1847, p. 2.

32. The nomination of Quincy was reported in the *Boston Daily Atlas* on December 2, 1847, p. 2 and December 4, 1847, p. 2. Parker's nomination was reported in the *Boston Daily Bee,* December 8, 1847, p. 2. The opposition to Quincy was discussed in an editorial in *ibid.,* December 13, 1847, p. 2.

Chapter 4

1. The election results were reported in the *Boston Evening Transcript,* December 14, 1847, p. 2.

2. Mayor Quincy's address on January 3rd is published in Boston City Register, *The Inaugural Addresses of the Mayors of Boston...,* 1894, p. 353–363.

3. The report of this petition was in the *Boston Evening Transcript,* January 14, 1848, p. 2. The "Special Police Notice" first appeared in the *Boston Daily Bee,* May 26, 1847, p. 3.

4. The report of the committee convened to hear the charges was published in *ibid.,* January 25, 1848, p. 2.

5. The association of William Farrar and Samuel K. Head is stated in *Boston Herald,* "The *Boston Herald*" 1878:31. That book, published more than 30 years later, commented on the feud, *ibid..* p.

18. Head purchased the newspaper on May 12, 1847, *ibid.*, p. 16. The article describing the *Herald's* support of the police was published in the *National Police Gazette* (New York, NY), January 30, 1847, p. 4.

6. The information on the *Herald's* election campaign was detailed in *Boston Herald*, "The *Boston Herald*" 1878:23– 24. The rejection of Head's petition to get the public advertising was in the *Boston Daily Bee*, February 18, 1848, p. 1. The best biography of William J. Snelling's career is Cohen, Gilfoyle and Lefkowitz, "*The Flash Press...*," 2008.

7. Kelley's attack on Snelling's review was published in the *Boston Traveler*, May 25, 1832, p. 3. Snelling's active role in attacking the gamblers was, including his recruiting of Amerige, in the *Norfolk Advertiser* (Dedham, MA), April 20, 1833, p. 2; *Boston Daily Advertiser*, April 24, 1833, p. 2; *ibid.*, April 26, 1833, p. 2. The description of Snelling as a "man stark mad" was in the *Lowell Mercury*, May 24, 1833, p. 2.

8. The length of time that Snelling spent in jail for his three convictions for libel is uncertain. Cohen, Gilfoyle and Lefkowitz, "The Flash Press," 2008:31 state that he was sentenced to 60 days in jail and a fine of $50. However, that was the sentence for one of the original cases in the Boston Municipal Court. Contemporary accounts of the Massachusetts Supreme Court, while they differ in details, all suggest he was sentenced to five and a half months in jail, *Boston Courier*, June 21, 1834, p. 2; *Boston Daily Advertiser*, June 21, 1834, p. 2.

9. Snelling's difficulties were reported in the *Boston Post* in a notice entitled "Police Court—The Fall of Genius" reprinted in the *Connecticut Courant* (Hartford, CT), February 25, 1837, p. 2.

10. Information on Snelling's activities in New York is based on Cohen, Gilfoyle and Lefkowitz, "*The Flash Press...*," 2008. The quote about the *Sunday Flash* is on p. 19–20. The first trial for obscenity was in *New York Journal of Commerce*, January 15, 1842, p. 2.

11. *Boston Herald*, May 3, 1848, p. 2. A search of the 13 Boston newspapers on the Genealogy Bank website for the name

Tukey in 1848 produced 306 references. From January through April, before the *Boston Herald* is preserved showed 76 references. From May through the end of the year, there were 230 references. The *Herald* accounted for 136 of these. In contrast, the other paper that mentioned Tukey was the *Boston Evening Transcript* which mentioned Tukey all of 28 times. It is clear that the editor of the *Boston Herald* was fixated on Tukey.

12. The pamphlet was published by the *Boston Herald* and entitled "A Narrative of the Life and Adventures of Francis Tukey, Esq., City Marshal of Boston." Original copies of the pamphlet are quite rare but it was consulted on microfilm as part of the *Making of Modern Law: Legal Treatises, 1800–1926* series published by Gale. The quotes from the pamphlet are on p. 3. The information on the notice Colesworthy had published is from the response in the *Boston Herald*, May 15, 1848, p. 2.

13. The relationship of Snelling and George Wilkes is reported in Cohen, Gilfoyle and Lefkowitz, "*The Flash Press...*," 2008:44. Snelling's death was described in *Boston Herald*, "The *Boston Herald*" 1878:28 and Head's withdrawal, *ibid..* p. 31.

14. The original show-up was reported in the *Boston Daily Bee*, April 13, 1848, p. 2 and the *Weekly Messenger* (Boston, MA), April 19, 1848, p. 1. The extent to which this process expanded is shown by one in 1851 which had 76 "rogues" exhibited to both the police and a large crowd of the public, Lane, *Policing the City*, 1967:66.

15. The account of the rescue of the foreman was in the *Boston Evening Times*, March 11, 1848, p. 2.

16. The original incident was reported in the *Boston Daily Times*, April 26, 1848, p. 2. Tukey's fine for driving too fast was in *Boston Daily Bee*, May 2, 1848, p. 2. The quote about Tukey paying his fine was from *Boston Daily Times*, May 3, 1848, p. 2. The first newspaper reference to the "omnibus war" was published in *ibid.*, May 23, 1848, p. 2 and was soon picked up by other newspapers in Boston.

17. A detailed profile of Horace King's enterprises was published in the *Boston*

Herald, October 22, 1849, p. 4. The quote about Tremont street was in the *Boston Herald,* March 13, 1848, p. 2. King's willingness to get his drivers licensed and to his substitution of two horse coaches was in the *Boston Daily Times,* May 27, 1848, p. 2.

18. Reports of the original drivers arrested were in *Boston Daily Bee,* May 20, 1848, p. 2; *Boston Daily Times,* May 20, 1848, p. 2; *Boston Evening Transcript,* May 20, 1848, p. 1. Further arrests on Monday were reported in *Boston Daily Atlas,* May 22, 1848, p. 2. This also contained Marshal Tukey's threat to arrest more drivers. Roxbury's response to the "war" was in *Boston Daily Times,* May 23, 1848, p. 2.

19. Further arrests were reported in the *Boston Daily Bee,* May 25, 1848, p. 2. The settlement of the cases was published in the *Boston Evening Transcript,* July 21, 1848, p. 2 and they reported further arrests on August 1, 1848, p. 2. The *Transcript* also described the compromise reached on November 4, 1848, p. 2.

20. The decision of the Massachusetts Supreme Court was reported in Cushing, Luther, ed., *Reports of Cases Argued ... in the Supreme Judicial Court of the Commonwealth of Massachusetts,* 1855, v. 2, pp. 562–576. The decision was printed in the *Boston Daily Bee,* March 13, 1849, p. 2.

21. The original petition was in the *Boston Evening Transcript,* May 16, 1848, p. 2. Pierce's application for a liquor license and Moses Grant's opposition to such licenses was in the *Boston Daily Bee,* March 30, 1847, p. 2. The raucous Temperance meeting was reported in the *Boston Daily Times,* May 13, 1847, p. 2. The *Boston Herald* publicized the meeting on May 25, 1848, p. 2 in an article on the omnibus war. The end result of the meeting was in the *Boston Evening Transcript,* May 27, 1848, p. 2.

22. The best description of the collapsed building was in *ibid.,* June 26, 1848, p. 2. Other important descriptions include the *Boston Courier,* June 26, 1848, p. 2 and the *Boston Daily Times,* June 26, 1848, p. 2.

23. The quote from the *Boston Herald* was published June 26, 1848, p. 2. A description of the gifts presented by the Dry Good Merchants was in the *Boston Evening Transcript,* August 18, 1848, p. 2. Tukey's reappointment was in the *Boston Daily Bee,* June 27, 1848, p. 2.

24. Tukey's being Chief Marshal of the Fourth of July celebration is from a notice published in the *Boston Courier,* July 4, 1848, p. 2. A summary of the efforts to bring water to Boston appeared in the *Boston Evening Times,* October 26, 1848, p. 2.

25. The *Boston Herald,* October 9, 1848, p. 4 printed the supposedly secret program. A letter to the editor first brought up the issue of the Irish; see *Boston Herald,* October 10, 1848, p. 4. This was further confirmed in the *Boston Evening Transcript,* October 18, 1848, p. 2.

26. The military objections were published in the *Boston Daily Bee,* October 19, 1848, p. 2. The resolution of problems with both the firemen and the military was reported in the *Boston Evening Transcript,* October 20, 1848, p. 2.

27. The quote concerning Tukey's organization of the procession is from a pamphlet published by the Common Council, Boston, Common Council, *Celebration of the Introduction of the Water of Cochituate Lake into the City of Boston,* 1848, p. 7. Descriptions of the procession and the program on the Common are from *Boston Evening Transcript,* October 26, 1848, p. 2 and the *Boston Daily Times,* October 26, 1848, p. 2–3. The Mayor's quote is from the *Boston Daily Times* while the description of the fountain was in the *Boston Evening Transcript.*

28. Quincy's declining to run for mayor was reported in the *Boston Evening Transcript,* November 15, 1848, p. 2. The biographical information on Bigelow was in State Street Trust Company, *"Mayors of Boston,"* 1914:23.

29. The first call for Tukey's removal was in the *Boston Herald,* November 15, 1848, p. 4. The committee of Tukey's friends and the *Herald's* secret knowledge was in the *Boston Herald,* November 15, 1848, p. 2. The placard is described *ibid.,* December 8, 1848, p. 2.

30. The vote totals were widely reported; e.g., *Boston Daily Bee,* December 12, 1848, p. 2. The quote is from the *Boston Herald,* December 12, 1848, 2.

Chapter 5

1. The first mention of the presentation to Quincy was in the *Boston Daily Bee*, January 3, 1849, p. 2. The article in the *Boston Herald* was on January 3, 1849, p. 2. The list of police officers and their donations were in the *Boston Herald*, January 4, 1849, p. 4.

2. Whipple's photograph of the City Fathers was reported in the *Boston Evening Transcript*, January 11, 1849, p. 2. The distribution of the Water Celebration pamphlet was reported first in the *Boston Daily Atlas* on January 30, 1849, p. 2. Other papers which acknowledged delivery of the pamphlet were the *Boston Daily Bee*, *Boston Evening Transcript* and the *Boston Investigator*.

3. The organization of the City government was reported in the *Boston Daily Bee*, January 2, 1849, p. 2. Mayor Bigelow's address was published in Boston City Register, *The Inaugural Addresses of the Mayors of Boston...*, 1894, p. 367–379. The quote about decreasing expenses was on p. 378.

4. Quincy's reference to the crowded streets is in Boston City Register, *The Inaugural Addresses of the Mayors of Boston...*, 1894, p. 324 and Bigelow made the comment on the expenses on p. 378.

5. Bigelow's quote about refusal to license was in *ibid.*, p. 373.

6. Catholic opposition to the public schools was discussed in O'Connor, *Fitzpatrick's Boston*, 1984, p. 112–114. For the regulation of newsboys see Chapter 2. The taking of truant boys by two constables was reported in the *Boston Courier*, October 7, 1847, p. 3. The editorial comment is from the *Boston Daily Bee*, October 11, 1847, p. 2.

7. Quincy's committee was reported in the *Boston Courier*, November 16, 1848, p. 2. Tukey's report was discussed in the *Boston Daily Bee*, March 5, 1849, p. 2, the *Christian Witness and Church Advocate* (Boston, MA), March 9, 1849, p. 2 and the *Christian Register* (Boston, MA), March 24, 1849, p. 2. The fate of the attendance bill was in the *Boston Semi-weekly Atlas*, April 28, 1849, p. 1.

8. Mayor Bigelow's remarks on cholera are in Boston City Register, *The Inaugural Addresses of the Mayors of Boston...*,

1894, p. 371. The report on nuisances in the city and the banning of swine keeping was in the *Boston Evening Transcript*, January 1, 1849, p. 4.

9. The City's preparations for combating cholera were detailed in the *Boston Daily Bee*, May 22, 1849, p. 2. The use of the police by the Board of Health was in Boston, Committee of Internal Health, *Report of the Committee of Internal Health on the Asiatic Cholera*, 1849:5–6. The role of the police was outlined in the *Boston Courier*, May 24, 1849, p. 4. The work of cleaning the streets was reported in the *Boston Evening Transcript*, May 18, 1849, p. 2.

10. False reports of cholera were reported in the *Boston Daily Bee*, May 19, 1849, p. 2 and the *Boston Evening Transcript*, May 31, 1849, p. 2. The case of William H. Mason was reported in the *Boston Herald*, May 21, 1849, p. 2. In the later map of all cholera cases, this is accounted as actual cholera.

11. The description of Edwards's death was reported in the *Boston Evening Transcript*, June 4, 1849, p. 2. Information on the *Argyle* and the passengers she carried was reported in the *Boston Daily Bee*, June 5, 1849, p. 2. The comments on who was sick were in the *Boston Courier*, June 7, 1849, p. 1.

12. The hiring of additional police was in the *Boston Herald*, June 5, 1849, p. 1. The distribution of chloride of lime was in *ibid.*, June 7, 1849, p. 2. The use of the gun house on Fort Hill for a hospital was in the *Boston Daily Bee*, June 6, 1849, p. 2. Preparation of the hospital building was described in the *Boston Semi-weekly Atlas*, August 11, 1849, p. 3.

13. The first report on Tukey's illness was in the *Boston Daily Times*, June 9, 1849, p. 2. The suggestion that he was recovering rapidly was in the *Boston Daily Bee*, June 11, 1849, p. 2. The comment on other police officers being sick was in the *Boston Courier*, June 11, 1849, p. 4.

14. Moulton's petition against Tukey was most prominently reported in the *Boston Herald*, May 8, 1849, p. 4. It also mentioned Blake's petition. On the same day, on p. 1, in a report on the Aldermen meeting, it added its assessment of the petition signers. Comments on the

Boston Mail appeared on May 9, 1849, p. 4 and on the *Boston Traveler* on May 10, 1849, p. 2. Hanscom's petition was reported in the *Boston Daily Bee*, June 12, 1849, p. 2. Wardwell's petition was in the *Boston Evening Transcript*, June 12, 1849, p. 2.

15. The report on the vote and the Mayor's blank vote was in the *Boston Daily Bee*, June 26, 1849, p. 2. The question of the constitutionality of Tukey's reappointment was in the *Boston Daily Times*, June 29, 1849, p. 1. The *Herald's* response was in the *Boston Herald*, June 26, 1849, p. 2.

16. His relapse was reported in the *Boston Evening Transcript*, June 25, 1849, p. 2. The subscription for a public bath house was reported in the *Springfield Republican*, June 27, 1849, p. 2. Participation in the parade was in the *Daily Atlas*, July 4, 1849, p. 2. Tukey's being sick and leaving his office is in the *Boston Courier*, August 6, 1849, p. 2.

17. The report on the purchase of the *Jacob Bell* as a tow boat was in the *Boston Evening Transcript*, April 19, 1849, p. 2. The only newspaper that reported Tukey being out of the city was the *Boston Herald*, July 11, 1849, p. 4 and July 14, 1849, p. 2. A description of both the *Jacob Bell* and the Cape Ann Pavilion is in the *Boston Daily Times*, June 29, 1849, p. 2. An extensive ad for the Cape Ann Pavilion was in the *Boston Daily Bee*, August 6, 1849, p. 3. The "Choleaphobia" quote is in the *Boston Evening Transcript*, August 11, 1849, p. 1. Tukey being at Rockport was in the *Boston Herald*, July 14, 1849, p. 2. The ad for Mount Pleasant House was in the *Daily Atlas*, July 1, 1850, p. 1.

18. Tukey's return to Boston and his weak condition were reported in the *Boston Courier*, August 6, 1849, p. 2. Statistics on the number of deaths by cholera are from Stone, "The Cholera Epidemic in Boston," 1849:299. Tukey's taking over the hospital was in the *Boston Evening Transcript*, July 3, 1849, p. 2. Regulations were published in the *Boston Herald*, August 6, 1849, p. 4. The information on Officer Ripley was from the *Catholic Observer* (Boston, MA), August 9, 1849, p. 6.

19. The report of the Committee on Internal Health was in the *Boston Daily*

Bee, August 17, 1849, p. 2. Tukey's clearance of the cellars and the need for housing for the poor was in the *Boston Evening Transcript*, August 21, 1849, p. 2.

20. The most reliable statistics on the epidemic would seem to be Boston, Committee of Internal Health, *Report of the Committee of Internal Health on the Asiatic Cholera*, 1849. However even in this report there are inconsistences. In discussing the number of deaths, the report states (p. 9) that there were "seventy-nine Bostonians." In the table of cases (p. 180) which lists place of birth, there were only 42 cases where the person was born in Boston. Apparently in considering the deaths, the definition of "Bostonian" was more than just birth.

21. The show up of Watson was reported in the *Christian Freeman and Family Visitor* (Boston, MA), May 18, 1849, p. 4. McDonald's show up was reported in the *Boston Semi-weekly Atlas*, May 23, 1849, p. 1. His previous history is in the *National Police Gazette* (New York, NY), February 17, 1849, p. 2; March 10, 1849, p. 2 and March 24, 1849, p. 2. McDonald's conviction and subsequent release was in the *Boston Daily Times*, June 16, 1849, p. 2. The fact that he skipped bail was reported in the *Boston Daily Bee*, January 16, 1849, p. 2. McDonald was later arrested in New York for pickpocketing, *Spectator* (New York, NY), July 5, 1849, p. 2.

22. The "show up" of Chauncey Larkin was reported in the *Boston Evening Transcript*, July 27, 1849, p. 2. The play was entitled *London Assurance* by Dion Boucicault. It was first produced in London in 1841 and a few months later was on the stage in New York. The description of the character of "Dazzle" was in *The New World: A weekly journal*. J. Winchester, publisher, New York, October 16, 1841, p. 254. The best report on Larkin's activities, based on the actual police report, was in the *Boston Semi-weekly Atlas*, July 28, 1849, p. 1. Additional information is in the *Boston Herald*, July 25, 1849, p. 4. The arrest of Larkin was detailed in the *Boston Herald*, July 27, 1849, p. 4 and the *Boston Daily Times*, July 28, 1849, p. 1. His "show up" was detailed in the *Boston Evening Transcript*, July 28, 1849, p. 2. The letter from Anthony Morse was

in the same paper. Larkin's previous exploits in New York are detailed in the *National Police Gazette* (New York, NY), June 12, 1847, p. 4 and June 26, 1847, p. 5. He continued to run his cons into the 1860s, *ibid.*, November 16, 1861, p. 4. Back in Boston, in 1862, he was arrested on a warrant from New York while posing as a Colonel in the army, *Boston Herald*, April 2, 1862, p. 4.

23. The pamphlet is entitled "The Life and Exploits of the Noted Criminal Bristol Bill." The original was published in Boston in 1850. That pamphlet does not seem to have survived. A later version was published in New York, also in 1850. The author of the document was listed as "Greenhorn" but other sources identify him as George Thompson. Like many such documents, the veracity of its stories are hard to assess.

24. The arrest of Margaret O'Connor was reported in the *Boston Evening Transcript*, July 31, 1849, p. 2. The failed escape attempt and the raid on the house was detailed in the *Boston Herald*, August 18, 1849, p. 4. The dramatic arrival of the telegram from Portland is recounted in the *Boston Daily Bee*, August 20, 1849, p. 2. Tukey's speech is recounted in the *Boston Daily Times*, August 20, 1849, p. 2. The description of the "show up" from Tukey's report is taken from the *Boston Daily Bee*, January 25, 1851, p. 1. The question of biasing the jury was presented in the *Boston Herald*, August 20, 1849, p. 3.

25. The Mayor's address was in the *Boston Courier*, September 13, 1849, p. 4. The quote about Tukey's efficiency was in the *Flag of Our Union* (Boston, MA), September 1, 1849, p. 3. The description of Tukey's popularity was in the *Boston Daily Bee*, November 12, 1849, p. 2.

26. An excellent and easy to read analysis of the Parkman murder is Collins, *Blood & Ivy*, 2018. Tukey's response to the disappearance is based on his testimony at the trial as reported in the *Boston Evening Transcript*, March 20, 1850, p. 2.

27. Webster's alleged payment for the mortgage and his report that Parkman was going to the bank in Cambridge was reported in the *Boston Herald*, November 26, 1849, p. 2. Mr. Hayden's remarks were

reported in the *Boston Evening Transcript*, November 26, 1849, p. 1. The issue with the bag that Dr. Parkman left at the grocery was known to Charles Kingsley, Parkman's agent, as early as Saturday, November 24th, Collins, "Blood & Ivy," 2018: 58.

28. That Tukey was suspicious of the Medical College is evident in that he had the building under watch even after it was searched, *Boston Herald*, December 1, 1849, p. 4.

29. Littlefield's suspicions and the actions he took are from his testimony at the trial as reported in the *Boston Evening Transcript*, March 22, 1850, p. 2.

30. The discovery of the body, the noises heard in the basement and the findings in the ashes of the furnace are from Tukey's testimony at the trial as reported in *ibid.*, March 20, 1850, p. 2.

31. The details of the arrest of John Webster was reported in the *Boston Herald*, March 19, 1850, p. 4. Webster's attempt to poison himself with strychnine is from Webster's confession as reported in the *Boston Evening Transcript*, July 2, 1850, p. 3.

32. The case of Sarah Furber, who died of a botched abortion, was in the *Boston Daily Times*, June 12, 1848, p. 2. Threats against the Medical College and the alert to the militia was reported in the *Boston Daily Bee*, December 3, 1849, p. 2.

33. Decision to keep Coroner's Jury deliberations private—*Boston Evening Transcript*, December 5, 1849, p. 2. For the Inquest verdict and the thanks to the Marshal and police see *ibid.*, December 14, 1849, p. 2.

34. The results of the Mayoral Election were reported in the *Boston Daily Bee*, December 11, 1849, p. 2.

Chapter 6

1. Mayor Bigelow's address was published in Boston City Register, *The Inaugural Addresses of the Mayors of Boston...*, 1894, p. 383–394. The Mayor's diatribe about juries, etc., was on p. 386–387.

2. Marshal Tukey's report was summarized in the *Boston Evening Transcript*, January 1, 1850, p. 4. The report he

did in 1847 was summarized in the *Boston Daily Bee*, October 5, 1847, p. 1.

3. Population statistics were from Handlin, *Boston's Immigrants*, 1970, p. 239, Table II. The increase in the number of police is from Lane, *Policing the City*, 1967:60–61.

4. *Boston Herald*, January 2, 1850, p. 4.

5. The initial report of the dinner was in the *Boston Daily Times*, January 7, 1850, p. 2. It was mentioned in the *Boston Herald*, January 8, 1850, p. 2. The statement that Tukey was not present was in the *Boston Daily Bee*, January 9, 1850, p. 2. The retraction was in the *Boston Daily Times*, January 9, 1850, p. 1.

6. Tukey's speech in the Dennis Scanlan case was in the *Boston Daily Bee*, January 16, 1850, p. 2.

7. Scanlan's conviction was reported in the *Boston Courier*, February 13, 1850, p. 2.

8. The Lieutenant Governor's letter to the editor was in the *Boston Courier*, January 19, 1850, p. 2. Tukey's reply was in *ibid.*, January 21, 1850, p. 2.

9. Marjoram's letter was published in *ibid.*, January 23, 1850, p. 2.

10. The story of the *California Packet* was closely followed by the Boston newspapers. Its launch was reported in the *Boston Semi-weekly Atlas*, December 12, 1849, p. 4. The ship's arrival in Boston was in the *Boston Courier*, January 18, 1850, p. 2. The quote was in the *Congregationalist* (Boston, MA), February 8, 1850, p. 3.

11. The announcement of the ball was in the *Boston Herald*, February 12, 1850, p. 4. The quote about the ball was in the *Boston Daily Bee*, February 15, 1850, p. 2. The ship's departure from Boston was reported in the *Boston Courier*, March 5, 1850, p. 2. Its arrival in San Francisco was in the *Daily Alta Vista* (San Francisco, CA), August 25, 1850, p. 3.

12. Notices of items shipped by Tukey to Lorenzo D. Brown in California were in *Sacramento Transcript*, November 11, 1850, p. 3, the *Daily Alta California* (San Francisco, CA), January 28, 1851, p. 3 and *ibid.*, April 7, 1852, p. 2.

13. A good summary of the trial is in Collins, *Blood & Ivy*, 2018. The three editions of the newspaper was reported in the *Boston Herald*, March 18, 1850, p. 2.

14. A description of the importance of the dental evidence is found in Bowers, *Forensic Dental Evidence: An Investigator's Handbook*, 2010:22–25. Dr. Keep's testimony was reported in the *Boston Evening Transcript*, March 21, 1850, p. 2.

15. Dr. Morton's testimony was reported in *ibid.*, March 28, 1850, p. 2.

16. Tukey's testimony about the letters was in Bemis, *Report of the Case of John W. Webster*, 1850:210–211. Testimony of the handwriting experts was reported in the *Boston Evening Transcript*, March 27, 1850, p. 2. Fuller's testimony about the cotton-wrapped twig was in *ibid.*, 1850:173. Matching the letter to the cut wrapping paper was reported in the *Boston Herald*, December 6, 1849, p. 4.

17. Tukey's testimony was in Bemis, *Report of the Case of John W. Webster*, 1850:46–51. A good description of the model was in the *Boston Herald*, March 20, 1850, p. 4. Professor Webster's confession was reported in the *Boston Evening Transcript*, July 2, 1850, p. 3.

18. The fire and Tukey's response was in *ibid.*, March 21, 1850, p. 2.

19. The story of O'Connor's arrest and the denial of bond money by Drury is in Thompson, "The Life and Exploits of the Noted Criminal Bristol Bill," 1850:46–47.

20. *Ibid.*, 51–58, 75–87.

21. The original report of Bulloch's crime was in *Savannah Republican*, March 4, 1850, p. 2. Butman's chase to Wales and Tukey's waiting on the pier was in the *New York Herald*, May 3, 1850, p. 5.

22. The report of Taylor's arrest in Boston was in the *Boston Courier*, May 18, 1850, p. 2. Starkweather's trip to Northampton and Chicopee was in *ibid.*, May 20, 1850, p. 2. The story of Milo A. Taylor is fully reported in the *Hampshire Gazette* (Northampton, MA), May 21, 1850, p. 2. Tukey's visit to Taylor was in *ibid.*, May 28, 1850, p. 2. The description of Tukey is in the *Springfield Republican*, May 22, 1850, p. 2.

23. Mayor Bigelow's suggestions about combining the departments was in his address published in Boston City Register, *The Inaugural Addresses of the Mayors of Boston...*, 1894, p. 383–394. The

make-up of the committee and Tukey's presence was reported in the *Boston Evening Transcript*, May 27, 1850, p. 2. Tukey is listed as being at the Willard Hotel on May 30th in the *Republic* (Washington, D.C.), May 30, 1850, p. 4. His arrival at the Astor House is in the *Commercial Advertiser* (New York, NY), June 5, 1850, p. 4. A description of the New York tour was in *ibid.*, June 7, 1850, p. 2. The presentation of the committee's report and its recommendations were in the *Boston Herald*, December 21, 1850, p. 2.

24. The best coverage of the Watchmen's dinner, and the quote from Tukey, was in the *Boston Herald*, June 27, 1850, p. 2. Tukey's place at the head table was reported in the *Boston Evening Transcript*, June 27, 1850, p. 1.

25. The vote and swearing in was reported in the *Boston Daily Atlas*, July 2, 1850, p. 2. The quote was from the *Boston Evening Transcript*, July 2, 1850, p. 2.

26. The most complete description of the picnic was in the *Boston Herald*, July 15, 1850, p. 2. Other details were in the *Boston Evening Transcript*, July 12, 1850, p. 2.

27. Tukey's leading the tour was reported in the *Boston Daily Times*, August 19, 1850, p. 1. The results of the evening's carousing was in *ibid.*, August 19, 1850, p. 2. The response in New York was in the *New York Herald*, August 20, 1850, p. 5.

28. The rumor that Tukey was being considered for the office seems to have been first reported in the *Springfield Republican*, September 19, 1850, p. 2. He is shown as checking in at the Willard Hotel in the *Republic* (Washington, D.C.), September 16, 1850, p. 3. He is listed as watching the demonstration on September 18th in the *Daily National Intelligencer* (Washington, D.C.), September 21, 1850, p. 3.

29. The first reference in Boston to "Lind mania" was in the *Boston Herald*, September 6, 1850, p. 2. The nominal price for a ticket was reported in *ibid.*, September 23, 1850, p. 2. Auction of the tickets and the prices was in the *Boston Daily Atlas*, September 26, 1850, p. 2.

30. The police preparations were in the *Boston Herald*, September 23, 1850, p. 2. Lind's arrival in Boston and her accommodations were in the *Boston Evening Transcript*, September 26, 1850, p. 2. The roping of Tremont Street was in the *Boston Courier*, September 28, 1850, p. 2. The quote on the police was in the *Boston Evening Transcript*, September 28, 1850, p. 2.

31. Estimates of the crowd in Bowdoin square were in the *Boston Courier*, September 30, 1850, p. 2 and the *Boston Daily Bee*, September 30, 1850, p. 2. The quote about the Marshal Tukey was in the latter article.

32. The original letter to the editor was in the *Boston Evening Transcript*, September 30, 1850, p. 2. Tukey's response was in *ibid.*, October 1, 1850, p. 2.

33. The arrest of an alleged runaway in New York under the Fugitive Slave Act was reported in the *Weekly Messenger* (Boston, MA), October 2, 1850, p. 2. The meeting in Boston of the fugitive slaves was in the *Boston Courier*, October 2, 1850, p. 2. The general meeting at Faneuil Hall was in the *Boston Evening Transcript*, October 15, 1850, p. 1. Ellen's flight from the city and William's resolve to see it through were in the *Boston Semi-weekly Atlas*, October 26, 1850, p. 2. Crafts' statement to Douglass was in the *Massachusetts Spy* (Worcester, MA), October 30, 1850, p. 2. The refusal of the police to help and Devens consulting a judge was in the *Emancipator and Republican* (Boston, MA), October 31, 1850, p. 2. Knight's interaction with Crafts was in the *Boston Evening Transcript*, October 29, 1850, p. 2. Knight's own, highly self-serving account of this transaction was in the *Emancipator and Republican* (Boston, MA), November 28, 1850, p. 1. The rumor about tar and feathering was in the *Boston Courier*, October 28, 1850, p. 2.

34. The arrest of Knight and the comments of Hughes were in the *Boston Herald*, October 28, 1850, p. 2. Subsequent arrests were reported in the *Boston Courier*, October 29, 1850, p. 2. The attempt to have the men forced out of their hotel and their change in attitude was in the *Boston Courier*, October 29, 1850, p. 2. The departure of the slave-catchers was in the *Boston Daily Atlas*, November 1, 1850, p. 3. The flight of the couple

to England was in the *Salem Register*, November 11, 1850, p. 2.

35. The story of Ingraham and his being chased by the mob was in the *Boston Daily Atlas*, November 14, 1850, p. 2. Reports suggest that Ingraham was looking for a fugitive slave in Boston, see *Boston Herald*, November 18, 1850, p. 2. However, according to Ingraham, while he was accused, that was never what he did, *Boston Times* reprinted in the *North American* (Philadelphia, PA), November 15, 1850, p. 1.

36. Thompson's arrival was reported in the *Boston Daily Bee*, October 30, 1850, p. 2. His attendance at the Free-soil meeting was in the *Boston Courier*, November 7, 1850, p. 2.

37. The meeting and its list of speakers was published in the *Liberator* (Boston, MA), November 8, 1850, p. 2. The comment on "attempts to speak" was in the *Boston Herald* November 7, 1850, p. 4. Comments on Thompson's harangues was in the *Boston Daily Bee*, November 15, 1850, p. 2. The quote about foreign interference was in the *Boston Evening Transcript*, November 13, 1850, p. 2.

38. The best description of what happened at the meeting was in the *Boston Courier*, November 16, 1850, p. 2. Quincy's speech about the police was in the *Boston Evening Transcript*, November 19, 1850, p. 2. The announcement by Adams of the end of the meeting was in the *Liberator* (Boston, MA), November 22, 1850, p. 2.

39. The verbal complaint against Tukey was reported in the *Boston Courier*, November 19, 1850, p. 2. The text of the memorial was in the *Boston Herald*, December 3, 1850, p. 4. The description of the hearing was in the *Liberator* (Boston, MA), December 20, 1850, p. 2. Other reports of the meeting were in the *Boston Evening Transcript*, December 10, 1850, p. 2 and the *Boston Herald*, December 10, 1850, p. 2. The decision of the Board of Aldermen was in the *Boston Daily Bee*, December 18, 1850, p. 2.

40. The meeting at the Baptist Church was in the *Boston Courier*, November 18, 1850, p. 2.

41. The result of the election and the mayor's addressing the crowd was in the *Boston Daily Bee*, December 10, 1850, p. 2.

Chapter 7

1. The policing of the Neck was reported in the *Boston Daily Bee*, January 1, 1851, p. 2. The threat to pull a chain across the road was in the *Congregationalist* (Boston, MA), January 3, 1851, p. 3.

2. Mayor Bigelow's address was published in Boston City Register, *The Inaugural Addresses of the Mayors of Boston...*, 1894, p. 397–406. The Mayor's discussion of the police and the night watch was on p. 402. The submission of the report and quotes from the text was in the *Boston Herald*, December 21, 1850, p. 2.

3. The first annual report of the Police Department was published on January 23rd, *Boston Evening Times*, January 23, 1851, p. 2. The full text of the report was published in the *Boston Daily Bee*, January 25, 1851, p. 1.

4. The reviews quoted here were in the *Boston Daily Bee*, January 24, 1851, p. 2 and the *Boston Recorder*, January 30, 1851, p. 4.

5. The notice of the men who were nominated and would be appointed as policemen was in the *Boston Daily Bee*, February 11, 1851, p. 2.

6. A concise biography of Savage is in Roth, *Historical Dictionary of Law Enforcement*, 2001:308. Further information is in Lane, *Policing the City*, 1967:116. Savage's book was Edward H. Savage, *Police Records and Recollections; or Boston By Gaslight*, 1873.

7. The description of Tukey's behavior and methods is from Savage, *Police Records and Recollections*, 1873:375–376.

8. The orders of the Board of Aldermen were in the *Boston Evening Transcript*, February 11, 1851, p. 1.

9. The text of the arrest warrant was in the *Boston Courier*, February 17, 1851, p. 2. Devens's trip to Washington was in the *Liberator* (Boston, MA), February 21, 1851, p. 2. Most of the description of what happened in this case is from a deposition made by U.S. Deputy Marshal Patrick Riley. The text of Deputy Riley's deposition is in the *Boston Herald*, February 17, 1851, p. 4.

10. The text of Tukey's letter to the Mayor is in the *Boston Evening Transcript*, February 17, 1851, p. 2.

11. Clay's petition was in the *Washington Daily Union*, February 18, 1851, p. 4. The text of the President's proclamation was in the *Washington Daily Globe*, February 19, 1851, p. 4. Some of the rumors were reported in the *Boston Evening Transcript*, February 21, 1851, p. 2.

12. The text of the ordinance authorizing the City Marshal to support the U.S. Officers was in the *Boston Courier*, February 19, 1851, p. 2. The transmittal of the ordinance to the President was in the testimony of Bigelow before the Massachusetts Senate reported in the *Boston Daily Atlas*, April 14, 1851, p. 2. The rescued man, Frederick Wilkins, was sent to Montreal, Canada where he eventually opened a barber shop, married and had children. As a result of his rescue, nine people, two white and seven black, were arrested for aiding in his rescue. All of the trials either ended in hung juries or acquittals.

13. Reports of the descent on the gamblers were in the *Boston Courier*, March 10, 1851, p. 2, the *Boston Daily Bee*, March 10, 1851, p. 2 and the *Boston Herald*, March 10, 1851, p. 2. A detailed list of the equipment seized at each location was in the *Boston Daily Bee*, March 10, 1851, p. 2. The trials were reported in the *Boston Evening Transcript*, March 10, 1851, p. 2.

14. Editorials on the descent were in the *Boston Daily Bee*, March 10, 1851, p. 2 and the *Boston Herald*, March 10, 1851, p. 2. The New York quote was from the *New York Day Book* as quoted in the *Boston Evening Transcript*, April 4, 1851, p. 2.

15. Tukey's personal raid on a gambling house was in the *Boston Daily Bee*, March 10, 1851, p. 2. The second raid on 29 Sudbury St. was in the *Boston Evening Transcript*, March 14, 1851, p. 2.

16. The nomination and dismissal of officers was reported in the *Boston Herald*, March 25, 1851, p. 2.

17. The issuance of the warrant to Byrnes was in the *Boston Herald*, April 4, 1851, p. 4. The arrest by Butman and his being stabbed was reported in the *Boston Daily Atlas*, April 4, 1851, p. 2. The excuse Butman gave to Simms for his arrest is uncertain. Some sources say it was for being drunk and noisy—see *Boston Statesman*, April 5, 1851, p.

2—while others state it was for the theft of a watch; see *Boston Daily Atlas*, April 14, 1851, p. 2.

18. Tukey's testimony was reported in *ibid.*, April 14, 1851, p. 2.

19. The placing of the chains and the Judges' reaction was in *ibid.*, April 14, 1851, p. 2.

20. Phillips' speech was reported in the *Boston Courier*, April 5, 1851, p. 2. Tukey's searching the crowd and finding weapons was in the *Boston Daily Atlas*, April 14, 1851, p. 2. Coburn's arrest of Tukey was in *ibid.*, April 8, 1851, p. 2. Randolph's arrest for assault was in the *Boston Evening Transcript*, April 8, 1851, p. 2.

21. A summary of all the early Fugitive Slave Cases is in Von Frank, *The Trials of Anthony Burns*, 1998. The story of the attempted rescue of Simms is on p. 28–29. A description of the police preparations is in Savage, *Police Records and Recollections*, 1873: 376–380. The police practicing with swords and doing maneuvers was in the *Boston Daily Atlas*, April 14, 1851, p. 2. The preparation of the deck cabin was in the *Boston Herald*, April 12, 1851, p. 2.

22. The decision and the removal of Simms was in the *Boston Evening Transcript*, April 12, 1851, p. 1. The quote is from Savage, *Police Records and Recollections*, 1873:380.

23. Channing's testimony was reported in the *Boston Daily Atlas*, April 14, 1851, p. 2.

24. The comments on preparations for the raid on Ann St. are from Savage, *Police Records and Recollections*, 1873:257.

25. The proceedings in the Police Court and the exchange between Tukey and the Judge was in the *Boston Herald*, April 24, 1851, p. 4. The appearance of the 15 fiddlers was in the *Boston Daily Atlas*, April 26, 1851, p. 2. The description of the charge was in *ibid.*, April 25, 1851, p. 2.

26. Savage, *Police Records and Recollections*, 1873:259.

27. Tukey's reappointment without dissent was in the *Boston Daily Atlas*, June 10, 1851, p. 2. The quote about his services to the city was in the *Flag of Our Union* (Boston, MA), June 21, 1851,

p. 3. The quarterly report for July 1851 was in the *Boston Courier*, July 15, 1851, p. 2. Comparison of crimes was with the report of the first six months of 1847, *Boston Daily Bee*, October 5, 1847, p. 1, and with the twelve months of 1849, *Boston Evening Transcript*, January 1, 1850, p. 4.

28. The hiring of special police and their division into squads of ten was in *ibid.*, September 15, 1851, p. 2. The "show up" and the quote from the *Commonwealth* was in the *Newburyport Herald*, September 8, 1851, p. 2.

29. The order of the procession and Tukey's place in it was reported in the *Boston Daily Bee*, September 20, 1851, p. 2. The horse that Tukey rode was described in the *Boston Herald*, September 20, 1851, p. 1. The comments made by the Canadians were in *ibid.*, September 23, 1851, p. 4. The quote from the Vermont newspaper was reprinted in the *Boston Daily Atlas*, September 29, 1851, p. 2.

30. The alliance between the Whigs and the Irish is described in Handlin, *Boston's Immigrants*, 1970:197. Further information on the political landscape was in Lane, *Policing the City*, 1967:75–77. The appointment of McGinniskin was reported in the *Boston Courier*, September 30, 1851, p. 2.

31. The article about foreigners on the police was in the *Boston Evening Transcript*, October 1, 1851, p. 2. The pseudo-quote from Monroe is in Stevens, *Hidden History of the Boston Irish*, 2008:42. Also in Wilhelm, *Wicked Victorian Boston*, 2017:72. Lane, *Policing the City*, 1967:105 reports that the Boston police did not get uniforms until 1858.

32. The vote reconsideration and Mayor Bigelow's remarks were in the *Boston Courier*, October 9, 1851, p. 2.

33. The removal of Oliver from his beat and the petition asking him to be put back is in the *Boston Herald*, November 10, 1851, p. 2. The presentation of the petition with 300 signatures and Tukey's letter were both in the *Boston Evening Transcript*, November 12, 1851, p. 1.

34. McGinniskin's sworn affidavit was in the *Boston Pilot*, November 22, 1851, p. 7. His conviction for rioting was reported in the *Bay State Democrat* (Boston, MA),

March 28, 1842, p. 2. A description of the cause of the riot was in the *Boston Courier*, February 28, 1842, p. 4. An interesting review of the dispute is in O'Connor, *Fitzpatrick's Boston*, 1984:37–39.

35. Tukey's final statement was in the *Boston Evening Transcript*, November 19, 1851, p. 3. The feelings of the police force on this issue were in Lane, *Policing the City*, 1967:75–79.

36. Tukey's insolvency case in 1851 is listed as Case #319 and the records are held in the Archives of the Massachusetts Supreme Judicial Court in Boston. The following discussion is based on those records. Tukey's land transactions are in the Suffolk County Deeds in the courthouse in Boston. The connection with the Vermont Central was stated by Tukey at his Faneuil Hall meeting, *Boston Herald*, January 31, 1853, p. 2. The obituary of Adelaide Tukey, which lists the effect of her father's insolvency was in the *New York Times*, February 7, 1910, p. 9.

37. The announcement of the marriage was in the *Boston Courier*, November 12, 1851, p. 2. A description of the case against Haycock is in Cushing, ed. *Reports of Cases Argued and Determined ... Massachusetts, Volume 5*, 1855:26–30. Haycock's journey to California is in the *Boston Daily Bee*, March 13, 1849, p. 2. The incident of his usurious loan is in *ibid.*, December 11, 1849, p. 2. Haycock's triumphant return to Boston was in the *Boston Evening Transcript*, May 16, 1850, p. 2. His death in Sacramento was in *ibid.*, December 7, 1850, p. 2. Tukey's reply to McGinniskin was dated November 17, 1851 from Baltimore and printed in the *Boston Daily Atlas*, November 19, 1851, p. 2.

38. That Mayor Bigelow declined renomination was reported in the *Boston Evening Transcript*, November 11, 1851, p. 2. The Whig choice for mayor and the actions of the Native American party were in the *Boston Courier*, November 24, 1851, p. 2. The letter to the editor by "22 Years in Boston" was in the *Boston Herald*, November 13, 1851, p. 4. Tukey's published refusal to have his name considered for mayor was in the *Boston Courier*, December 6, 1851. p. 3.

39. The results of the election on

December 8th were in the *Boston Herald*, December 9, 1851, p. 2. The selection of Seaver by the Whigs was in the *Boston Courier*, December 15, 1851, p. 2. The results of the second election were reported in the *Boston Evening Transcript*, December 18, 1851, p. 2. The meeting of the "adopted citizens" was in *ibid.*, December 23, 1851, p. 2. The police getting involved in the election was in Savage, *Police Records and Recollections*, 1873:91 and Lane, *Policing the City*, 1967:77. The vote totals in the *Boston Evening Transcript*, December 26, 1851, p. 2 show Seaver with a majority of one vote. The *Boston Daily Atlas*, December 25, 1851, p. 2 gave Seaver a majority of 33 votes while the *Boston Statesman*, December 27, 1851, p. 2 gave him a majority of 14 votes.

Chapter 8

1. The aid from the police to the Irish poor is in Lane, *Policing the City*, 1967:76. The report of Tukey taking in the two Irish children was in both the *Boston Post*, July 21, 1846, p. 2 and the *Boston Semi-weekly Atlas*, July 22, 1846, p. 2.

2. The vote of the Native American Party meeting for their nomination for mayor was reported in the *Boston Courier*, November 24, 1851, p. 2. Tukey's published refusal to have his name considered for mayor was in *ibid.*, December 6, 1851. p. 3.

3. Charges of Tukey's opposition to certain Aldermen and Common Council members was in the *Boston Daily Atlas*, January 12, 1852, p. 2. The support of the Irish was acknowledged *ibid.*, December 25, 1851, p. 2. The quote is from Savage, *Police Records and Recollections*, 1873:91.

4. The story of McGinniskin's dismissal and reinstatement was in the *Boston Evening Transcript*, January 7, 1852, p. 2. Tukey's refusal to accept the lost money from McGinniskin was in the *Boston Daily Atlas*, January 9, 1852, p. 2. The editor's quote was in the *Boston Evening Transcript*, January 9, 1852, p. 2. McGinniskin would remain a policeman until after the Mayoral election of 1854, when the Native American Party

candidate was elected, Stevens, *Hidden History of the Boston Irish*, 2008:45.

5. The organization of the government and the text of Mayor Seaver's address was in the *Boston Semi-weekly Atlas*, January 7, 1852, p. 1.

6. The text of the 1852 annual report was in the *Boston Daily Bee*, January 20, 1852, p. 1.

7. The questions on liquor were reported in *Boston Evening Transcript*, November 4, 1851, p. 1. Tukey's answers to the questions on liquor sales was in *ibid.*, November 11, 1851, p. 2. Tukey's induction into the Sons of Temperance was in the *Boston Herald*, February 7, 1852, p. 4.

8. The subscription being raised was in the *Boston Daily Atlas*, February 13, 1852, p. 2. The soiree and presentation was in the *Boston Daily Bee*, March 6, 1852, p. 2. McGinniskin's illness was in *ibid.*, March 10, 1852, p. 2.

9. The illness of Tukey and Earle was in the *Boston Evening Transcript*, April 12, 1852, p. 2. The *Boston Daily Times*, May 4, 1852, p. 2 reported that Tukey rode out for the first time that day. However, he had a relapse and was out sick again, *Boston Herald*, May 7, 1852, p. 4.

10. The granting of licenses was reported in the *Boston Daily Times*, May 4, 1852, p. 2 and the *Boston Herald*, May 11, 1852, p. 2. The intention of getting around the new law was expressed in the *Boston Recorder*, July 22, 1852, p. 2.

11. The dismissal of the Night Police was in the *Boston Evening Transcript*, May 18, 1852, p. 2. The lack of opposition was reported in Lane, *Policing the City*, 1967:78. The *Boston Herald* editorial was published May 24, 1852, p. 2. The *Boston Daily Times* editorial was published May 22, 1852, p. 2. The petition for the restoration was in the *Boston Herald*, May 18, 1852, p. 4.

12. Tukey's letter to the Mayor and Board of Aldermen was in the *Boston Daily Bee*, December 29, 1852, p. 2. That it was an attempt to get Tukey to resign was recognized in the *Boston Daily Times*, June 4, 1852, p. 2.

13. Roxbury's attempt to eliminate the office of City Marshal was in the *Boston Herald*, February 29, 1852, p. 2. The passage of the new ordinance and Mr.

Allen's question were in the *Boston Daily Times*, June 25, 1852, p. 2.

14. Tukey's declining the office was in the *Boston Herald*, June 30, 1852, p. 4. The lack of an appointment and the quote on delinquency was in the *Boston Daily Times*, July 1, 1852, p. 2. Tukey's functioning as the Chief of Police was in the *Boston Herald*, July 1, 1852, p. 2.

15. The meeting was reported in the *Boston Evening Transcript*, July 14, 1852, p. 2. The quote about Nourse was in *Gleason's Pictorial Drawing Room Companion*, 3(8):128, August 21, 1852. The *Boston Journal* quote was reprinted in the *Salem Register*, July 15, 1852, p. 2.

16. Tukey's interactions with the Mayor and Aldermen was reported in the *Boston Daily Bee*, December 29, 1852, p. 2. His introduction of Nourse to the assembled force was in the *Boston Evening Transcript*, July 17, 1852, p. 2 and the *Boston Semi-weekly Atlas*, July 21, 1852, p. 1.

17. The debate in the Common Council was reported in the *Boston Evening Transcript*, July 16, 1852, p. 2. Tukey's presence at the Temperance Convention and Rev. Clark's remarks were in the *Boston Herald*, July 16, 1852, p. 2. The posters about Tukey were listed in the *Boston Evening Transcript*, July 16, 1852, p. 2.

18. Tukey's ad was in a number of different papers but always the same text. The first appearance was in the *Boston Herald*, July 15, 1852, p. 2. The ad then appeared almost every day until March 30, 1852.

19. Tukey's address to the meeting was in the *Boston Herald*, October 19, 1852, p. 4. The Union Whig ticket was shown in *ibid.*, November 1, 1852, p. 4. Tukey's work on the committee was in the *Boston Daily Bee*, November 2, 1852, p. 2.

20. The quote about independence of party was from a letter of Dr. Smith accepting the nomination, in the *Boston Herald*, December 4, 1852, p. 2. The convention nominating Smith was in the *Boston Daily Bee*, December 4, 1852, p. 2. The editorial was in the *Boston Daily Atlas*, December 6, 1852, p. 2. The vote totals were in the *Boston Evening Transcript*, December 14, 1852, p. 2.

21. The filing of the petition was reported in the *Boston Herald*, December 15, 1852, p. 4. The decision by the City Government was in the *Boston Daily Bee*, December 16, 1852, p. 2.

22. Tukey's letter to Mayor Seaver was in the *Boston Herald*, December 13, 1852, p. 2. The comment about shooting wild shots was in the *Boston Daily Bee*, December 18, 1852, p. 2.

23. The text of the report is in Boston, Committee on Ordinances, *Report on the Watch and Police Departments*, 1852. The debate about the report was in the *Boston Evening Transcript*, December 24, 1852, p. 2. That Jewell and Haskell were the prime movers was in the *Boston Herald*, December 24, 1852, p. 4.

24. The quote about feathers about to fly was in the *Boston Daily Bee*, December 25, 1852, p. 2. The text of the memorial was in *ibid.*, December 29, 1852, p. 2. The tabling of the memorial was in the *Boston Evening Transcript*, December 28, 1852, p. 1.

25. The public meeting was held in Faneuil Hall and reported in the *Boston Herald*, January 31, 1853, p. 2.

26. The discussion of the role of the Police was in Boston, Committee on Ordinances, *Report on the Watch and Police Departments*, 1852.

27. Alderman Perry's death was reported in the *Boston Evening Transcript*, January 6, 1853, p. 2. The quote regarding "an army of radicals" was from the editor of the *Boston Courier*, January 31, 1852, p. 2. The quote about being found faithless was in the *Boston Daily Atlas*, January 28, 1852, p. 2.

28. The petition for the meeting and the ad for it were in the *Boston Daily Bee*, January 28, 1852, p. 2.

29. The description of the meeting is based on three contemporary reports all published on January 31, 1852 and in the *Boston Herald*, p. 2, the *Boston Daily Bee*, p. 2 and the *Boston Courier*, p. 2.

30. Quotes from the *Boston Courier*, January 31, 1852, p. 2, and the *Boston Daily Atlas*, January 31, 1852, p. 2.

31. Results of the election were published in the *Boston Herald*, January 31, 1853, p. 4.

32. Tukey's first trip to Washington was reported in the *Washington Evening Star*, February 24, 1853, p. 2.

His admittance to the bar of the U.S. Supreme Court was in the *Republic* (Washington, D. C.), February 26, 1853, p. 4. The second trip to Washington was in *ibid.*, March 15, 1853, p. 4. His participation in the auction was in the *New York Herald*, March 22, 1853, p. 8. The opposition to non-residents was expressed in the *Daily Alta California* (San Francisco, CA), April 4, 1853, p. 2.

33. A good summary of reaching the gold fields in California is in Maxwell-Long, *Daily Life During the California Gold Rush*, 2014.

34. The description of the travelling party was in the *Boston Daily Bee*, March 30, 1853, p. 2.

35. The Tukeys were reported to be on the *Georgia* in the *Boston Daily Bee*, April 9, 1853, p. 2. The letter in the *Buffalo Republic* was reprinted in *ibid.*, May 3, 1853, p. 2. The arrival in California was in the *Sacramento Daily Union*, May 7, 1853, p. 1.

Chapter 9

1. The letter was reported in the *Boston Daily Bee*, June 8, 1853, p. 2. Carsilla's sickness and that they arrived in Sacramento on June 1st was in a letter from Tukey to Josiah Quincy, Jr., written June 14, 1854 in the Quincy Family Papers, Massachusetts Historical Society, Boston.

2. Jesse Haycock's building a house was in the *Boston Daily Atlas*, December 9, 1850, p. 2. The description of the house was from an ad in the *Daily Democratic State Journal* (Sacramento, CA), October 1, 1855, p. 3. Tukey's first ad for his law office was in the *Sacramento Daily Union*, September 2, 1853, p. 2.

3. The Sunday school celebration was reported in the *Democratic State Journal* (Sacramento, CA), July 9, 1853, p. 2 and the *Pacific* (San Francisco, CA), July 15, 1853, p. 2.

4. The organization of the Eureka Engine Company was reported in the *Sacramento Daily Union*, August 30, 1853, p. 2. The advertisement for meeting at Tukey's office was *ibid.*, August 16, 1853, p. 2. The subscription and how the money was used was from a letter from

Tukey to Josiah Quincy, Jr., written June 14, 1854 in the Quincy Family Papers, Massachusetts Historical Society, Boston. In an ad published in the *Sacramento Daily Union*, September 5, 1853, p. 2 Tukey is listed as the foreman. The firemen's competition was in *ibid.*, September 12, 1853, p. 2. The presentation of the trumpet was in *ibid.*, September 29, 1853, p. 2.

5. The number of children in school was cited in the *Sacramento Daily Union*, September 5, 1853, p. 2. The School Board advertised that it was opening a school on August 1st, *ibid.*, July 22, 1853, p. 2. By the end of the year there were still no public schools, *ibid.*, December 20, 1853, p. 2. The first public school in the city was opened on February 20, 1854, *ibid.*, February 27, 1854, p. 2. Tukey became School Superintendent in April 1855, *ibid.*, April 20, 1855, p. 3.

6. Babson's life was well summarized in his obituary published by the American Institute of Architects, Schulze, "Seth Babson, F. A. I. A.," *Quarterly Bulletin of the American Institute of Architects* Vol. 8, No. 2 (July 1907), pp. 108–109. A description of the Auburn Plan is in Caron, *A Century in Captivity*, 2006:119. That Babson's plan was based on the Charles Street Jail was in the *Sacramento Daily Union*, June 5, 1854, p. 2.

7. The description of Babson's plan was in *ibid.*, May 30, 1854, p. 2. The acceptance of his plan by the County Court was in *ibid.*, May 25, 1854, p. 2. The ultimate decision to go with another plan was in *ibid.*, July 31, 1854, p. 3.

8. Tukey's letter to Josiah Quincy, Jr., written June 14, 1854 in the Quincy Family Papers, Massachusetts Historical Society, Boston. A description of the controversy surrounding Broderick and the politics of California at the time is Purcell, "Senator David C. Broderick of California," *Studies: An Irish Quarterly Review*, Vol. 28, No. 111 (Sep. 1939), pp. 415–431. The earliest organization of the New England Society appears to be in San Francisco in 1850, *Daily Alta California* (San Francisco, CA), October 13, 1850, p. 2. Tukey as Chief Marshal was in the *Sacramento Daily Union*, December 13, 1853, p. 2.

9. An early description of the Orleans

Hotel is in the *Sacramento Daily Union*, October 28, 1850, p. 2. Descriptions of the event were published on December 23, 1853 in *ibid.*, p. 2 and the *Democratic State Journal* (Sacramento, CA), p. 2. That Tukey responded to the Massachusetts toast was in *ibid.*, December 24, 1853, p. 2.

10. Information on the land titles of Sacramento and their resolution was in Hurtado, *John Sutter*, 2006:314.

11. The primary report on the 1854 fire was in the *Sacramento Daily Union*, July 14, 1854, p. 2. A secondary report was in the *Daily Placer Times and Transcript* (San Francisco, CA), July 15, 1854, p. 3.

12. The survival of the Kreaner & Quivey Co. was in the *Sacramento Daily Union*, July 14, 1854, p. 2. The rebuilding in brick was discussed *ibid.*, July 22, 1854, p. 2. The rebuilding of the Congregational Church was in *ibid.*, August 3, 1854, p. 3. The examination of the fire house and its rebuilding was in *ibid.*, July 21, 1854, p. 3.

13. Tukey's total loss was in the *Daily Placer Times and Transcript* (San Francisco, CA), July 15, 1854, p. 3. The description of the buildings was in the *Sacramento Bee*, July 20, 1857, p. 3. The date of the building construction was bracketed by a report in the *Sacramento Daily Union*, August 5, 1854, p. 3.

14. The creation of the School Board was in *ibid.*, March 27, 1855, p. 3. The Democratic Convention was reported in *ibid.*, March 30, 1855, p. 2.

15. The various tickets for election were printed in *ibid.*, April 2, 1855, p. 2. The results of the election was in *ibid.*, April 3, 1855, p. 2. First school commissioners' notice was in *ibid.*, April 18, 1855, p. 21. The notice of the examination was in *ibid.*, April 30, 1855, p. 2. The ad for renting the house was in the *Daily Democratic State Journal* (Sacramento, CA), October 1, 1855, p. 3. His resignation was reported in the *Sacramento Daily Union*, February 12, 1856, p. 3.

16. Tukey arrived in New York on June 27th on the steamship *Illinois* and was part of a passenger committee suing the captain for overcrowding on the trip from Aspinwall, *Evening Mirror* (New York), July 3, 1856, p. 3. Tukey's

nomination for Suffolk County Sheriff was in the *Boston Herald*, September 17, 1856, p. 3. The organization of the parade was in the *Boston Traveler*, October 14, 1856, p. 3. A detailed description of the procession was in *ibid.*, October 16, 1856, p. 4.

17. Tukey's address to the convention was reported in the *Boston Herald*, October 20, 1856, p. 2. A very anti-Tukey description was in a letter to the editor in the *Boston Morning Journal*, October 21, 1856, p. 4.

18. Earle's death was reported in the *Boston Traveler*, March 30, 1857, p. 2. Tukey's participation in the funeral was in *ibid.*, April 2, 1857, p. 4.

19. The report of the burglary was in the *Sacramento Daily Union*, February 20, 1857, p. 2. The earlier fire was in the *Daily Democratic State Journal* (Sacramento, CA), February 19, 1857, p. 2. The suggestion that someone was out to get Tukey was in the *Sacramento Bee*, February 21, 1857, p. 3. A good description of the July fire is in the *Daily Democratic State Journal* (Sacramento, CA), July 20, 1857, p. 2. The estimate of Tukey's loss is in the *Sacramento Bee*, July 20, 1857, p. 3.

20. Tukey's reason for leaving Boston was in the *Boston Daily Bee*, August 25, 1857, p. 3. His journey to California was in the *Daily Democratic State Journal* (Sacramento, CA), September 15, 1857, p. 2. A good reference for the steamship *Central America* is Klare, *The Final Voyage of the "Central America," 1857*, 1992.

21. Tukey's contemplation of a brick building was in the *Sacramento Daily Union*, September 26, 1856, p. 2. The commencement of the work was in *Sacramento Bee*, September 19, 1857, p. 3. The architect was mentioned in *Sacramento Daily Union*, April 19, 1883, p. 4. The ad for the bricks was in *Sacramento Bee*, September 21, 1857, p. 2. The excavation of the basement was in *ibid.*, September 24, 1857, p. 3. The description of the building was in the *Sacramento Daily Union*, April 19, 1883, p. 4.

22. Advertisements for the employment office and the jewelry store were in the *Sacramento Bee*, December 22, 1857, p. 3. The saloon advertisement was in the *Daily Democratic State Journal* (Sacramento, CA), February 23, 1858, p. 2. The

rumor about the courts moving in was in the *Sacramento Daily Union*, October 12, 1857, p. 2. The Grand Jury room was reported in the *Sacramento Bee*, July 20, 1858, p. 1. The location of the Sacramento Public Library was in *ibid.*, February 8, 1858, p. 3. The meeting of the California Agricultural Society was reported in the *Sacramento Daily Union*, March 1, 1859, p. 2.

23. The formation of the Sacramento Union Club was in *ibid.*, April 30, 1861, p. 2. Tukey's appointment to the executive committee was in *ibid.*, May 21, 1861, p. 3. The number of members was in *ibid.*, May 17, 1861, p. 2. Tukey was listed as a speaker in the *Sacramento Daily Bee*, May 27, 1861, p. 3. The number of people at the meeting was in the *Sacramento Daily Union*, May 31, 1861, p. 3. Notice of Tukey as the Chief Marshal was in the *Sacramento Daily Bee*, June 29, 1861, p. 2.

24. The printed program was in *ibid.*, June 29, 1861, p. 2. The spiking of the canon was in *ibid.*, July 5, 1861, p. 3. The description of the celebration was in *ibid.*, July 5, 1861, p. 3 and in the *Sacramento Daily Union*, July 6, 1861, p. 1.

25. For Tukey as a Republican delegate see the *Sacramento Daily Bee*, June 1, 1861, p. 3.

26. Tukey's appointment as chairman and his speech were in the *Sacramento Daily Union*, June 5, 1861, p. 3. His selection as candidate for Police Judge was in *ibid.*, July 20, 1861, p. 3. The election results were in *ibid.*, September 9, 1861, p. 2. Tukey's appointment to the levee board was in *ibid.*, March 19, 1862, p. 2. His appointment as Assistant Assessor was in the *Sacramento Bee*, September 22, 1862, p. 2. His role as chairman of the County Central Committee was in *ibid.*, August 4, 1862, p. 2. Selected candidate for Assembly, *ibid.*, June 5, 1863, p. 3 and elected, *ibid.*, September 15, 1863, p. 2.

27. Gillis's arrest in Sacramento and Tukey's bringing him to San Francisco was in the *Daily Alta California* (San Francisco, CA), October 11, 1862, p. 1.

The Fourth of July antics were detailed in the *Sacramento Daily Union*, October 13, 1862, p. 4. Gillis's drunkenness on the occasion was in the *Sacramento Bee*, July 6, 1861, p. 2.

28. Tukey's election was reported in *ibid.*, September 15, 1863, p. 2. His appointment to the Judiciary and Education committees was in *ibid.*, December 12, 1863, p. 3. As chairman of the Committee on the State Prison see *Daily Alta California* (San Francisco, CA), January 27, 1864, p. 1. The bill for the prison at Folsom was in the *Sacramento Bee*, April 7, 1864, p. 2. The committee on the Agricultural College was in the *Sacramento Daily Union*, December 12, 1863, p. 1.

29. A good description of the issuance of greenbacks and the opposition to them is in Rothbard, *A History of Money and Banking in the United States: The Colonial Era to World War II*. 2002. The question of loyalty was discussed in the *Daily Alta California* (San Francisco, CA), August 2, 1864, p. 2.

30. Tukey's per diem bill was in the *Stockton Independent*, December 16, 1863, p. 2. The seven bills were detailed in the *Sacramento Daily Union*, January 9, 1864, p. 2.

31. The San Francisco meeting was in the *Daily Alta California* (San Francisco, CA), February 5, 1864, p. 1. The debate over inviting Cheesman to speak was in the *Sacramento Daily Union*, February 8, 1864, p. 1. The report of his speech was in *ibid.*, February 9, 1864, p. 3. The failure to repeal the Specific Contracts Act was reported in the *Los Angeles Star*, March 5, 1864, p. 1.

32. Tukey's stand on the Pacific Railroad was in the *Sacramento Daily Union*, April 2, 1864, p. 1.

33. Tukey speaking at a Union meeting was in the *Sacramento Bee*, November 4, 1864, p. 3. His selection as a candidate for Assemblyman was in *ibid.*, May 29, 1865, p. 3. His death was reported in the *Sacramento Daily Union*, November 25, 1867, p. 2.

References Cited

Almy, James F.
  1887—"A History of Methodism in Salem." *Essex Institute Historical Collections*, 24:275–301.
Anonymous
  1848—"A Narrative of the Life and Adventures of Francis Tukey, Esq., City Marshal of Boston." Boston: Boston Herald Office. In *Making of Modern Law: Legal Treatises, 1800–1926*. Electronic reproduction. Farmington Hills, Mich.: Thomson Gale, 2004.
Bacon, Edward M., and George E. Ellis
  1886—*Bacon's Dictionary of Boston*. Houghton, Mifflin and Company, Boston, MA.
Bemis, George
  1850—*Report of the Case of John W. Webster... Indicted for the Murder of George Parkman*. Charles C. Little and James Brown, Boston, MA.
Boston, City Record
  1975—*Boston's 45 Mayors: from John Phillips to Kevin H. White.*, City of Boston Printing Section, Boston, MA.
Boston, City Register
  1894—*The Inaugural Addresses of the Mayors of Boston, 1822–1851.* Rockwell & Churchill, City Printer, Boston, MA.
Boston, Committee of Internal Health
  1849—*Report of the Committee of Internal Health on the Asiatic Cholera, together with a Report of the City Physician on the Cholera Hospital.* J. H. Eastburn, City Printer, Boston, MA.
Boston, Committee on Ordinances
  1852—*Report on the Watch and Police Departments*, City Document 63, City of Boston, MA.
Boston, Common Council
  1848—*Celebration of the Introduction of the Water of Cochituate Lake into the City of Boston, October 25, 1848.* J. H. Eastburn, City Printer, Boston, MA.
Boston Herald
  1878—*The Boston Herald and Its History. Boston Herald*, Boston, MA.
Bowers, C. Michael
  2010—*Forensic Dental Evidence: An Investigator's Handbook.* Academic Press, Burlington, MA.
Caron, Denis R.
  2006—*A Century in Captivity: The Life and Times of Prince Mortimer, a Connecticut Slave.* University of New Hampshire Press, Lebanon, NH.
Carson, Gerald
  1957—*Cornflake Crusade: From the Pulpit to the Breakfast Table.* Rinehart & Company, New York, NY.

Chandler, Peleg W., editor
    1840—*The Law Reporter.* volume II, Weeks, Jordan & Co., Boston, MA.
Child, Lydia Maria
    1835—*American Frugal Housewife Dedicated to Those Who Are Not Ashamed of Economy.* 16th edition. Carter, Hendee, and Co., Boston, MA.
Civitello, Linda
    2017—*Baking Powder Wars: The Cutthroat Food Fight That Revolutionized Cooking.* University of Illinois Press, Urbana, IL.
Clark, Solomon
    1882—*Antiquities, Historicals and Graduates of Northampton.* Steam Press of Gazette Printing Company, Northampton, MA.
Cohen, Patricia C., Timothy J. Gilfoyle and Helen Lefkowitz
    2008—*The Flash Press: Sporting Male Weeklies in 1840s New York.* University of Chicago Press, Chicago, IL.
Collins, Paul
    2018—*Blood & Ivy: The 1849 Murder that Scandalized Harvard.*—W. W. Norton, New York, NY.
Coquillette, Daniel R., and Bruce A. Kimball
    2015—*On the Battlefield of Merit: Harvard Law School the First Century.* Harvard University Press, Cambridge, MA.
Cushing, Luther, ed.
    1855—*Reports of Cases Argued and Determined in the Supreme Judicial Court of the Commonwealth of Massachusetts.* v. 2. Little, Brown, Boston, MA.
    1855—*Reports of Cases Argued and Determined in the Supreme Judicial Court of the Commonwealth of Massachusetts.* v. 5. Little, Brown, Boston, MA.
    1865—*Reports of Cases Argued and Determined in the Supreme Judicial Court of the Commonwealth of Massachusetts.* v. 57. Little, Brown, Boston, MA.
Cutler, Joseph
    1853—*The Insolvent Laws of Massachusetts, with Notes of Decisions.* Metcalf and Company, Cambridge, MA.
Davis, William T.
    1900—*History of the Judiciary in Massachusetts.* Boston Book Company, Boston, MA.
Duis, Perry R.
    1999—*The Saloon: Public Drinking in Chicago and Boston, 1880–1920.* University of Illinois Press, Urbana, IL.
Elliot, Samuel A.
    1936—"Being Mayor of Boston a Hundred Years Ago." *Proceedings of the Massachusetts Historical Society*, vol. 66, 1936, pp. 154–173.
Escobar, Robert
    2018—*Saps, Blackjacks and Slungshots: A History of Forgotten Weapons.* Gatekeeper Press, Columbus, OH.
Gleason, Frederick
    1851—"City Marshal of Boston." *Gleason's Pictorial Drawing-Room Companion.* Boston, MA, 1(2):25.
    1852—"Gilbert Nourse, Chief of Police of Boston." *Gleason's Pictorial Drawing-Room Companion.* Boston, MA, 3(8):128.
Hamilton, Luther, ed.
    1854—*Memoirs, Speeches and Writings of Robert Rantoul, Jr.* John P. Jewett & Co., Boston, MA.
Hampel, Robert L.
    2013—"15 Gallon Law." In *Alcohol and Drugs in North America: A Historical Encyclopedia*, Vol. 1, pp. 255–57. David M, Fahey and Jon S. Miller, editors, ABC-CLIO, Santa Barbara, CA.
Handlin, Oscar
    1970—*Boston's Immigrants, 1790–1880.* Atheneum, New York.

Harvard Law School
1842—*A Catalogue of the Students of Law in Harvard University: From the Establishment of the Law School, to the End of the First Term in the Year 1842.* Metcalf, Keith and Nichols, Cambridge, MA.
1845—*A Catalogue of the Students of Law in Harvard University: From the Establishment of the Law School, to the End of the First Term in the Year 1845.* Metcalf, Keith and Nichols, Cambridge, MA.
1918—*The Centennial History of Harvard Law School.* Harvard Law School Association, Cambridge, MA.
Harvard University
1842—*A Catalogue of the Officers and Students of Harvard University for the Academical Year 1842–43.* Metcalf, Keith and Nichols, Cambridge, MA.
Hurtado, Albert L.
2006—*John Sutter: A Life on the North American Frontier.* University of Oklahoma Press, Norman, OK.
Iacobbo, Karen, and Michael Iacobbo
2004—*Vegetarian America.* Praeger Publishers, Westport, CT.
Klare, Normand E.
1992—*The Final Voyage of the "Central America," 1857: The Saga of a Gold Rush Steamship, the Tragedy of Her Loss in a Hurricane and the Treasure which is Now Recovered.* Arthur H. Clark, Spokane, WA.
Knights, Peter R.
1991—*Yankee Destinies: The Lives of Ordinary Nineteenth-Century Bostonians.* University of North Carolina Press, Chapel Hill, NC.
Krout, John A.
1925—*The Origins of Prohibition.* Alfred A. Knopf, New York, NY.
Lane, Roger
1967—*Policing the City: Boston 1822–1885.* Harvard University Press, Cambridge, MA.
Laxton, Edward
1996—*The Famine Ships: The Irish Exodus to America.* Henry Holt, New York, NY.
Massachusetts General Court
1848—*Private and Special Statutes of the Commonwealth of Massachusetts, from January 1838, to May 1848 : revised and published by authority of the Legislature, in conformity to a resolve, passed April 26, 1847. vol. VIII.* Dutton & Wentworth, Boston, MA.
Maxwell-Long, Thomas
2014—*Daily Life During the California Gold Rush.* Greenwood Press, Santa Barbara, CA.
Metcalf, Theron, ed.
1822—*The General Laws of Massachusetts, from the Adoption of the Constitution, to February, 1822: With the Constitutions of the United States and of this Commonwealth, Together with Their Respective Amendments.* Wells & Lilly and Cummings & Hilliard, Boston, MA.
1847—*Reports of Cases Argued and Determined in the Supreme Judicial Court of Massachusetts.* Volume 9, Charles C. Little and James Brown, Boston, MA.
Nackenoff, Carol
1994—*The Fictional Republic: Horatio Alger and American Political Discourse.* Oxford University Press, New York, NY.
O'Connor, Thomas H.
1984—*Fitzpatrick's Boston: John Bernard Fitzpatrick, Third Bishop of Boston.* Northeastern University Press, Boston, MA.
Perry, Edwin A.
1878—*The Boston Herald and Its History.* Boston, MA.
Pope, Charles H.
1888—*A History of the Dorchester Pope Family, 1634–1888.* Privately published, Boston, MA.

Purcell, Richard J.
    1939—"Senator David C. Broderick of California." *Studies: An Irish Quarterly Review*, Vol. 28, No. 111 (Sep. 1939), pp. 415–431.
Reed, G. Walter, and William L. Willis
    1923—*History of Sacramento County, California : with biographical sketches of the leading men and women of the county who have been identified with its growth and development from the early days to the present.* Historic Record Co., Los Angeles, CA.
Roth, Michael P.
    2001—*Historical Dictionary of Law Enforcement.* Greenwood Publishing Group, Westport, CT.
Rothbard, Murray N.
    2002—*A History of Money and Banking in the United States: The Colonial Era to World War II.* Ludwig von Mises Institute, Auburn, AL.
Savage, Edward H.
    1873—*Police Records and Recollections; or Boston By Gaslight for Two Hundred and Forty Years.* John P. Dale & Co., Boston, MA.
Schulze, Henry A
    1907—"Seth Babson, F. A. I. A." *Quarterly Bulletin of the American Institute of Architects*, Vol. 8, No. 2, July 1907, pp. 108–109.
Seaburg, Carl
    2003—*The Ice King: Frederic Tudor and his Circle.* Massachusetts Historical Society, Boston, MA.
Smith, Andrew F.
    2009—*Eating History: 30 Turning Points in the Making of American Cuisine.* Columbia University Press, New York, NY.
State Street Trust Company.
    1914—*Mayors of Boston: An Illustrated Epitome of Who the Mayors Have Been and What They Have Done.* Privately Published by the State Street Trust Company, Boston, MA.
Stearns, Robert E. C.
    1890—"On the Nishinam Game of 'Ha' and the Boston Game of 'Props' " *American Anthropologist* 3:353–358.
Stevens, Paul
    2008—*Hidden History of the Boston Irish.* History Press, Charleston, SC.
Stone, James W.
    1849—"The Cholera Epidemic in Boston." *Boston Medical and Surgical Journal*, 41(15):296–299.
Thompson, George
    1850—*Life and Exploits of the Noted Criminal, Bristol Bill.* M.J. Ivers & Co. New York, NY.
Tukey, Francis
    1854—"Letter to Josiah Quincy, Jr." Ms. in the Massachusetts Historical Society, "Quincy Family Papers," Boston, MA.
Von Frank, Albert J.
    1998—*The Trials of Anthony Burns: Freedom and Slavery in Emerson's Boston.* Harvard University Press, Cambridge, MA.
Wilhelm, Robert
    2017—*Wicked Victorian Boston.* History Press, Charleston, SC.
Yale University
    1880—*Obituary Record of Graduates of Yale College Deceased from June 1870, to June 1880.* Tuttle, Morehouse & Taylor, New York, NY.

Index